Asset Recovery Handbook

Asset Recovery Handbook

A Guide for Practitioners

Jean-Pierre Brun
Larissa Gray
Clive Scott
Kevin M. Stephenson

STAR Stolen Asset Recovery Initiative
The World Bank • UNODC

© 2011 The International Bank for Reconstruction and Development / The World Bank
1818 H Street NW
Washington DC 20433
Telephone: 202-473-1000
Internet: www.worldbank.org
E-mail: feedback@worldbank.org

1 2 3 4 13 12 11 10

This volume is a product of the staff of the International Bank for Reconstruction and Development / The World Bank. The findings, interpretations, and conclusions expressed in this volume do not necessarily reflect the views of the Executive Directors of The World Bank or the governments they represent. The World Bank does not guarantee the accuracy of the data included in this work.

The maps in this book were produced by the Map Design Unit of The World Bank. The boundaries, colors, denominations, and any other information shown on these maps do not imply, on the part of The World Bank Group, any judgment on the legal status of any territory, or any endorsement or acceptance of such boundaries.

Rights and Permissions
The material in this publication is copyrighted. Copying and/or transmitting portions or all of this work without permission may be a violation of applicable law. The International Bank for Reconstruction and Development / The World Bank encourages dissemination of its work and will normally grant permission to reproduce portions of the work promptly.

For permission to photocopy or reprint any part of this work, please send a request with complete information to the Copyright Clearance Center Inc., 222 Rosewood Drive, Danvers, MA 01923, USA; telephone: 978-750-8400; fax: 978-750-4470; Internet: www.copyright.com.

All other queries on rights and licenses, including subsidiary rights, should be addressed to the Office of the Publisher, The World Bank, 1818 H Street NW, Washington, DC 20433, USA; fax: 202-522-2422; e-mail: pubrights@worldbank.org.

ISBN: 978-0-8213-8634-7
eISBN: 978-0-8213-8635-4
DOI: 10.1596/978-0-8213-8634-7

Library of Congress Cataloging-in-Publication Data
Brun, Jean-Pierre, 1962-
    Asset recovery handbook : a guide for practitioners / Jean-Pierre Brun and Larissa Gray.
        p. cm.
    Includes bibliographical references and index.
    ISBN 978-0-8213-8634-7 — ISBN 978-0-8213-8635-4 (electronic)
    1. Forfeiture—Criminal provisions. 2. Searches and seizures. I. Gray, Larissa. II. Title.
    K5107.B788 2011
    345'.0773—dc22
                                                                            2010048779

Contents

Figures

Tables

Preface

Developing countries lose between US$20 to US$40 billion each year through bribery, misappropriation of funds, and other corrupt practices. Much of the proceeds of corruption find "safe haven" in the world's financial centers. These criminal flows are a drain on social services and economic development programs, contributing to the further impoverishment of the world's poorest countries. The victims include children in need of education, patients in need of treatment, and all members of society who contribute their fair share and deserve assurance that public funds are being used to improve their lives. But corruption affects us all by undermining confidence in governments, banks, and companies in both developed and developing economies.

The international community has responded to the challenge and, in principles and through international agreements, is now moving forward. The G20 has put the fight against corruption at the forefront of its efforts to improve global integrity and accountability. The Stolen Asset Recovery (StAR) Initiative was launched in September 2007 by the World Bank and the United Nations Office on Drugs and Crime (UNODC) to promote the ratification and implementation of the United Nations Convention against Corruption (UNCAC), and specifically its chapter 5, which provides the first comprehensive and innovative framework for asset recovery.

Many developing countries have already sought to recover stolen assets. A number of successful high-profile cases with creative international cooperation have demonstrated that asset recovery *is* possible. However, to date, only US$5 billion in stolen assets have been recovered. What we need now is more visible, tangible progress in forcefully prosecuting bribery cases, and systematic recovery of proceeds of corruption.

However, recovering proceeds of corruption is complex. The process can be overwhelming for even the most experienced of practitioners. It is exceptionally difficult for those working in the context of failed states, widespread corruption, or with limited resources. We must support their efforts as they grapple with the strategic, organizational, investigative, and legal challenges of recovering stolen assets, whether through criminal confiscation, nonconviction based confiscation, civil actions, or other alternatives.

We hope that the guide will prove useful for law enforcement officers, prosecutors, investigating judges, lawyers, and other experts. We also expect that it will be helpful to those making policy decisions regarding legislation and management of resources devoted to fighting corruption, and we look forward to using the handbook to provide technical assistance and promote capacity building in countries interested in the StAR Initiative.

Ngozi N. Okonjo-Iweala
Managing Director, The World Bank

Yury Fedotov
Executive Director, UNODC

Acknowledgments

This handbook is the result of special collaborative efforts from colleagues around the world. Their time and expertise were invaluable in developing a practical tool to assist practitioners in recovering the proceeds and instrumentalities of corruption.

This publication was written by Jean-Pierre Brun (team leader, Financial Market Integrity Unit, World Bank), Larissa Gray (Financial Market Integrity Unit), Kevin Stephenson (Financial Market Integrity Unit), and Clive Scott (United Nations Office on Drugs and Crime [UNODC]), with the participation of Nina Gidwaney (Financial Market Integrity Unit).

The authors are especially grateful to Jean Pesme (manager, Financial Market Integrity Unit, Financial and Private Sector Development Network) and Adrian Fozzard (Stolen Asset Recovery [StAR] Initiative coordinator) for their ongoing support and guidance on this project.

The team benefited from many insightful comments during the peer review process, which was co-chaired by Jean Pesme and Tim Steele (senior governance specialist, StAR Secretariat). The peer reviewers were Raymond Baker (director, Global Financial Integrity), Yara Esquivel (Integrity Vice Presidency, World Bank), Frank Fariello (Legal Department, World Bank), Agustin Flah (Legal Department, World Bank), Jeanne Hauch (Integrity Vice Presidency, World Bank), Lindy Muzila (UNODC), and Mutembo Nchito (prosecutor, Zambia).

As part of the drafting and consultation process, practitioners' workshops were held in Vienna, Austria (May 2009) and Marseille, France (May 2010). Practitioners brought experience conducting criminal confiscation, non-conviction based confiscation, civil actions, investigations, asset tracing, international cooperation and asset management—from both civil and common law jurisdictions, and from both developed and developing countries. The people participating (from both public and private sectors) were Yves Aeschlimann (Financial Market Integrity Unit), Jean-Marc Cathelin (France), France Chain (Organisation for Economic Co-operation and Development [OECD]), Hamza Chraiti (Switzerland), Anne Conestabile (OECD), Margaret Cotter (International Monetary Fund), William Cowden (United States), Maxence Delorme (France), Nick de Villiers (South Africa), Adrian Fajardo (Mexico), Frank Filippeli (United States), Clara Garrido (Colombia), John Gilkes (United States), Dorothee A. Gottwald (UNODC),

Guillermo Jorge (Argentina), Vitaliy Kasko (Ukraine), William Loo (OECD), Marko Magdic (Chile), Olaf Meyer (Germany), Holly Morton (United Kingdom), Elnur Musayev (Azerbaijan), Shane Nainappan (United Kingdom), Nchima Nchito (Zambia), Jean Fils Kleber Ntamack (Cameroon), Pedro Pereira (International Centre for Asset Recovery), Stephen Platt (Jersey), Frederic Raffray (Guernsey), Linda Samuel (United States), Jean-Bernard Schmid (Switzerland), Salim Succar (Haiti), Jose Ugaz (Peru), Gary Walters (United Kingdom), Jean Weld (United States), Simon Williams (Canada), and Annika Wythes (UNODC).

The handbook also benefited from the contributions of Theodore S. Greenberg (Financial Market Integrity Unit), David M. Mizrachi (Panama), and Felicity Toube (United Kingdom).

A special thanks also to Thelma Ayamel for arranging the logistics of the workshops in Vienna and Marseille; and to Maria Orellano and Miguel Nicolas de la Riva for their administrative support.

Jean-Pierre Brun
Task Team Leader
Financial Market Integrity Unit
World Bank

Acronyms and Abbreviations

BIC	Bank identifier code
CARIN	Camden Assets Recovery Inter-Agency Network
CHAPS	Clearing House Automated Payments System
CHIPS	Clearing House Interbank Payments System
CTR	Currency transaction report
ECHR	European Court of Human Rights
EWHC (Ch.)	England and Wales High Court (Chancery Division)
FATF	Financial Action Task Force
FCPA	Foreign Corrupt Practices Act
Fedwire	Fedwire Funds Service
FIU	Financial intelligence unit
GDP	Gross domestic product
IBC	International business corporation
ICSID	International Centre for Settlement of Investment Disputes
LLC	Limited Liability Company
MLA	Mutual legal assistance
NCB	Non-conviction based
OECD	Organisation for Economic Co-operation and Development
PEP	Politically exposed person
PTC	Private trust company
RICO	Racketeer Influenced and Corrupt Organizations
StAR	Stolen Asset Recovery Initiative
STR	Suspicious transaction report; Suspicious activity report
SWIFT	Society for Worldwide Interbank Financial Telecommunications
UAE	United Arab Emirates
UNCAC	United Nations Convention against Corruption
UNODC	United Nations Office on Drugs and Crime
UNTOC	United Nations Convention against Transnational Organized Crime
WDF	World Duty Free Company Limited

Introduction

The theft of public assets from developing countries is an immense development problem. The amount of money stolen from developing and transition jurisdictions and hidden in foreign jurisdictions each year is approximately $20–$40 billion—a figure equivalent to 20–40 percent of flows of official development assistance.[1] The societal costs of corruption far exceed the value of assets stolen by public leaders. Corruption weakens confidence in public institutions, damages the private investment climate, and ruins delivery mechanisms for such poverty alleviation programs as public health and education.[2]

Recognizing the serious problem of corruption and the need for improved mechanisms to combat its devastating impact and facilitate the recovery of corruption proceeds, the international community introduced a new framework in the United Nations Convention against Corruption (UNCAC). Chapter V of the convention provides this framework for the return of stolen assets, requiring states parties to take measures to restrain, seize, confiscate, and return the proceeds of corruption. To do so, they may use various mechanisms, such as:

- direct enforcement of freezing or confiscation orders made by the court of another state party;[3]
- non-conviction based asset confiscation, particularly in cases of death, flight, or absence of the offender or in other cases;[4]
- civil actions initiated by another state party, allowing that party to recover the proceeds as plaintiff;[5]
- confiscation of property of a foreign origin by adjudication of an offense of money laundering or other offenses;[6]
- court orders of compensation or damages to another state party and recognition by courts of another state party's claim as a legitimate owner of assets acquired through corruption;[7]
- spontaneous disclosure of information to another state party without prior request;[8] and
- international cooperation and asset return.[9]

---

1. World Bank, *Stolen Asset Recovery (StAR) Initiative: Challenges, Opportunities, and Action Plan* (Washington, DC, 2007), 9.
2. Ibid.
3. United Nations Convention against Corruption (UNCAC), art. 54(1)(a) and 54(2)(a).
4. UNCAC, art. 54(1)(c).
5. UNCAC, art. 53.
6. UNCAC, art. 54(1)(b) and 54(2)(b).
7. UNCAC, art. 53(b) and (c).
8. UNCAC, art. 56.
9. UNCAC, art. 55 and 57.

Even with this framework, the practice of recovering stolen assets remains complex. It involves coordination and collaboration with domestic agencies and ministries in multiple jurisdictions with different legal systems and procedures. It requires special investigative techniques and skills to "follow the money" beyond national borders and the ability to act quickly to avoid dissipation of the assets. To ensure effectiveness, the competent authority ("the authority") must have the capacity to launch and conduct legal proceedings in domestic and foreign courts or to provide the authorities in another jurisdiction with evidence or intelligence for investigations (or both). All legal options—whether criminal confiscation, non-conviction based confiscation, civil actions, or other alternatives—must be considered. This process may be overwhelming for even the most experienced practitioners. It is exceptionally difficult for those working in the context of failed states, widespread corruption, or limited resources.

The complexity of the process highlights the need for a practical tool to help practitioners navigate the process. With this in mind, the Stolen Asset Recovery Initiative, a joint initiative of the United Nations Office of Drugs and Crime and the World Bank focused on encouraging and facilitating more systematic and timely return of stolen assets, has developed this *Asset Recovery Handbook: A Guide for Practitioners*. Designed as a how-to manual, the handbook guides practitioners as they grapple with the strategic, organizational, investigative, and legal challenges of recovering assets that have been stolen by corrupt leaders and hidden abroad. It provides common approaches to recovering stolen assets located in foreign jurisdictions, identifies the challenges that practitioners are likely to encounter, and introduces good practices. By consolidating into a single framework the information dispersed across various professional backgrounds, the handbook will enhance the effectiveness of practitioners working in a team environment.

Methodology

To develop the *Asset Recovery Handbook* as a practical tool to help practitioners navigating the issues, laws, and theory, the Stolen Asset Recovery Initiative drew on those people who have practical day-to-day experience in one or more of the core areas of asset recovery. Participants included law enforcement, financial investigators, investigating magistrates, prosecutors, lawyers in private practice, and asset managers. They brought experience—from developed and developing jurisdictions and from civil and common law systems—in conducting criminal confiscation, non-conviction based asset confiscation, civil actions, investigations, asset tracing, international cooperation, and asset management. They have worked with other national agencies as well as with foreign counterparts. Being familiar with some of the challenges in this regard, they have developed their own methods and ideas for overcoming those challenges.

The overall format of the handbook and key topics for consideration were agreed on by a group of practitioners at a workshop held in Vienna, Austria, in May 2009.[10] These

---

10. Participating practitioners in the May 2009 Vienna workshop brought experience from practice in Argentina, Azerbaijan, Canada, Colombia, Costa Rica, France, Guernsey, Jersey, Peru, South Africa, Switzerland, Ukraine, United Kingdom, United States, and Zambia.

were developed by the authors into a draft version, and then presented and discussed at a second practitioners' workshop held one year later in Marseille, France.[11] The second workshop was followed by additional contributions and consultations, and the final version was agreed to by the expanded group.

How the Handbook Can Be Used

The *Asset Recovery Handbook* is designed as a quick-reference, how-to manual for practitioners—law enforcement officials, investigating magistrates, and prosecutors—as well as for asset managers and those involved in making policy decisions in both civil and common law jurisdictions. Given diverse audiences and legal systems, it is important that readers keep in mind that a practice or strategy that has worked in one jurisdiction may not work in another. Likewise, an investigative technique that is permitted in one jurisdiction may not be permitted—or may have different procedural requirements—in another. In addition, jurisdictions may use different terminology to describe the same legal concept (for example, some jurisdictions use "confiscation" and others use "forfeiture") or procedure (some jurisdictions' assets may be "seized," whereas others' may be "restrained," "blocked," or "frozen").[12] Or different jurisdictions may assign different roles and responsibilities to those people who are involved in asset recovery: in some jurisdictions, investigations are conducted by an investigating magistrate; in others, by law enforcement authorities or prosecutors.

The handbook attempts to point out these differences where they exist, and it highlights how different concepts or practices may offer similar solutions to the same challenges. However, the handbook is not designed to be a detailed compendium of law and practices. Each practitioner therefore should read the handbook in the context of his or her specific jurisdiction's legal system, law enforcement structures, resources, legislation, and procedures—without being restrained by the terminology or the concepts used to illustrate the challenges and tools for successful recovery of assets. The practitioner should also consider the context of the legal system, law enforcement structures, resources, legislation, and procedures of the specific jurisdiction where the asset recovery procedures will be sought.

The primary purpose of this handbook is to facilitate asset recovery in the context of grand corruption, particularly as outlined in chapter V of UNCAC. Nonetheless, asset confiscation and recovery can and should be applied to a wider range of offenses—particularly,

---

11. Practitioners participating in the May 2010 Marseille workshop brought experience from Argentina, Azerbaijan, Brazil, Cameroon, Chile, Colombia, France, Germany, Guernsey, Haiti, Peru, South Africa, Switzerland, Ukraine, United Kingdom, United States, and Zambia.
12. For example, in South Africa's Prevention of Organised Crime Act, 1998, "confiscation" is defined as value-based orders made pursuant to chapter V of the act. In other jurisdictions, these orders are described as "pecuniary penalty orders" (for example, in federal and many state confiscation laws in Australia). In Mexico, the term "forfeiture" is preferred because this refers to the proceeds and instrumentalities of crime; "confiscation," on the other hand, refers to the assets of an individual. In Jersey, "forfeiture" is used with the instrumentalities of crime, and "confiscation" relates to the proceeds of crime.

the asset confiscation provisions set out in the United Nations Convention against Narcotic Drugs and Psychotropic Substances (Vienna) and the United Nations Convention against Transnational Organized Crime.

The handbook is organized into nine chapters, a glossary, and 10 appendixes of additional resources. Chapter 1 provides a general overview of the asset recovery process and legal avenues for recovery, along with practical case examples. Chapter 2 presents a host of strategic considerations for developing and managing an asset recovery case, including gathering initial sources of facts and information, assembling a team, and establishing a relationship with foreign counterparts for international cooperation. Chapter 3 introduces the techniques that practitioners may use to trace assets and analyze financial data, as well as to secure reliable and admissible evidence for asset confiscation cases. The provisional measures and planning necessary to secure the assets prior to confiscation are discussed in chapter 4; and chapter 5 introduces some of the management issues that practitioners will need to consider during this phase. Confiscation systems are the focus of chapter 6, including a review of the different systems and how they operate and the procedural enhancements that are available in some jurisdictions. On the issue of international cooperation, chapter 7 reviews the various methods available, including informal assistance and mutual legal assistance requests; and guides practitioners through the entire process. Finally, chapters 8 and 9 discuss two additional avenues for asset recovery—respectively, civil proceedings and domestic confiscation proceedings undertaken in foreign jurisdictions.

The glossary defines many of the specialized terms used within the handbook. Because jurisdictions often use different terminology to describe the same legal concept or procedure, the glossary provides examples of alternative terms that may be used.

The appendixes contain additional reference tools and practical resources to assist practitioners. Appendix A provides an outline of offenses where criminal prosecution is concerned. Appendix B presents a detailed list and descriptions of commonly used corporate vehicle terms. For those reviewing suspicious transaction reports, appendix C provides a sample financial intelligence unit report. Appendix D offers a checklist of some additional considerations for planning the execution of a search and seizure warrant. Appendixes E and G, respectively, provide a sample production order for financial institutions and a sample financial profile form. Appendix F outlines the serial and cover payment methods used by correspondent banks in relation to electronic fund transfers, and it discusses the new cover payment standards that became effective in November 2009. Appendix H offers discussion points that practitioners may use to begin communications with their foreign counterparts. With respect to mutual legal assistance requests, Appendix I provides an outline for a letter of request, with key drafting and execution tips. Finally, Appendix J provides a broad range of international and country-specific Web site resources.

1. Overview of the Asset Recovery Process and Avenues for Recovering Assets

One of the first considerations in an asset recovery case is the development of an effective strategy for both obtaining a criminal conviction (if possible) and recovering the proceeds and instrumentalities of corruption. Practitioners must be aware of the various legal avenues available for recovering assets, as well as some of the factors or obstacles that may lead to the selection of one avenue over another. This chapter introduces the general process for asset recovery and the various recovery avenues (most of which are discussed in greater detail in subsequent chapters).

1.1 General Process for Asset Recovery

Whether pursuing assets through criminal or non-conviction based (NCB) confiscation or through proceedings in a foreign jurisdiction or through a private civil action, the objectives and fundamental process for recovery of assets are generally the same. Figure 1.1 illustrates this process.

1.1.1 Collection of Intelligence and Evidence and Tracing Assets

Evidence is gathered and assets are traced by law enforcement officers under the supervision of or in close cooperation with prosecutors or investigating magistrates, or by private investigators or other interested parties in private civil actions. In addition to gathering publicly available information and intelligence from law enforcement or other government agency databases, law enforcement can employ special investigative techniques. Some techniques may require authorization by a prosecutor or judge (for example, electronic surveillance, search and seizure orders, production orders, or account monitoring orders), but others may not (for example, physical surveillance, information from public sources, and witness interviews). Private investigators do not have the powers granted to law enforcement; however; they will be able to use publicly available sources and apply to the court for some civil orders (such as production orders, on-site review of records, prefiling testimony, or expert reports). Criminal investigative techniques and tracing are discussed in detail in chapter 3, and investigative techniques in civil actions are discussed in chapter 8.

FIGURE 1.1 Process for Recovery of Stolen Assets

Collecting Intelligence and Evidence and
Asset Tracing
(Domestically and in foreign jurisdictions using MLA)

↓

Securing the Assets
(Domestically and in foreign jurisdictions using MLA)

↓

Court Process
(To obtain conviction [if possible], confiscation, fines,
damages, and/or compensation)

↓

Enforcing Orders
(Domestically and in foreign jurisdictions using MLA)

↓

Return of Assets

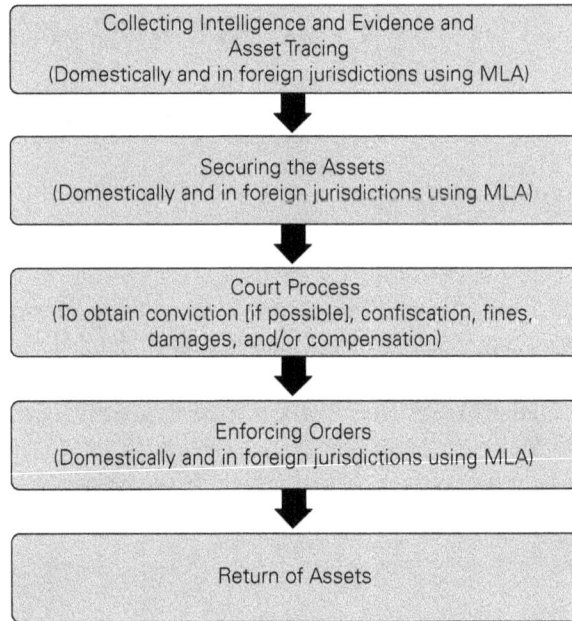

Source: Authors' illustration.
Note: MLA = mutual legal assistance.

1.1.2 Securing the Assets

During the investigation process, proceeds and instrumentalities subject to confiscation must be secured to avoid dissipation, movement, or destruction. In certain civil law jurisdictions, the power to order the restraint or seizure of assets subject to confiscation may be granted to prosecutors, investigating magistrates, or law enforcement agencies. In other civil law jurisdictions, judicial authorization is required. In common law jurisdictions, an order to restrain or seize assets generally requires judicial authorization, with some exceptions in seizure cases. Asset restraint and seizure is discussed in detail in chapter 4; restraint in private civil actions is discussed in chapter 8. Systems to manage assets will also need to be in place (see chapter 5).

1.1.3 International Cooperation

International cooperation is essential for the successful recovery of assets that have been transferred to or hidden in foreign jurisdictions. It will be required for the gathering of evidence, the implementation of provisional measures, and the eventual confiscation of the proceeds and instrumentalities of corruption. And when the assets are confiscated, cooperation is critical for their return. International cooperation includes "informal assistance," mutual legal assistance (MLA) requests, and extradition.[13] Informal assistance

---

13. For the purposes of this handbook, "informal assistance" is used to include any type of assistance that does not require a *formal* MLA request. Legislation permitting this informal, practitioner-to-practitioner

is often used among counterpart agencies to gather information and intelligence to assist in the investigation and to align strategies and forthcoming procedures for recovery of assets. An MLA request is normally a written request used to gather evidence (involving coercive measures that include investigative techniques), obtain provisional measures, and seek enforcement of domestic orders in a foreign jurisdiction. International cooperation is addressed in chapter 7.

1.1.4 Court Proceedings

Court proceedings may involve criminal or NCB confiscation or private civil actions (each described below and in subsequent chapters); and will achieve the recovery of assets through orders of confiscation, compensation, damages, or fines. Confiscation may be property based or value based. Property-based systems (also referred to as "tainted property" systems) allow the confiscation of assets found to be the proceeds or instrumentalities of crime—requiring a link between the asset and the offense (a requirement that is frequently difficult to prove when assets have been laundered, converted, or transferred to conceal or disguise their illegal origin). Value-based systems (also referred to as "benefit" systems) allow the determination of the value of the benefits derived from crime and the confiscation of an equivalent value of assets that may be untainted. Some jurisdictions use enhanced confiscation techniques, such as substitute asset provisions or legislative presumptions to assist in meeting the standard of proof. Chapter 6 describes these and other confiscation issues; chapter 8 describes private civil actions.

1.1.5 Enforcement of Orders

When a court has ordered the restraint, seizure, or confiscation of assets, steps must be taken to enforce the order. If assets are located in a foreign jurisdiction, an MLA request must be submitted. The order may then be enforced by authorities in the foreign jurisdiction through either (1) directly registering and enforcing the order of the requesting jurisdiction in a domestic court (direct enforcement) or (2) obtaining a domestic order based on the facts (or order) provided by the requesting jurisdiction (indirect enforcement).[14] This will be accomplished through the mutual legal assistance process (described above and in chapter 7). Similarly, private civil judgments for damages or compensation will need to be enforced using the same procedures as for other civil judgments.

1.1.6 Asset Return

The enforcement of the confiscation order in the requested jurisdiction often results in the confiscated assets being transferred to the general treasury or confiscation fund of

---

assistance may be outlined in MLA legislation and may involve "formal" authorities, agencies, or administrations. For a description of this type of assistance and comparison with the MLA request process, see section 7.2 of chapter 7.

14. See United Nations Convention against Corruption (UNCAC), art. 54 and 55; United Nations Convention against Transnational Organized Crime (UNTOC), art. 13; United Nations Convention against Narcotic Drugs and Psychotropic Substances, art. 5; and the Terrorist Financing Convention, art. 8. For restraint or seizure, see UNCAC, art. 54(2).

the requested jurisdiction (not directly returned to the requesting jurisdiction).[15] As a result, another mechanism will be needed to arrange for the return of the assets. If UNCAC is applicable, the requested party will be obliged under article 57 to return the confiscated assets to the requesting party in cases of embezzlement of public funds or laundering of such funds, or when the requesting party reasonably establishes prior ownership. If UNCAC is not applicable, the return or sharing of confiscated assets will depend on domestic legislation, other international conventions, MLA treaties, or special agreements (for example, asset sharing agreements). In all cases, total recovery may be reduced to compensate the requested jurisdiction for its expenses in restraining, maintaining, and disposing of the confiscated assets and the legal and living expenses of the claimant.

Assets may also be returned directly to victims, including a foreign jurisdiction, through the order of a court (referred to as "direct recovery").[16] A court may order compensation or damages directly to a foreign jurisdiction in a private civil action. A court may also order compensation or restitution directly to a foreign jurisdiction in a criminal or NCB case. Finally, when deciding on confiscation, some courts have the authority to recognize a foreign jurisdiction's claim as the legitimate owner of the assets.

If the perpetrator of the criminal action is bankrupt (or companies used by the perpetrator are insolvent), formal insolvency procedures may assist in the recovery process. All of these mechanisms are explained further in chapters 7, 8, and 9.

A number of policy issues are likely to arise during any efforts to recover assets in corruption cases. Requested jurisdictions may be concerned that the funds will be siphoned off again through continued or renewed corruption in the requesting jurisdictions, especially if the corrupt official is still in power or holds significant influence. Moreover, requesting jurisdictions may object to a requested country's attempts to impose conditions and other views on how the confiscated assets should be used. In some cases, international organizations such as the World Bank and civil society organizations have been used to facilitate the return and monitoring of recovered funds.[17]

---

15. Stolen Asset Recovery (StAR) Initiative Secretariat, "Management of Confiscated Assets" (Washington, DC, 2009), http://www.worldbank.org/star.

16. UNCAC, art. 53 requires that states parties take measures to permit direct recovery of property.

17. In 2007, the U.S. Department of Justice filed a civil confiscation action against a U.S. citizen indicted in 2003 for allegedly paying bribes to Kazakh officials for oil and gas deals. The action was for approximately $84 million in proceeds. The American citizen agreed to transfer those proceeds to a World Bank trust fund for use on projects in Kazakhstan. See "U.S. Attorney for S.D.N.Y, Government Files Civil Forfeiture Action Against $84 Million Allegedly Traceable to Illegal Payments and Agrees to Conditional Release of Funds to Foundation to Benefit Poor Children in Kazakhstan," news release no. 07-108, May 30, 2007, http://www.usdoj.gov/usao/nys/pressreleases/May07/pictetforfeiturecomplaintpr.pdf; World Bank, "Kazakhstan BOTA Foundation Established," news release no. 2008/07/KZ, June 4, 2008, http://siteresources.worldbank.org/INTKAZAKHSTAN/News%20and%20Events/21790077/Bota_Establishment_June08_eng.pdf.

1.2 Legal Avenues for Achieving Asset Recovery

The legal actions for pursuing asset recovery are diverse. They include the following mechanisms:

- domestic criminal prosecution and confiscation, followed by an MLA request to enforce orders in foreign jurisdictions;
- NCB confiscation, followed by an MLA request or other forms of international cooperation to enforce orders in foreign jurisdictions;
- private civil actions, including formal insolvency process;
- criminal prosecution and confiscation or NCB confiscation initiated by a foreign jurisdiction (requires jurisdiction over an offense and cooperation from the jurisdiction harmed by the corruption offenses); and
- administrative confiscation.

The availability of these avenues, either domestically or in a foreign jurisdiction, will depend on the laws and regulations in the jurisdictions involved in the investigation, as well as international or bilateral conventions and treaties. Box 1.1 outlines the various laws relevant to practitioners pursuing these avenues. In addition, there are other legal, practical, or operational realities that will influence the avenue selected. Some of these strategic considerations, obstacles, and case management issues are discussed in chapter 2.

1.2.1 Criminal Prosecution and Confiscation

When authorities seeking to recover stolen assets decide to pursue a criminal case, criminal confiscation is a possible means of redress. Practitioners must gather evidence, trace and secure assets, conduct a prosecution against an individual or legal entity, and obtain a conviction. After obtaining a conviction, confiscation can be ordered by the court. In some jurisdictions, particularly common law jurisdictions, the standard of proof for confiscation will be lower than the standard required for obtaining the conviction. For example, "balance of probabilities" will be needed for confiscation, whereas "beyond a reasonable doubt" will be required for a conviction. Other jurisdictions apply the same standard to both conviction and confiscation. See figure 2.1 in section 2.6.5 for an explanation of the standards of proof. Generally, unless enhanced confiscation provisions apply, confiscation legislation will provide for confiscation of proceeds and instrumentalities that are directly or indirectly traceable to the crime.[18]

---

18. The form and operation of "enhanced confiscation provisions" are discussed in more detail in chapter 6. Enhancements include substitute asset provisions that permit confiscation of assets not connected with a crime if the original proceeds have been lost or dissipated, presumptions about the unlawful use or derivation of assets in certain circumstances, presumptions about the extent of unlawful benefits flowing from certain offenses, and the reversal of the onus and burden of proof in certain circumstances.

BOX 1.1   Legal Framework for Asset Recovery

Legislation and procedures (domestic and foreign jurisdictions):

- Confiscation provisions (criminal, NCB, administrative);
- MLA;
- Criminal law provisions and codes of procedures (corruption, money laundering);
- Private (civil) law provisions and codes of procedure; and
- Asset sharing laws.

International conventions and treaties[a]

- UNCAC;
- United Nations Convention against the Illicit Traffic in Narcotic Drugs and Psychotropic Substances;
- UNTOC;
- Organisation for Economic Co-operation and Development Convention on Combating Bribery of Foreign Public Officials in International Business Transactions;
- Southeast Asian Mutual Legal Assistance in Criminal Matters Treaty;
- Inter-American Convention against Corruption;
- Council of Europe Convention on Laundering, Search, Seizure and Confiscation of the Proceeds of Crime (1990) and the revised Council of Europe Convention on Laundering, Search, Seizure and Confiscation of the Proceeds of Crime and on the Financing of Terrorism (2005);
- Council of the European Union Framework Decision 2003/577/JHA on the Execution in the European Union of Orders Freezing Property or Evidence;
- Council of the European Union Framework Decision 2006/783/JHA on the Application of the Principle of Mutual Recognition to Confiscation Orders;
- Southern African Development Community Protocol against Corruption (2001);
- African Union Convention on Preventing and Combating Corruption and Related Offenses (2003);
- Commonwealth of Independent States Conventions on Legal Assistance and Legal Relationship in Civil, Family and Criminal Matters;
- Scheme Relating to Mutual Assistance in Criminal Matters within the Commonwealth (the Harare Scheme);
- Mercosur Mutual Legal Assistance in Criminal Matters Treaty (Dec. No. 12/01); and
- Bilateral MLA treaties.

a. See appendix J for available Web site resources.

International cooperation, including informal assistance and requests for MLA, will be used throughout the process to trace and secure assets in foreign jurisdictions, as well as to enforce the final order of confiscation.[19]

A benefit of criminal prosecution and confiscation is the societal recognition of the criminal nature of corruption and the accountability of the perpetrator. Further, penalties of imprisonment, fines, and confiscation serve to deter future offenders. In addition, criminal investigators generally have the most aggressive means of gathering information and intelligence, including access to data from law enforcement agencies and financial intelligence units (FIUs), use of provisional measures and coercive investigative techniques (such as searches, electronic surveillance, examination of financial records or access to documents held by third parties), as well as grand juries or other means of compelling testimony or evidence. And, in most jurisdictions, MLA is provided only in the context of criminal investigations. However, significant barriers may exist to obtaining a criminal conviction and confiscation: insufficient evidence; lack of capacity or political will; or the death, flight, or immunity of the perpetrator. Furthermore, the conduct giving rise to the request may not be a crime in the jurisdiction where the relief is being sought. These and other barriers are discussed in chapter 2.

1.2.2 Non-Conviction Based Confiscation

Another type of confiscation gaining traction throughout the world is confiscation without a conviction, referred to as "NCB confiscation."[20] NCB confiscation shares at least one common objective with criminal confiscation—namely, the recovery and return of the proceeds and instrumentalities of crime. Likewise, deterrence and depriving corrupt officials of their ill-gotten gains are other societal equities realized by NCB confiscation.

NCB confiscation differs from criminal confiscation in the procedure used to confiscate the assets. A criminal confiscation requires a criminal trial and conviction, followed by the confiscation proceedings; NCB confiscation does not require a trial or conviction, but only the confiscation proceedings. In many jurisdictions, NCB confiscation can be established on a lower standard of proof (for example, the "balance of probabilities" or "preponderance of the evidence" standard), and this helps ease the burden on the authorities. Other (mainly civil law) jurisdictions require a higher standard of proof—specifically, the same standard required to obtain a criminal conviction.

---

19. UNCAC, art. 54(1)(a); UNTOC, art. 13(1)(a); and United Nations Convention against Narcotic Drugs and Psychotropic Substances, art. 5(4)(a) require states parties to take measures to give effect to foreign orders.

20. Jurisdictions include Anguilla, Antigua and Barbuda, Australia, some of the provinces of Canada (Alberta, British Columbia, Manitoba, Ontario, Quebec, Saskatchewan), Colombia, Costa Rica, Fiji, Guernsey, Honduras, Ireland, Isle of Man, Israel, Jersey, Liechtenstein, New Zealand, the Philippines, Slovenia, South Africa, Switzerland, Thailand, the United Kingdom, the United States, and Zambia. International conventions and multilateral agreements also have introduced NCB confiscation. See UNCAC, art. 53(1)(c) and recommendation 3 of the Financial Action Task Force 40+9 Recommendations.

However, because NCB confiscation is not available in all jurisdictions, practitioners may have difficulty obtaining MLA to assist with investigations and to enforce NCB confiscation orders. NCB confiscation is discussed in greater detail in chapter 6.

1.2.3 Private Civil Action

Authorities seeking to recover stolen assets have the option of initiating proceedings in domestic or foreign civil courts to secure and recover the assets and to seek damages based on torts, breach of contract, or illicit enrichment.[21] The courts of the foreign jurisdiction may be competent if a defendant is a person (individual or business entity) living or incorporated in the jurisdiction (personal jurisdiction), if the assets are within or have transited the jurisdiction (subject matter jurisdiction), or if an act of corruption or money laundering was committed within the jurisdiction. As a private litigant, the authorities seeking redress can hire lawyers to explore the potential claims and remedies (ownership of misappropriated assets, tort, disgorgement of illicit profits, contractual breaches). The civil action will entail collecting evidence of misappropriation or of liabilities based on contractual or tort damages. Frequently, it is possible to use evidence gathered in the course of a criminal proceeding in a civil litigation. It is also possible to seek evidence with the assistance of a court prior to filing an action.

The plaintiff usually has the option to petition the court for a variety of orders, including the following:

- Freezing, embargo, sequestration, or restraining orders (potentially with worldwide effect) secure assets suspected to be the proceeds of crime, pending the resolution of a lawsuit laying claim to those assets. In some jurisdictions, interim restraining orders may be issued pending the outcome of a lawsuit even before the lawsuit has been filed, without notice and with extraterritorial effect. These orders usually require the posting of a bond, guarantee, or other undertaking by the petitioner.
- Orders against defendants oblige them to provide information about the source of their assets and transactions involving them.
- Orders against third parties for disclosure of relevant documents are useful in obtaining evidence from banks, financial advisers, or solicitors, among others.
- "No-say" (gag) orders prevent banks and other parties from informing the defendants of a restraint injunction or disclosure order.
- Generic protective or conservation orders preserve the status quo and prevent the deterioration of the petitioner's assets, legal interests, or both. Such orders usually require showing the likelihood of success on the merits and an imminent risk in delaying a decision.

The principal disadvantages of litigating in a foreign jurisdiction are the cost of tracing assets and the legal fees entailed in obtaining relevant court orders. However, the litigant

---

21. UNCAC art. 53(a) calls on states parties to permit another state party to initiate a civil action in domestic courts.

has more control in pursuing civil proceedings and assets in the hands of third parties and may have the advantage of a lower standard of proof. For example, civil cases in common law jurisdictions usually are decided on a "balance of probabilities" or "preponderance of the evidence" standard.

Similarly, arbitration proceedings related to international contracts obtained through bribes or illicit advantages awarded to corrupt officials may open promising avenues, including the cancellation of contracts, and potential claims for torts or damages. These avenues are discussed in greater detail in chapter 8.

1.2.4 Actions Initiated by Foreign Jurisdictions

Authorities seeking to recover stolen assets may choose to support a criminal or NCB confiscation proceeding that has been initiated in another jurisdiction against the corrupt official, associates, or identified assets. At the conclusion of the proceedings, the state or government may be able to obtain a portion of the recovered assets through orders of the foreign courts or pursuant to legislation or agreements.[22] This will require that the foreign authority has jurisdiction; the capacity to prosecute and confiscate; and, most important, the willingness to share the proceeds. The initiation of an action by a foreign authority may take place in one of two ways:

1. Authorities in the jurisdiction harmed by corruption may ask the foreign authorities to open their own case. This may be accomplished by filing a complaint or, even more simply, by sharing incriminating evidence and a case file with authorities of the foreign jurisdiction. In all cases, the foreign authorities ultimately have the discretion to pursue or ignore the case. If authorities pursue it, the jurisdiction harmed by the offenses will need to cooperate with the foreign authorities to ensure they have the necessary evidence.
2. Foreign authorities may open a case independent of request from the jurisdiction harmed by corruption. Foreign authorities may receive information linking a corrupt official to their jurisdiction—whether through a newspaper article, a suspicious transaction report (STR), or a request for informal assistance or MLA—and decide to investigate money laundering or foreign bribery activities undertaken within their national territory.

The involvement of the victim—including a state or government that has been harmed by corruption offenses—in the proceedings is generally encouraged in most jurisdictions; however, it generally is limited to discussions with practitioners and does not extend to actual standing in the proceedings. In some civil law jurisdictions, however, it may also be possible for the victim to participate in foreign proceedings as a private prosecutor or as a civil party to the proceedings. In both civil and common law jurisdictions, it may be possible to recover assets from these proceedings through court-ordered compensation, restitution, or damages as a party harmed by corruption offenses or as a legitimate owner in confiscation proceedings.

---

22. UNCAC art. 53(b) and 53(c) require states parties to take measures to permit direct recovery.

This avenue is an interesting option if the jurisdiction seeking redress does not have the legal basis, capacity, or evidence to pursue an international investigation on its own. Moreover, if the limitation period rules out the prosecution of the initial corruption charges, it may be possible to investigate offenses of money laundering or possession of stolen assets in other jurisdictions. On the other hand, the jurisdiction that has been harmed by corruption offenses has no control over the proceedings, and success largely depends on the foreign authorities' priorities. In addition, unless the return of the assets is ordered by the court, it will be dependent on asset sharing agreements or the authorities' ability to return the assets on a discretionary basis (see section 9.4 in chapter 9).

1.2.5 Administrative Confiscation

Unlike criminal or NCB confiscation, which requires court action, administrative confiscation generally involves a non-judicial mechanism for confiscating assets used or involved in the commission of the offense. It may occur by operation of statute, pursuant to procedures set out in regulations, and is typically used to address uncontested confiscation cases. The confiscation is carried out by an authorized agency (such as a police unit or a designated law enforcement agency), and often follows a process similar to that traditionally used in customs smuggling cases. The procedures usually require notice to persons with a legal interest in the asset and publication to the public at large. Generally, administrative confiscation is restricted to low-value assets or certain classes of assets. For example, legislation may permit the confiscation of any amount of cash, but prohibit the confiscation of real property. Another variation on this type of confiscation, called "abandonment" by some jurisdictions, employs a similar procedure. Another non-judicial means to recover assets is through taxation of the illicit profits (see box 1.2).

1.3 Use of Asset Recovery Avenues in Practice: Three Case Examples

Outlined below are three short case examples that demonstrate how the various avenues discussed throughout this chapter have been used to recover assets in practice. Each case involved several jurisdictions and incorporated a number of different strategic approaches, depending on the circumstances of the case, the avenues available in the domestic and foreign jurisdictions, or repatriation arrangements.

1.3.1 Case of Vladimiro Montesinos and His Associates

Following televised videos that showed Vladimiro Montesinos (personal adviser to Peru's president Alberto Fujimori and de facto chief of Peru's intelligence service) bribing an elected opposition congressman in September 2000, funds were traced to several jurisdictions, including the Cayman Islands, Luxembourg, Switzerland, and the United States. Ultimately, more than $250 million was recovered from Switzerland and the United States and from local banks in Peru.

Alternative Means of Recovering Assets

Taxation of Illicit Profits

A public official or an executive from a state-owned company who receives bribes, misappropriated funds, or stolen assets may be liable for income taxes on this illicit income. In such a case, authorities do not have to prove the illicit origin of assets. It is sufficient to prove that they represent undisclosed revenue. The authorities simply prove that the taxpayer has made a taxable gain or received taxable income and that he or she is liable for the appropriate amount of taxes, including interest and penalties if the tax was not paid on time. Therefore, the evidentiary burden is less than in a civil recovery case. Given the fact that this approach generally does not involve court proceedings, this mechanism is potentially cheaper and faster than civil recovery or criminal proceedings.

Fines and Compensation Orders in Criminal Trials

In criminal cases, the court may order the defendant to pay fines, compensation to the victim, or both. Such orders may accompany confiscation orders, or may be ordered in lieu of confiscation orders. Although fines or compensation orders may be easier to achieve than a separate proceeding for confiscation, the enforcement of such orders is likely to be more difficult. Enforcement of fines and compensation orders may proceed through civil courts, whereas confiscation orders will be enforced against assets that have been previously restrained. In addition, the amount of the fine may be limited by statute and therefore insufficient on its own to meet the recovery being sought.

For the $48 million of assets in Switzerland, two options were discussed with the Swiss investigating magistrate: The Peruvian authorities could prosecute the offenders domestically for corruption and then seek recovery of the assets through MLA requests and signed waivers. Or Switzerland could pursue drug trafficking and related money laundering offenses that were involved in the case. With the second option, recovery would be reduced because Peru would have to share a percentage of the assets with Switzerland. Peru decided to pursue the first option. To lay the groundwork, Peruvian authorities introduced legislation permitting guilty pleas (plea agreements) and other forms of cooperation.[23] In return for a reduced criminal sentence or dismissal of proceedings, defendants provided useful information regarding known or unidentified crimes and unknown evidence, access to the proceeds of crime, or testimony against key figures. In addition, defendants signed waivers authorizing the foreign banks that held their money to transfer it to the Peruvian government accounts. Several million dollars were recovered through the use of these waivers.

---

23. Referred to as the "Efficient Collaboration Act" (Law 27.378).

For the assets allegedly in the Cayman Islands, Peru hired local lawyers to assist with pursuit of $33 million transferred through a Peruvian bank. Peruvian authorities also met with the FIU to seek its assistance. After several months of financial analysis, Peru discovered that the money had never been sent to the Cayman Islands, but had remained in the Peruvian bank. A back-to-back loan scheme had been used to simulate the "transfer" to the Cayman bank and the "return" to the Peruvian bank. When this was discovered, the funds in the Peruvian bank were seized.

In the United States, Victor Venero Garrido, an associate of Montesinos, was arrested in coordination with the Peruvian authorities; his apartment was seized; and $20 million was frozen. Another $30 million of Montesinos' funds held in the name of a front man were also frozen. NCB confiscation proceedings in California and Florida were used to recover the funds, and the entire amount was repatriated to Peru. The repatriation agreement with the United States was conditioned on the investment of the money in human rights and anticorruption efforts.

In Peru, more than $60 million was recovered by Peruvian authorities seizing and confiscating properties, vehicles, boats, and other assets through approximately 180 criminal proceedings involving more than 1,200 defendants.

1.3.2 Case of Frederick Chiluba and His Associates

In 2002, a task force was established in Zambia to investigate corruption allegations against the former president Frederick Chiluba and his associates during the period 1991–2001, to assess whether criminal proceedings could be brought, and to determine the best options for recovering assets. In 2004, the attorney general of Zambia initiated a civil suit in the United Kingdom to recover funds transferred to London and across Europe between 1995 and 2001 to fund the former president's expensive lifestyle—including a residence valued at more than 40 times his annual salary.[24] These proceedings were launched in addition to ongoing criminal proceedings in Zambia.

Three factors informed the decision to launch the civil action in addition to the criminal proceedings: First, most of the defendants were located in Europe, making domestic criminal prosecution and confiscation impossible in a number of cases.[25] Second, most of the evidence and assets were located in Europe, which made a European venue a more favorable option. And, third, specifically with respect to the cases whereas domestic criminal prosecution and confiscation was possible, successful international cooperation through an MLA request was unlikely. Zambia lacked the bilateral or multilateral agreements, procedural safeguards, capacity, and experience necessary to collect evidence and enforce confiscation orders across Europe. Instead, court orders obtained in a European jurisdiction would be easier to enforce in jurisdictions that were parties to the Brussels Convention on recognition of foreign court decisions in Europe.

---

24. *Attorney General of Zambia v. Meer Care & Desai & Others*, [2007] EWHC 952 (Ch.) (U.K.).
25. Zambia did not have NCB confiscation legislation at that time; however, it was adopted subsequently.

London was chosen as the European venue because most of the funds diverted from Zambia had passed through two law firms and bank accounts in the United Kingdom, and the attorney general of Zambia was able to establish jurisdiction over defendants in jurisdictions that were parties to the Brussels Convention. Finally, it was anticipated that decisions obtained from courts in the United Kingdom would also be enforceable in Zambia when they were registered before the courts.

The High Court of London found sufficient evidence of a conspiracy to transfer approximately $52 million from Zambia to a bank account operated outside ordinary government business—the "Zamtrop account"—and held at the Zambia National Commercial Bank in London. Forensic experts traced the monies received in the Zamtrop account back to the ministry of finance. They also substantially traced the funds leaving the Zamtrop account, and they revealed that $25 million was misappropriated or misused. In addition, the High Court found no legitimate basis for payments of about $21 million made by Zambia pursuant to an alleged arms deal with Bulgaria and paid into accounts in Belgium and Switzerland.

The Court held that the defendants conspired to misappropriate $25 million from the Zamtrop account and $21 million from the arms deal payments. The Court also held that the defendants had broken the fiduciary duties they owed to the Zambian Republic or dishonestly assisted in such breaches. As a result, the defendants were held liable for the amounts and assets corresponding to misappropriated funds.

1.3.3 Case of Diepreye Alamieyeseigha

In the case involving Diepreye Peter Solomon Alamieyeseigha, former governor of Bayelsa State, Nigeria, this jurisdiction was able to recover $17.7 million through domestic proceedings and through cooperation with authorities in South Africa and the United Kingdom.

In September 2005, Alamieyeseigha was first arrested at Heathrow Airport by the London Metropolitan Police on suspicion of money laundering. An investigation revealed that Alamieyeseigha had $2.7 million stashed in bank accounts and in his home in London, as well as London real estate worth an estimated $15 million. Alamieyeseigha was released on bail and subsequently left the jurisdiction in November 2005, returning to Nigeria.

In Nigeria, he claimed immunity from prosecution. He was subsequently removed from office by Bayelsa State's lawmakers, and thereby lost his immunity. Later in November 2005, Nigeria's Economic and Financial Crimes Commission charged him with 40 counts of money laundering and corruption, and it secured a court order restraining assets held in Nigeria.

For assets in the United Kingdom, close cooperation between the Commission and the London Metropolitan Police's Proceeds of Corruption Unit was crucial. The $1.5 million in cash seized from Alamieyeseigha's London home was confiscated under the Proceeds of Crime Act on the basis of a court order that the assets represented proceeds of crime. In May 2006, the court ordered the funds repaid to Nigeria, and the transfer was made a few weeks later. For the bank accounts, the process was more challenging because assets and evidence were located in the Bahamas, the British Virgin Islands, the Seychelles, South Africa, and the United Kingdom. Nigerian authorities recognized that requesting assistance from these jurisdictions could take considerable time and that orders from Nigerian courts would not necessarily be executed. In addition, the pursuit of legal proceedings in each of these jurisdictions was a daunting prospect because the Nigerian authorities had little evidence linking Alamieyeseigha to these assets and linking the assets to acts of corruption.

As a result, Nigerian authorities decided to bring civil proceedings in the United Kingdom and simultaneously pursue criminal proceedings in Nigeria. To secure evidence, the Nigerian authorities obtained a disclosure order for the evidence compiled by the Metropolitan Police in the course of its investigation.[26] Nigeria was able to use this evidence together with Alamieyeseigha's income and asset declaration[27] to obtain a worldwide restraint order covering all assets owned directly or indirectly by Alamieyeseigha and a disclosure order for documents held at banks and by Alamieyeseigha's associates.

In parallel with those proceedings, the South African Asset Forfeiture Unit initiated NCB confiscation proceedings against Alamieyeseigha's luxury penthouse. Funds were returned to Nigeria following the sale of the property in January 2007.

Before a Nigerian high court in July 2007, Alamieyeseigha pleaded guilty to six charges of making false declaration of assets and caused his companies to plead guilty to 23 charges of money laundering. He was sentenced to two years in prison, and the court ordered the confiscation of assets in Nigeria. Alamieyeseigha's guilty pleas effectively voided his defense in the civil proceedings in the London High Court; and, in December 2007, the Court issued a summary judgment confiscating property and a bank account in the United Kingdom. A judgment in July 2008 led to the confiscation of the remaining assets in Cyprus, Denmark, and the United Kingdom.

---

26. The Nigerian application for disclosure was not contested by the Metropolitan Police. This departed from the usual practice: the police usually do not concede to providing evidence gathered through criminal investigations to assist private parties pursuing civil claims.
27. The declaration was filed in 1999 when Alamieyeseigha was first elected state governor. It indicated that he had assets amounting to just over half a million dollars and an annual income of $12,000.

2. Strategic Considerations for Developing and Managing a Case

Successful asset recovery requires a comprehensive plan of action that incorporates a number of important steps and considerations. Practitioners will need to gather and assess the facts to understand the case; assemble a team; identify key allies; communicate with foreign practitioners; grapple with the legal, practical, and operational challenges[28]; and ensure effective case management. Each facet will help practitioners select the most appropriate legal avenue for recovering assets—whether criminal or non-conviction based (NCB) confiscation followed by a mutual legal assistance (MLA) request for enforcement, private civil action, or a request that authorities in another jurisdiction pursue criminal or NCB confiscation. Experience has demonstrated that whereas a criminal *conviction* is always important to combat and deter corruption, criminal *confiscation* may not be the best option for asset recovery. Some authorities will use a combination of the avenues to pursue confiscation.[29] Alternatively, the presence of obstacles may warrant consideration of another legal avenue. In cases involving multiple jurisdictions, a number of different avenues may be pursued—for example, domestic confiscation followed by an MLA request for enforcement in one jurisdiction and private civil recovery in another.

This chapter reviews some of the initial actions and some of the issues that practitioners will have to consider in selecting an avenue for asset recovery. It is important for practitioners to persevere and to think creatively in developing and implementing a strategy: perhaps there is an innovative way to resolve an issue, such as introducing new legislation or a different approach. Practitioners should also be conscious that decision making is an ongoing and iterative process: because pragmatism is essential, the first choices should be reviewed regularly to check that they are still appropriate in light of case developments.

2.1 Gathering Facts: Initial Sources of Information

To launch an asset recovery investigation, authorities analyze leads from diverse sources of information discussed below. They may also choose to undertake some preliminary

---

28. The Stolen Asset Recovery (StAR) Initiative is currently undertaking a study of the barriers to asset recovery. The expected publication date is early-2011. The study will be available at www.worldbank.org/star. See also "Best Practices: Confiscation (Recommendations 3 and 38)," adopted by the plenary of the Financial Action Task Force (FATF) in February 2010. The document is available at http://www.fatf-gafi.org/dataoecd/39/57/44655136.pdf.

29. In the United States, for example, prosecutors often use NCB confiscation procedures to freeze or seize property and have the NCB case "stayed" during criminal proceedings. If the defendant is convicted, criminal confiscation will be used to confiscate the defendant's interest in the property.

investigations, as outlined in chapter 3. Potential sources of information include the following:

- **Criminal complaints (communications) and proceedings.** Reports of fraud, corruption, theft, or other offenses filed by victims (including individuals, companies, and jurisdictions harmed by corruption offenses) or government agencies (such as regulatory authorities, anticorruption agencies, tax authorities, and financial intelligence units [FIUs]) are vital sources of information. In addition, investigations into other criminal activities may reveal corruption. For example, a search or communication intercept in a drug case could yield evidence of bribery activities.
- **FIU reports.** Money laundering legislation obliges financial institutions, regulatory authorities, and some nonfinancial businesses and professions (such as lawyers, accountants, dealers in precious metals and stones, and trust and company service providers) to file suspicious transaction or activity reports (STRs) with FIUs and to be particularly vigilant concerning politically exposed persons— namely, senior government officials, their family members, and close associates.[30] Some jurisdictions also require the filling of currency transactions reports (CTRs) for certain transactions. On receipt of an STR or a CTR from a reporting entity, an FIU may launch an investigation and relay the completed report to local law enforcement or prosecutors. The FIU may also transmit the information to a foreign FIU through the Egmont Group, a network of FIUs. For more information on using FIUs in initiating and investigating asset recovery cases, see box 2.1, and section 3.3.2 of chapter 3.
- **Civil or administrative proceedings.** Civil or administrative proceedings, such as a brokerage report, regulator sanctions against a financial institution, or sanctions against a company by an international or regional development bank, may reveal corrupt activities. Many complaints, although not specifically citing corruption, lead to the discovery of such misconduct on investigation. A complaint about missing or defective materials, for instance, could indicate that defective goods were accepted by a procurement official in exchange for bribes. Similarly, complaints filed by contractors alleging unfair treatment in a bidding process also merit attention.
- **MLA requests.** Requesting jurisdictions may include in their requests a lot of detailed information on individuals and bank accounts that may lead the requested jurisdiction to open a domestic case for money laundering. Information shared through tax exchange agreements also may be useful.
- **Spontaneous disclosures.** Foreign competent authorities and FIUs may spontaneously provide the authorities in another jurisdiction with information on corruption activities that have taken place in the other jurisdiction or have involved one of its nationals. Such information may also be passed through formal or informal practitioner networks (see section 7.3.5 of chapter 7).

---

30. See United Nations Convention against Corruption (UNCAC), art. 52(1) and (2); and recommendations 6, 13, and 16 of the FATF 40+9 Recommendations.

BOX 2.1   Role and Contribution of FIUs in Asset Recovery Cases

FIUs are agencies responsible for collecting STRs from financial institutions and other reporting entities, conducting analysis, and disseminating the resulting intelligence to local competent authorities (typically, law enforcement agencies and prosecutors and foreign FIUs) to combat money laundering and terrorist financing. They may be helpful partners for asset recovery practitioners in initiating a case and conduct an investigation in a number of ways:

- **Proactive sharing of intelligence with law enforcement and prosecutors.** Where an FIU analysis reveals money laundering or other criminal activity, FIUs will proactively provide intelligence reports to local law enforcement or prosecutors. Where appropriate, FIUs will also provide intelligence reports to foreign FIUs bilaterally, often through the Egmont Group's secure Web site. That information is analyzed further and may be passed to foreign law enforcement and prosecutors.
- **Provision of ancillary intelligence.** Most FIUs maintain a central database of all STRs, CTRs, cross-border currency reports, intelligence reports, and any queries received from law enforcement agencies or foreign FIUs. The intelligence received and stored may not have been sufficient on its own to warrant a report to law enforcement; however, it may be useful to law enforcement officials in understanding the activity of an investigation's targets, identifying associates, and forming links with the investigations of other agencies.
- **Expertise in financial matters.** Financial intelligence analysts are familiar with financial services and products and with money laundering typologies, and they are experienced in analyzing financial records and flows. Such expertise is critical throughout an investigation and prosecution, and FIUs may be a helpful resource in this regard.
- **Personal contacts and networks.** FIUs will have contacts in financial institutions, other domestic agencies, and foreign FIUs (through the Egmont Group) that may be helpful resources for practitioners.
- **Ability to institute an administrative freeze.** Some FIUs are able to restrain funds for a brief period of time (see section 7.3.4), thereby helping practitioners quickly preserve assets prior to the obtaining of a formal court order.

Practitioners have found FIUs to be most effective as partners. Such a relationship requires a two-way sharing of relevant intelligence between the FIU and the practitioner: both upstream and downstream rather than a one-way flow of intelligence from the FIU to the practitioner. Practitioners have found that such a practice increases the intelligence available to FIUs and ultimately improves the financial analysis that the FIUs produce.

- **Auditors.** Companies are commonly subject to annual audits of their financial statements, and individuals are audited by tax agencies. Similarly, governments usually establish auditing or regulatory agencies (for example, offices of inspectors general, courts, inspection agencies, and specialized accounting offices) to oversee government departments or state-owned companies. These audits frequently uncover discrepancies between movements of funds and actual business transactions, thereby signaling possible corrupt activities. In particular, examination of financial documents relating to revenues or expenses may reveal patterns of fictitious billing typical of corruption and bribery cases.

- **Whistle-blowers.** Initial referrals for investigation may come from employees or individuals who suspect malfeasance within their institutions or who are hoping for lenient treatment for their own crimes.[31]

- **Media and civil society reports.** Suspicious activity or arrests of foreign officials on corruption charges are often relayed by the news media or through reports of civil society and nongovernmental organizations. Such reports may trigger an investigation directly or may prompt the filing of an STR that leads to an investigation.

- **Asset and income declarations by public officials.** Many jurisdictions oblige public officials to disclose information regarding their assets and income.[32] These declarations may highlight significant increases in assets that are inconsistent with an individual's declared income or even falsification of declared income. Comparing declared assets against those assets used by public officials may point toward illicit enrichment.

- **Intelligence services.** Information may be received from an intelligence agency or through intelligence services located in another government agency (for example, law enforcement or a regulatory authority).

- **Proactive investigations.** Practitioners may also actively seek information from potential sources. They may monitor the activities of sensitive industries or those susceptible to money laundering and corruption, such as natural resource extraction or arms dealing.

2.2 Assembling a Team or Unit, Task Forces, and Joint Investigations with Foreign Authorities

Particularly in large, complex cases, it will be important to assemble a multidisciplinary team or unit to ensure the effective handling of the case and eventual confiscation. This team likely will comprise a range of individuals, including financial investigators and experts in financial analysis, forensic accountants, law enforcement officers, prosecutors, and asset managers. Experts may be appointed from the private sector or seconded

---

31. Many jurisdictions have incorporated whistle-blower protections and procedures into legislation. Haiti, for example, enshrined the concept—referred to as "public outcry"—in its 1987 constitution. See also UNCAC, art. 33.

32. UNCAC art. 8(5), 52(5), and 52(6) require states parties to consider establishing such systems; and there are approximately 114 jurisdictions with systems in place for disclosure to an ethics office, anticorruption body, or other government department. See Theodore S. Greenberg, Larissa Gray, Delphine Schantz, Carolin Gardner, and Michael Lathem, *Politically Exposed Persons: Preventive Measures for the Banking Sector* (Washington, DC: World Bank, 2010), 42; Ruxandra Burdescu, Gary J. Reid, Stuart Gilman, and Stephanie Trapnell, *Stolen Asset Recovery—Income and Asset Declarations: Tools and Trade-offs* (Washington, DC: StAR Initiative, conference edition released November 2009). Documents are available at www.worldbank.org/star.

from other agencies, such as a regulatory authority, the FIU, a tax authority, an auditing agency, or the office of an inspector general. Depending on its jurisdiction and circumstances, the case will likely involve investigative and prosecutorial teams and may expand to a joint task force of the relevant agencies or a joint investigation with another jurisdiction.[33]

2.2.1 Investigative and Prosecutorial Teams

Investigative teams should include individuals with the expertise necessary to analyze significant volumes of financial, banking, and accounting documents, including wire transfers, financial statements, and tax or customs records. They should also include investigators with experience in gathering business and financial intelligence; identifying complex illegal schemes; following the money trail; and using such investigative techniques as electronic surveillance, wiretapping, search warrants, and witness interviews. In some cases, it may be useful or necessary to appoint experts or consultants who bring technical expertise in financial analysis, forensic accounting, and computer forensics.

Prosecutors also require similar expertise and experience to effectively present the case in court. Special prosecutors may be appointed in cases involving high-ranking officials to prevent conflicts of interest, to guarantee independent investigations, and to ensure that the process is credible.

Normally, a high-ranking prosecutor should lead the investigation or follow investigations conducted by the investigating magistrate or law enforcement because the prosecutor ultimately is responsible for presenting the case to the court. He or she must ensure that law enforcement agencies collect the necessary evidence to establish the offenses, provisional measures, and confiscation.[34] In addition, the prosecutor acts as an interface with judges when law enforcement officers need judicial authorization to use special investigative tools, such as wiretapping, searches, arrests, and plea agreements.

The law enforcement or prosecution agencies having primary responsibility for the specific offenses involved in a case often have the capacity to gather and present the evidence required for the purpose of confiscation. Where possible, there is also merit in creating specialized confiscation investigation and prosecution units to support primary criminal investigation teams. Experience suggests that it can be difficult when law enforcement officers and prosecutors are responsible for both the specific offense and the confiscation. In some jurisdictions, for example, criminal prosecutors are not assigned until the investigation is largely complete—a point too late for the purposes of asset confiscation. In addition, criminal investigators and prosecutors have large

---

33. The term "investigative teams" includes investigations or intelligence gathering that takes place before and after the initiation of charges against the defendant. In some jurisdictions, the term "investigation" is used exclusively for investigations that follow the initiation of formal charges.

34. In some civil law jurisdictions, investigating magistrates may lead the investigations from the beginning of the case until its final adjudication; however, prosecutors can appeal their decisions.

caseloads and tend to give priority to obtaining the criminal conviction, not necessarily the confiscation.

With the establishment of specialized confiscation units, confiscation investigators and prosecutors develop the specialized skills needed to present evidence effectively for the purpose of enforcing confiscation laws. Confiscation investigators will generally go farther than will criminal investigators in identifying and tracing assets for the purpose of confiscation, and they are well placed to undertake international inquiries to follow assets that have left the jurisdiction. If such an approach is taken, confiscation practitioners must work closely with their counterparts pursuing the criminal prosecution. Failure to do so can have negative consequences for the criminal case—and that, in turn, is likely to affect confiscation efforts.

The team may be based in anticorruption agencies that have the authority to investigate, prosecute, or both; or in regular law enforcement and prosecutorial agencies. Wherever the team is situated, it will be critical that investigators and prosecutors are granted, in law, the authority to investigate or prosecute (or both) the offenses and to confiscate the proceeds and instrumentalities of those offenses.[35]

2.2.2 Joint Task Forces

Authorities may consider forming joint task forces that comprise the various agencies, law enforcement authorities, and private sector actors who have an interest in the prosecution or recovery of assets (or both). A joint task force may include representatives from departments of tax, customs, justice, foreign affairs, treasury, and immigration; as well as participants from the FIU, the regulatory authority, the central authority, and the asset management authority. Such task forces facilitate exchange of information and skills and assist in discussions and reviews of the latest developments in the case. It will be important to clarify the respective roles of the team members and other law enforcement authorities to avoid confusion or rivalries among the agencies.

2.2.3 Joint Investigations with Foreign Authorities

In demanding and difficult investigations requiring coordinated action with other jurisdictions, a joint investigation or agency task force involving authorities in other jurisdictions should be considered.[36] Where permitted, a joint investigation avoids duplicating efforts and can facilitate cooperation, the exchange of information, and the development of a common strategy (that is, a case may be pursued in one jurisdiction or multiple jurisdictions). It can avoid some of the pitfalls of making an MLA request (such as alerting the targets to the investigation and losing time with subsequent appeals) because the

---

35. Generally, foreign jurisdictions will refuse to grant MLA to investigations or prosecutions led by non-judicial agencies or agencies not authorized at law.
36. UNCAC, art. 49, and United Nations Convention against Transnational Organized Crime (UNTOC), art. 19, call on states parties to consider establishing joint investigations on a case-by-case basis.

practitioners are all working with a common purpose. Where there are multiple venues with ongoing litigation, a joint investigation (and case conferences) may help ensure that the various litigants are informed of what is happening in the other jurisdictions. Where capacity and the domestic legal framework for provisional measures and confiscation are weak in one jurisdiction, a joint investigation can facilitate skills transfer among members or permit the pursuit of the matter in the jurisdiction with the more efficient and effective legal framework.

Nevertheless, joint investigations can be difficult to coordinate, and practitioners will need to consider whether the conditions for a successful joint investigation are present. They should verify the existence of appropriate legal frameworks that enable competent authorities to conduct joint investigations in the absence of an MLA request, the gathering of evidence by foreign practitioners in the host jurisdiction, and the direct sharing of information. Because each participating authority must have jurisdiction over an offense, laws that provide extraterritorial jurisdiction are helpful. In addition, practitioners should confirm the presence of sufficient resources, proper training, security measures for operational information, and an environment of trust and commitment. Finally, the parties will need to agree on a common purpose, duration, and procedures; and on how information collected will be used. Such agreements may be set out in a memorandum of understanding.

2.3 Establishing Contact with Foreign Counterparts and Assessing Ability to Obtain International Cooperation

Establishing a liaison with foreign practitioners early in the case can help assess potential difficulties, build a strategy, obtain preliminary information and informal assistance, confirm requirements for MLA requests, and create goodwill in the international cooperation process. Making connections with law enforcement attachés or liaison magistrates posted to embassies is a good way to ensure contact with the authorities in foreign jurisdictions. In larger cases, face-to-face meetings with counterparts have proved essential to successful international cooperation. Direct contact helps demonstrate political will and facilitate discussions of obstacles, strategies, and needed assistance. Some authorities have opted to convene a case conference or workshop that involves representatives from each of the foreign authorities having a potential interest in the case. This tactic is particularly effective in cases that involve a number of jurisdictions or where resource constraints may limit foreign travel. An alternative is to travel to the foreign jurisdiction. Section 7.1 describes this process and possible points of contact in greater detail.

Differences in legal traditions (common law versus civil law) and among confiscation systems (value-based versus property-based systems) create challenges and frustrations in cooperating with foreign jurisdictions. Terminology tends to be different as do the procedures used, evidentiary burdens, and time required to obtain assistance. For example, some civil law jurisdictions can restrain or seize assets more easily because prosecutors or investigating magistrates have this power and can take swift action (in contrast to common law jurisdictions that require an application before a court). A value-based confiscation system will need only evidence that the assets are linked to a person who has been accused or convicted of a crime, whereas a property-based confiscation system demands proof of the connection between the asset and the offense. Use of incorrect terminology or failure to meet the necessary evidentiary requirements can lead to confusion, delay, and even the refusal of assistance. This handbook attempts to highlight some of these differences; however, it will be important to use personal contacts on a continuing basis to learn about the other systems and confirm the proper course of action.

Authorities pursuing an international asset recovery effort should verify as soon as possible whether they can meet the conditions for obtaining informal assistance and MLA from foreign jurisdictions, or whether there may be obstacles in obtaining such assistance. A potential obstacle to MLA is meeting dual criminality requirements—namely, that the conduct underlying the request for assistance is criminalized in both jurisdictions. Because dual criminality should be reviewed on the basis of conduct, not terminology, it may be overcome by providing facts or evidence that support offenses acceptable to the requested jurisdiction. For example, if the requested jurisdiction does not have laws against illicit enrichment, practitioners will have to supply facts supporting another crime that is an offense in the requested jurisdiction. Box 2.2 outlines more

---

BOX 2.2   Obstacles to International Cooperation

The following obstacles may compromise efforts toward international cooperation:

- Legal obstacles, including insufficient laws and procedures on international cooperation, enforcement of foreign orders, return of assets, lack of legal authority to cooperate informally, limited ability to provide assistance before the filing of criminal charges, statutory time limits for investigations and prosecutions in the requesting jurisdiction that may not allow sufficient time for the MLA process, and laws that require disclosure to the asset holder;
- Need to meet the dual criminality requirement and provide the necessary undertakings (for example, reciprocity, limits on use of information, or payment of costs or damages);
- Reasons for refusal, including essential interests, nature of penalty, ongoing proceedings in the requested jurisdiction, lack of due process in the requesting jurisdiction, and specific crimes (such as tax evasion)[a];
- Length of process (delay) due to formalities, processing times, and appeals;
- Evidentiary requirements that are too difficult to meet (for example, a request may be considered a "fishing expedition" because it is overbroad and lacks sufficient details to identify the bank account concerned); and
- Differences in confiscation systems that may lead to problems in enforcement.

a. It is uncertain whether tax evasion is covered under the United Nations Convention against Corruption.

specific examples of problems that may be encountered, and chapter 7 discusses these issues in greater detail.

If MLA requests for enforcement of domestic provisional measures and confiscation orders will not be granted, then the other avenues must be considered. It may be possible to use NCB confiscation or civil law actions (including formal insolvency processes) to recover the stolen assets or provide the case materials and evidence to support a prosecution in a foreign jurisdiction.

2.4 Securing Support and Adequate Resources

The demonstrated and credible intent of political actors, civil servants, and mechanisms of the state to combat corruption and recover assets—referred to as "political will"—is a necessary precondition for asset recovery. Without political will and the support of government leaders, lack of resources and political interference may become major obstacles in developing a case.[37] Practitioners will need to identify allies and build support for the case, both at the political level and among the various agencies. Strong public support developed with the help of the media (particularly investigative journalists) and nongovernmental organizations can help generate or maintain high-level political will. Regular progress reports to senior political officials in which needs and resources are discussed may help enhance and maintain commitments. Likewise, practitioners will need to take efforts to minimize possible interferences, particularly if potential targets are political allies or personal friends of government officials. These alliances may extend into other jurisdictions and lead to problems with international cooperation or to tipping off the targets.

In addition to securing political and public support, adequate funding for each stage of the asset recovery effort should be ensured—preferably through legislation. Asset recovery investigations may be overwhelming for a developing jurisdiction because they require a team of practitioners with the ability to analyze bank records, trace and secure funds in foreign jurisdictions, draft proper MLA requests, and eventually obtain a final confiscation order.

If the authorities are seeking to conduct a domestic investigation and prosecution, there may be foreign jurisdictions that are willing to contribute personnel (for example, a mentor), funding, or training for practitioners. Even civil actions may not be out of reach: some jurisdictions have helped fund private civil actions against corrupt officials who have misappropriated assets from a low-capacity jurisdiction, and private law firms have accepted cases on a pro bono or contingency-fee basis.

In the absence of political support and adequate resources for a domestically led investigation and recovery through confiscation or a civil action, authorities may decide to

---

37. For a discussion of how the lack of political will can impede asset recovery, see the forthcoming study described in footnote 28.

provide the case materials and evidence to foreign authorities (assuming jurisdiction) to assist in foreign proceedings.

2.5 Assessing Legislation and Considering Legal Reforms

It will be important for the authorities to determine whether adequate and effective laws are in place, both domestically and in the foreign jurisdiction.[38] This will include legislation on the various legal avenues, as well as asset management and international cooperation (see chapter 5 on asset management and chapter 7 on international cooperation). Confiscation, for example, might result from general legislation providing for confiscation of proceeds or instrumentalities of crime, or from provisions applying to a specific offense. In both cases, authorities should make sure that confiscation related to the crimes they investigate is legally possible.

When legislation on a particular legal avenue is insufficient, an alternative avenue may have to be considered. Or it may be possible in some jurisdictions to apply new procedures to crimes committed before the laws were enacted. As an example, introducing plea agreements allowing peripheral defendants to plead guilty to a lesser charge or with a recommendation of a sentence lighter than the maximum may encourage cooperation in locating evidence relating to more important targets. That is what happened in Peru in the context of the Montesinos case (see box 2.3). Because ex post facto legislation or

---

38. The Internet and contact with foreign practitioners can be helpful resources for foreign legislation. Some jurisdictions will publish laws and guidance on government Web sites. See appendix J for some examples. Other resources for legislation include the International Money Laundering Information Network (http://www.imolin.org) and the UNCAC Knowledge Management Consortium and the Legal Library (to be released in late-2010 at http://www.unodc.org).

procedures are likely to face constitutional scrutiny, it is important at the outset that practitioners consider the adequacy and constitutionality of the laws.[39]

2.6 Addressing Legal Issues and Obstacles

In the early phases of an asset recovery case, practitioners will need to assess potential legal issues and obstacles and consider options for addressing them. This will include issues with jurisdiction, immunities enjoyed by suspect officials, statute of limitations, return provisions, and applicable standards of proof.

2.6.1 Jurisdiction

Jurisdiction is the practical authority granted to legal authorities to investigate, prosecute, adjudicate, and enforce legal matters.[40] Before an action is launched, authorities must verify that courts can claim jurisdiction.

In criminal proceedings, territorial jurisdiction over offenses committed by domestic or foreign offenders within the national territory will be critical. Jurisdiction over the person may also allow the authorities to claim jurisdiction for crimes committed by their nationals or incorporated entities in a foreign jurisdiction. In some jurisdictions, the commission of a single element of the crime on national territory will be sufficient, even if other elements were committed in a foreign jurisdiction. Consider, for example, a situation in which the corruption offense was committed in a foreign jurisdiction, but money was laundered using domestic banks and intermediaries. Some authorities will claim jurisdiction even if some peripheral acts related to the offense have "touched" their territory. In the absence of both territorial and personal jurisdiction, the offenses can only be prosecuted by the authorities in the foreign jurisdiction (see section 9.1 in chapter 9 for a more detailed discussion of jurisdictional issues).[41]

A challenge with cases that are multijurisdictional is that a foreign authority with jurisdiction may decide (or be obligated) to start its own case. And it may do so based on the information provided by the requesting jurisdiction during informal assistance and the submission of an MLA request. Because such action could derail a domestic case by alerting the targets or suspending an MLA request, it will be important for practitioners to be aware of the issue, identify when it is applicable, and undertake necessary

---

39. For example, the retroactivity of NCB confiscation laws has been raised in cases in Liechtenstein, Thailand, and the United States. See Theodore S. Greenberg, Linda M. Samuel, Wingate Grant, and Larissa Gray, *Stolen Asset Recovery—A Good Practices Guide to Non-Conviction Based Asset Forfeiture* (Washington, DC: World Bank, 2009), 45–46.
40. UNCAC, art. 42; UNTOC, art. 15; and the United Nations Convention against Narcotic Drugs and Psychotropic Substances, art. 5 oblige states parties to adopt the measures necessary to establish jurisdiction over the offenses, in accordance with the convention.
41. This is true, for example, if a foreign national misappropriates assets from a foreign subsidiary of a state-owned company and if the money laundering activities were conducted in foreign jurisdictions.

coordination to ensure that both cases eventually proceed without difficulty. Chapter 9 provides additional detail on proceedings initiated by foreign authorities.

2.6.2 Immunities Enjoyed by Officials

Immunity from prosecution enables some public officials to avoid prosecution for criminal offenses. In most jurisdictions, immunities incorporated into domestic laws or constitutional provisions are referred to as "national immunities." In addition, there are "international immunities" that apply in all jurisdictions under customary international law and treaties, including functional and personal immunity. Functional immunity is granted to foreign officials performing acts of state (for example, a head of state or head of government, a senior cabinet member, a foreign minister, and a minister of defense); personal immunity shields some foreign officials (particularly heads of state and diplomatic and consular agents) from arrest and criminal, civil, or administrative proceedings (typically, while in office). Functional immunity may protect foreign officials after they leave office, whereas personal immunities normally cease at that time.

If the asset recovery action concerns a head of state, a member of parliament, a judge, or other high-ranking authority, practitioners must consider the immunities enjoyed by these officials.[42] In particular, practitioners should confirm the extent of the immunity (for example, whether it is national or international, functional or personal; and whether it shields the official from criminal, civil, or administrative liability); the possibility that the immunity can be waived; and, if necessary, the opportunity to lodge charges against other individuals implicated in the crimes, including family members, accomplices, and those people involved in the laundering of funds. Some jurisdictions have changed immunity laws to allow prosecution but not actual incarceration of an official.[43] In some cases, a jurisdiction may not recognize the national immunities of another jurisdiction, and it may proceed with a prosecution for money laundering or foreign bribery.[44] Even international immunities have been set aside in cases involving the restraint and seizure of assets held in foreign financial institutions.[45] If the success of criminal proceedings appears to be doubtful, but civil liability can be established, avenues including NCB confiscation and civil proceedings should be explored.

---

42. UNCAC, art. 30 requires states parties to maintain an appropriate balance between immunities and the possibility of effectively investigating, prosecuting, and adjudicating offenses.

43. Law 25.320 of 2000 (Argentina), http://www1.hcdn.gov.ar/dependencias/dip/textos%20actualizados/25320%20Ley%20de%20fueros.pdf.

44. The United Kingdom has prosecuted Nigerian governors for corruption-related money laundering offenses in circumstances where national immunities were in force. See David Chaikin and J. C. Sharman, *Corruption and Money Laundering: A Symbiotic Relationship* (New York: Palgrave Macmillan, 2009), 89–90.

45. In a case involving the bribery of Kazakh officials by an American businessman, the Swiss Federal Tribunal refused to unfreeze $84 million held in Swiss bank accounts, despite Kazakh claims that the money was protected by the doctrine of sovereign immunity. David Chaikin, "International Anti-Money Laundering Laws: Improving External Accountability of Political Leaders," *U4 Brief* 4 (August 2010): 2–3. The funds were eventually confiscated by the United States using NCB confiscation (see footnote 17).

2.6.3 Period of Prescription or Statute of Limitations

In most jurisdictions, it is impossible to initiate criminal or civil proceedings once a certain period of time has passed since the commission of the offense—the "period of prescription" or the "statute of limitations." The time period varies among jurisdictions and with the severity of the offense—that is, the more severe offenses generally allow for lengthier limitation periods.[46] Because the period begins after the commission of the offense, the start of the time period may be delayed or suspended (tolled) in the event of offenses that continue to occur over a period of time.[47] In addition, the clock may be suspended or even restarted by certain events, including investigations by law enforcement, the commencement of formal proceedings, or the flight of the offender. Moreover, in some jurisdictions, the start of the limitation period may be delayed until the offense is discovered or until after the public official has left office.[48] For example, if fictitious invoices and false accounting conceal bribes paid to an intermediary, the statute would not start to run until after the discovery of the fraud. The concept of "discovery" will be mandated under statute or by courts; determining the actual date at which discovery occurred will frequently be adjudicated before the court.

The expiry of the limitation period presents a challenge for practitioners, and it is even more acute in cases of corruption: the misappropriation of assets or evidence of bribery is often not discovered until long after the corrupt official has left office. In addition to obstacles arising from the short duration of the limitation periods and from some jurisdictions' lack of discovery provisions, some jurisdictions require that the predicate offense for money laundering be within the limitation period. In addition to remaining mindful of the applicable limitation periods, officials seeking to recover stolen assets should:

- identify offenses that apply a more favorable limitation period (for example, embezzlement, money laundering, and possession of stolen assets);
- research laws or court decisions that delay the start of a limitation period until discovery of the crime or until the public official has left office, or that suspend the limitation period if assets or the corrupt official are located outside the jurisdiction;
- verify whether specific actions by prosecutors or law enforcement agencies have suspended or restarted the time limitation;

---

46. For example, a prosecution for homicide may have no limitation period, whereas a prosecution for theft may be limited to a five-year period following the offense.

47. Under the "continuing offense doctrine" in the United States, if the offense is continuous, then the practical effect of its ongoing nature is to extend the statute "beyond its stated term." *Toussie v. United States,* 397 U.S. 112, 114, 90 S.Ct. 858, 25 L.Ed.2d 156 (1970). "Conspiracy ... is the prototypical continuing offense." *United States v. Jaynes,* 75 F.3d 1493, 1505 (10th Cir., 1996).

48. In Argentina, for example, the period starts for all defendants after the public official has left office (Criminal Code [Argentina], art. 67). France and the United Kingdom also apply the principle of discovery, as does the United States in NCB cases (Title 19, United States Code, sec. 1621).

- explore all legal avenues—including criminal and NCB confiscation, civil actions, a request that a foreign authority initiate proceedings—to determine the most favorable time limitation[49]; and
- consider continuing the investigation because criminal investigations of an offense for which the statute of limitations has expired may lead to the discovery of another offense that is not statute barred.

2.6.4 Legislative Provisions on Asset Return

In choosing between foreign and domestic criminal proceedings or other avenues, it is important to consider how this decision will influence the amount of assets to be recovered. Embezzled or laundered public funds recovered pursuant to the United Nations Convention against Corruption must be returned to the requesting jurisdiction.[50] In addition, some jurisdictions will return assets where confiscation was the result of the direct enforcement of a foreign order and there is a treaty in place. Assets may also be returned directly to the legitimate owner or jurisdiction harmed by corruption offenses through a court order for damages or compensation. However, if the assets were confiscated outside these parameters—perhaps through a domestic money laundering case conducted by foreign authorities—the amount of return will depend on the sharing agreement in place or the prerogative of the requested jurisdiction.[51] Furthermore, foreign proceedings may be limited to money laundering offenses, and that may be a barrier to confiscating the proceeds from predicate or related offenses, particularly in jurisdictions that only confiscate assets linked to the offenses that form the basis of the confiscation (see section 6.2.2 of chapter 6).

2.6.5 Standards of Proof

Practitioners must also consider whether the evidence is sufficient to meet the standards of proof required for tracing, provisional measures, confiscation, civil actions, or conviction—both domestically and, where applicable, in foreign jurisdictions. Although the applicable standard will vary among jurisdictions, it is generally true that the more intrusive the investigative technique or measure, the higher the evidentiary standard of proof.

---

49. In the United States, the statute of limitations for NCB confiscation—unlike the statute of limitations for criminal prosecutions—begins to run from the discovery of the offense giving rise to the confiscation action; it can be suspended if the property is located beyond U.S. borders (Title 19, United States Code, sec. 1621).

50. UNCAC art. 57(3) requires return of assets to the requesting state party in case of embezzlement or laundering of public funds when executed in accordance with the convention.

51. This was one of the factors that influenced Peru's decision in the Montesinos case to conduct a domestic case to pursue assets in Switzerland. Although it was possible to have Switzerland prosecute parts of the case in Switzerland under drug legislation, asset sharing laws at that time would have allowed only a portion of the funds to be returned to Peru. Following strategy discussions with Switzerland, Peru decided to conduct domestic cases and use MLA and legislative waivers to recover a larger portion of the funds. For additional details, see section 1.3.1 of chapter 1.

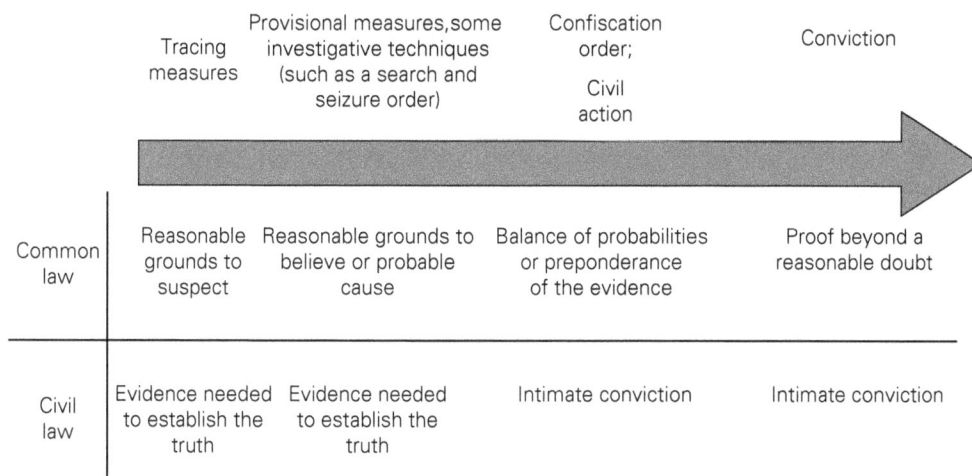

FIGURE 2.1 Standards of Proof

	Tracing measures	Provisional measures, some investigative techniques (such as a search and seizure order)	Confiscation order; Civil action	Conviction
Common law	Reasonable grounds to suspect	Reasonable grounds to believe or probable cause	Balance of probabilities or preponderance of the evidence	Proof beyond a reasonable doubt
Civil law	Evidence needed to establish the truth	Evidence needed to establish the truth	Intimate conviction	Intimate conviction

Source: Authors' illustration.

For practitioners involved in cases that require international cooperation, it will be important to understand that common and civil law jurisdictions differ in the terminology used and the way that the standard of proof is understood. In most common law jurisdictions, a conviction requires proof "beyond a reasonable doubt," and the confiscation (whether NCB or criminal) requires the lower "balance of probabilities" or "preponderance of the evidence" standard that is normally applied in civil (private law) proceedings. In most civil law jurisdictions, the standard of proof is the same for a conviction, a criminal or NCB confiscation, or a finding for the plaintiff in a civil proceeding—namely, an "intimate conviction" of the truth of the evidence. Common law jurisdictions apply a probabilistic approach to assessing the evidence; that is, the quantifiable likelihood of the occurrence of the event expressed as an odds or percentage. Civil law jurisdictions focus more on the judge's subjective impression. Figure 2.1 illustrates the different standards of proof that apply, from investigative techniques to conviction or confiscation.

Practitioners should be aware of these distinctions to ensure that evidence sufficient to meet the applicable standard is provided. Where evidence is insufficient to meet the standard of proof required under one approach, practitioners may have the option to consider another avenue. For example, the inability to establish a criminal conviction "beyond a reasonable doubt" will prevent criminal confiscation. Nevertheless, it may be possible to recover the proceeds and instrumentalities of corruption through a private civil action or through NCB proceedings, domestically or in a foreign jurisdiction, if different standards of proof are applied.

2.7 Identifying All Liable Parties

In most jurisdictions, parties who knowingly facilitated the transfer of proceeds of corruption or who received illicit assets may be held liable under various civil or criminal statutes, including complicity, conspiracy, willful blindness, negligence, and fraudulent abstentions or omissions. This is particularly true for legal entities and their directors, as well as bankers, financial managers, real estate agents, notaries, and lawyers who deliberately fail to make reasonable inquiries. In some jurisdictions, courts may not accept claims of lack of knowledge when consultancy fees are not proportionate to services rendered or are paid to agents with no relevant technical expertise. Other jurisdictions will hold the parent company liable for acts committed by a subsidiary if there is direct involvement by the parent's employees and officers.[52]

Targeting receiving or facilitating parties may have two major advantages: First, it may increase chances of claiming restitution or compensation from entities or individuals other than the corrupt official. Second, it is sometimes possible to obtain information and cooperation from third parties or co-conspirators. However, practitioners must consider the potential disadvantages of complicating the management of the case and diluting resources.

2.8 Specific Considerations in Criminal Cases

Outlined below are a number of additional considerations for practitioners in pursuing criminal cases.

2.8.1 Identifying Applicable Criminal Offenses

Bribery is not the only possible charge to consider in plotting strategy for stolen asset recovery proceedings. Figure 2.2 outlines some of the charges that practitioners should consider lodging.

Corruption frequently involves the commission of several criminal offenses. In selecting the offenses to pursue, practitioners will have to consider the following aspects: the facts of the case; whether the direct or circumstantial evidence fulfills elements of the offenses; the use of procedural aids, such as rebuttable presumptions[53]; the likelihood of conviction; sentencing interests; the public interest; and, where applicable, the ability to obtain foreign assistance and enforcement.

---

52. Working Group on Bribery in International Business Transactions, "Typologies on the Role of Intermediaries in International Business Transactions" (Organisation for Economic Co-operation and Development, 2009).

53. A number of jurisdictions employ rebuttable presumptions that effectively assist the prosecution or plaintiff in meeting the burden of proof. For example, if the prosecution establishes the defendant's involvement in organized crime, the defendant's assets are presumed to be the proceeds of criminal activity (unless the defendant can overcome the presumption). For additional examples, see section 6.3.1 of chapter 6.

FIGURE 2.2   Criminal Charges to Consider

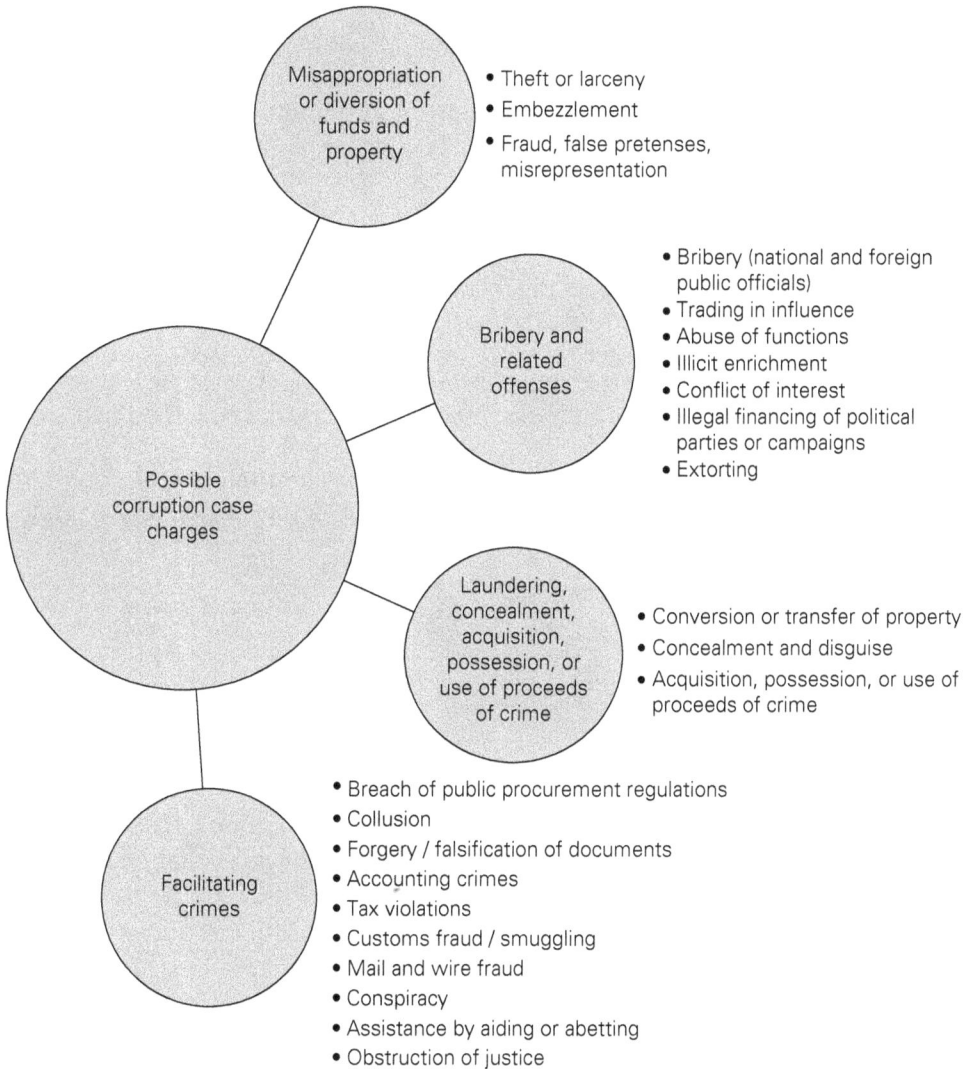

Source: Authors' illustration.
Note: Descriptions of the terms used in this figure may be found in appendix A of this volume.

In addition to the more obvious offenses of corruption, practitioners should consider other offenses that could increase the opportunity for securing a conviction. These offenses include conspiracy, aiding and abetting, receipt or possession of proceeds of crime, or money laundering.[54] Money laundering may be the most effective offense to pursue, particularly in jurisdictions that allow self-laundering and do not require proof

---

54. In France, tax or false accounting offenses, embezzlement, or breach of trust—offenses frequently associated with corrupt activities—may be easier to prove than bribery.

Prosecution of Accounting, Records, and Internal Control Provisions in the United Kingdom and the United States

In *United States v. Siemens*,[a] authorities discovered that bribes were paid to public officials to secure government contracts. Bribes were accounted for as payments to consultants, who subsequently channeled them to the public officials. Siemens and its subsidiaries in Argentina, Bangladesh, and República Bolivariana de Venezuela pleaded guilty to charges of conspiracy and violations of books and records and internal controls provisions in a plea agreement that resulted in a $450 million fine.

In a case involving BAE Systems, the company bribed several public officials to secure arms sales in different jurisdictions. Eventually, BAE Systems reached a settlement with the United Kingdom and the United States.[b] In the United States, the company pleaded guilty to charges of conspiring to make false statements in connection with regulatory filings, and it agreed to pay a $400 million fine and make additional commitments concerning ongoing compliance. In the United Kingdom, the company pleaded guilty to failure to keep reasonably accurate accounting records, and agreed to pay a £30 million (approximately $47 million) financial order.

a. *U.S. Department of Justice. v. Siemens Aktiengesellshaft, Siemens S.A. (Argentina), Siemens Bangladesh Ltd., Siemens S.A. (Venezuela)*, sentencing memorandum Dec. 12, 2008, http://www.siemens.com/press/pool/de/events/2008-12-PK/DOJ2.pdf. See also Title 18, United States Code, sec. 371; and Title 15, United States Code, sec. 78(b)(2)(B), 78m(b)(5), and 78ff(a).
b. "BAE Systems plc," news release, February 5, 2010, http://www.sfo.gov.uk/press-room/latest-press-releases/press-releases-2010/bae-systems-plc.aspx. See also *U.S. v. BAE Systems*, sentencing memorandum February 22, 2010, No. 1:10-cr-00035 (D.D.C. 2010) (U.S.), http://www.justice.gov/criminal/pr/documents/03-01-10%20bae-sentencing-memo.pdf.

of all elements of the predicate offense to obtain a conviction.[55] Box 2.4 offers examples from the United Kingdom and the United States. Practitioners should be aware that such decisions may affect proceedings in foreign jurisdictions, and they should try to coordinate with foreign counterparts.

The offense of illicit enrichment has been a particularly useful tool for prosecuting corrupt officials in a number of jurisdictions, such as Argentina, Brazil, and Colombia.[56] It penalizes public officials for any significant increase in their declared assets that is not reasonably corroborated by their lawful income. Effectively, it eases the burden on the prosecution, which otherwise would be required to establish the various elements of a corruption offense (that is, the occurrence of a corrupt act, derivation of a benefit, and so forth). Some jurisdictions will not recognize illicit enrichment as a criminal offense, but will have incorporated it into civil or administrative legislation.[57] Where illicit

---

55. In Belgium, defendants involved in financial transactions may be convicted of money laundering if there is sufficient evidence that they knew that assets were of illicit origin. Prosecutors do not have to establish the elements of the predicate offense.

56. UNCAC art. 20 and Inter-American Convention against Corruption art. 9 require states parties to consider adopting provisions.

57. Some jurisdictions that have illicit enrichment as a criminal offense will use civil avenues to pursue recovery of the assets.

enrichment is criminalized, practitioners must be aware that its use may introduce obstacles to international cooperation in jurisdictions that do not have the offense because of a lack of dual criminality (see section 7.4.2 of chapter 7).

2.8.2 Anticipating Evidentiary Challenges

Practitioners will need to consider the challenges in establishing the specific elements of the offense to the required standard of proof (see examples of these challenges in box 2.5). In some jurisdictions, there may be rebuttable presumptions that will assist

---

BOX 2.5	Examples of Challenges in Establishing the Elements of the Offense

Bribery and trafficking in influence. May require proof that the bribe was offered, promised, or paid as part of a "corruption pact" (agreement on terms of the bribe and quid pro quo in advance) between the briber and the public official. Securing this proof will be difficult if the investigation is conducted well after the fact. In addition, when bribes are paid overseas by subsidiaries or intermediaries, prosecutors may need to prove that managers or directors at headquarters knew or intended that the subsidiary or the intermediary would commit this crime. Defendants may claim that employees who paid bribes to foreign public officials acted in their personal capacity, flouting corporate guidelines.

Illicit enrichment. Will necessitate an assessment of an individual's concealed assets or income.

Theft or embezzlement. May not apply to real property, services, or intangible assets.

Money laundering. Usually requires proof of the commission of a predicate offense, and proof of transactions or schemes organized to conceal or disguise the illegal origin, ownership, or control of assets.

Forgery or falsification. May require evidence that the falsified documents have legal significance or consequences. Other documents are frequently not considered to be subject to forgery. In certain jurisdictions, accounting offenses only apply to published accounting statements.

Criminal liability of legal entities. May not apply, depending on the jurisdiction or the specific offense.

Fraud. When committed over a long period, the activity may involve hundreds or even thousands of individual offenses. Prosecution of such offenses can be cumbersome or difficult. Use of sample or representative charges may have adverse consequences on related confiscation proceedings. For additional information on use of representative charges, see section 6.2.2 of chapter 6.

For additional explanation of these offenses, see appendix A of this handbook.

prosecutors in establishing these elements, whether for the offense or during the confiscation stage (see section 6.3 of chapter 6).

A review of the challenges relating to different offenses should be conducted on a case-by-case basis. As an example, illicit enrichment may be easier to prove than bribery in the absence of written documentation of bribes and quid pro quo during the course of the preliminary investigation.[58] On the other hand, if practitioners uncover such evidence, bribery will become the easier offense to prove—especially given that illicit enrichment still requires the prosecution to gather information on the lifestyle and assets of the defendant.

2.8.3 Inability to Obtain a Conviction

In most jurisdictions, it is impossible to adjudicate a criminal case in the absence of the defendant, such as in cases of flight or death. In a few civil law jurisdictions, it may be possible to proceed with a criminal trial in absentia if the person is a fugitive. However, convictions in these cases may not be final because due process requires that court decisions be subject to appeal by the fugitive if he or she is apprehended. In addition, some confiscation laws contain absconding provisions that permit the law to continue to operate, even in the event of the flight or death of the defendant.

If the defendant is a fugitive, authorities should consider obtaining extradition of the fugitive in the context of multilateral and bilateral conventions or the legislation of the jurisdiction to which the fugitive has fled (or both). Extradition can be a very long and frustrating process involving numerous court decisions and appeals to higher courts. In addition, if some of the criminal offenses that are the basis of the request are denied by the extraditing country, the specialty principle forces the requesting country to cease the investigation or prosecution of these offenses. Alternative options include filing a complaint with the foreign authorities (leading to criminal or NCB confiscation in the foreign jurisdiction) or initiating domestic NCB confiscation proceedings. If the defendant is deceased, authorities may consider a private civil action against the estate of the decedent (in domestic or foreign courts) or domestic or foreign NCB confiscation.

The authorities may not have sufficient evidence to meet the standard of proof required to establish a conviction. In these circumstances, practitioners should explore whether there may be sufficient evidence to proceed through a private civil action or NCB confiscation (see section 2.6.5 above concerning standards of proof).

2.9 Implementing a Case Management System

To increase efficiency, accountability, and transparency, it will be important that proper policies and procedures are in place to ensure that offenders are appropriately charged,

---

58. Note that prosecution for illicit enrichment may cause difficulties in meeting the dual criminality requirement for MLA in some jurisdictions. See section 7.4.2 of chapter 7 for additional information.

that evidence is properly gathered and passed from law enforcement to prosecutors to courts, and that the due process rights of the offender are respected. Noncompliance with confidentiality or due process requirements may lead to nullification of the domestic case, loss of credibility, and failure to obtain international cooperation from foreign jurisdictions. Some examples of important policies and procedures are discussed below.

2.9.1 Strategic Planning and Leadership

Whereas strategies must be set at the beginning of the case, authorities should ensure that decision making is an ongoing and fluid process. Unanticipated difficulties or challenges may arise at any moment in the asset recovery effort and may call for new investigative methods or the exploration of other avenues. To ensure maximum flexibility, frequent reviews of the case should bring together policy makers, law enforcement officers, prosecutors, investigating magistrates, asset managers, and representatives of other participating agencies. These meetings should be based on precise, updated, and accurate reports or records detailing recent decisions and their rationale; and time should be devoted to anticipating potential challenges or opportunities. Many jurisdictions have found it useful to have one case manager appointed—a person who is responsible for coordinating meetings, making final decisions, ensuring resources, and so forth.

2.9.2 Timing and Coordination

The case should be planned to ensure that investigative measures and MLA requests are coordinated with provisional measures and arrests to prevent the dissipation or movement of assets or the flight of a target. Where assets will be seized, asset management issues must be assessed as part of the planning process. Mechanisms should also be in place to provide for the safety of key witnesses, law enforcement officials, attorneys, or judges concerned with high-profile cases. This coordination is particularly important in the initial phase of the investigation when gathering basic information, requesting documents, interviewing witnesses, and submitting MLA requests may alert potential targets and give them a chance to destroy or conceal documentary evidence, influence key witnesses, move or hide assets, gain political support, and flee to foreign jurisdictions.

That risk should be assessed constantly and minimized by careful choices of covert investigative techniques in the early phases of the investigation—for example, physical and electronic surveillance, monitoring of mail and trash, or use of informants. When more overt techniques are needed (such as searches of houses or businesses, orders for seizure or production of documents, or interviews of targets and witnesses), it will be important to consider coordinating those activities with the timing of arrests and restraint or seizure of assets. For additional information on these issues, see sections 3.3 (investigative measures), 3.1 and 4.3 (timing provisional measures), 4.2.2 and chapter 5 (asset management).

2.9.3 File Organization and Report Writing

Files should be organized to ensure that deadlines relevant to the case are met: for example, charges are laid within the prescription period and extensions of provisional measures, preventive detention of targets, or other temporary remedies are in place. The case file should include assets targeted for recovery, graphics demonstrating the flow of financial transactions, explanations for calculations of criminal proceeds (made in accordance with domestic legislation), criminal records of targets, and summaries of testimonial and documentary evidence.

Evidence should be numbered, logged, and stored in a secured location, along with records of the chain of custody between seizure and storage. Although these preparations are very time consuming and may appear to impede the development of the case, they are necessary to ensure the integrity of the evidence or chain of custody.

Report writing is an important aspect of criminal investigation work that is often ignored or given lower priority. In asset recovery investigations, however, report writing takes on an even greater importance because the investigations can be lengthy, complex, and multijurisdictional. Accurate, timely, and concise reports will assist, for example, in drafting the necessary background information to meet evidentiary requirements in MLA requests for evidence. It is imperative that practitioners document their findings periodically throughout the entire investigation, as well as after significant events. Reports should be written in a clear and concise manner, preferably on the same day as the event being described; and should include all relevant information and events. They should be reviewed and approved by a supervisor as soon as possible.

2.9.4 Addressing Media Inquiries

Corruption cases, particularly those involving high-profile officials, are likely to attract substantial media attention. Practitioners must be prepared to deal with these inquiries; otherwise, the inadvertent release of confidential information is likely to have disastrous consequences on a case.

In most jurisdictions, responsibility for addressing the media will lie with the attorney general or director of a relevant government agency (for example, public affairs personnel or the department of justice). Typically, a senior official in the local office or, in large cases, a senior member of the team is designated as the media contact point. These individuals should be properly trained and familiar with applicable guidance and procedures (if available), such as ways of addressing the media through press releases or conferences, the types of information that may be disclosed in an ongoing investigation, and coordination with national counterparts on issues of national or regional importance. In some cases, practitioners have found it helpful to designate a contact point for procedural (not substantive) information—an individual who can explain how the system of justice operates. Ultimately, care must be taken to avoid any statement that would prejudice a legal proceeding against a target.

3. Securing Evidence and Tracing Assets

One of the biggest challenges in an asset confiscation case is producing the evidence that links the assets to the criminal activities (property-based confiscation) or proving that assets are a benefit derived from an offense committed by the target (value-based confiscation).[59] To establish this link (also referred to as the "nexus" or a "paper trail"), practitioners must identify and trace assets or "follow the money" until the link with the offense or location of the assets can be determined.

However, it is often the case that the assets have been moved around the world, using schemes that involve offshore centers, corporate vehicles, and a variety of financial transactions in an effort to launder the funds and obscure this paper trail. In addition, cases are often document-intensive "paper cases" that are time-consuming and complicated and that require multiple skills. These skills include the abilities to understand what information can be obtained from financial institutions; obtain relevant information through traditional investigative techniques; analyze bank statements, business records, financial documents, and contracts; pierce the corporate veil to determine the ultimate beneficial owners; assemble corroborative evidence through interviews of witnesses or targets; coordinate with foreign authorities; and organize the information in a comprehensive and coherent manner.[60]

The purpose of this chapter is to introduce some of the techniques that practitioners can use to trace assets and analyze financial data, and to secure reliable and admissible evidence for asset confiscation cases. The techniques discussed may also be helpful in gathering evidence to prove the elements of the offenses that are under investigation.

3.1 Introducing a Plan and Important Considerations

Experience has demonstrated that it is important to trace assets at the early stages of an investigation, simultaneously with the investigation into the offenses of corruption, money laundering, and so forth. Establishing a framework or investigative plan is an important first step in navigating tracing efforts.

---

59. For a discussion of property-based and value-based confiscation systems, see chapter 6.
60. Some jurisdictions have created specialized units of investigators that trace assets while other investigators focus on gathering evidence of the criminal offenses or unlawful conduct. These groups typically work in close cooperation, and the unit tracing assets only performs actions that will not compromise the criminal investigation.

The overall plan or approach often depends on whether the preliminary evidence points to corrupt activities, money laundering, or both. For corruption, law enforcement officials investigate the corrupt activities and then follow the money trail to identify and recover the proceeds and instrumentalities of crime. In the case of money laundering, practitioners begin by analyzing financial transactions to link them to corruption or other offenses. Specific steps are likely to include the identification of persons, companies, and assets involved in the case and the connections between them; and an analysis of the assets and financial flows.

Particularly in large cases involving significant activity and volumes of documentation, practitioners will find it helpful to set priorities and focus on specific types of documents or accounts or on a particular time frame. For example, securing, obtaining, and analyzing bank account documentation that can be interpreted and mapped out easily is most useful in money laundering cases where practitioners need to show links between individuals and companies and to understand the money flow. However, in the case of an individual living off cash bribes, the more important evidence may be witness statements of business associates, employees, and neighbors; title information; and tax records.

There are also a few important considerations to keep in mind when planning and conducting an asset recovery investigation. First, when tracing assets through the financial sector, it is important to remember that proceeds of corruption may be commingled with other assets not linked to the offense, may change form, and may flow through various channels. Even if such proceeds change form (for example, $1 million is deposited into one account and portions are subsequently wired to different bank accounts or used to purchase property), the proceeds may be confiscated.[61]

Second, experience has demonstrated that a corrupt official does not hold assets or bank accounts in his or her own name. Instead, assets are held by other individuals or companies to disguise the official's role as the beneficial owner—the natural person who ultimately owns or controls the assets or the bank accounts. It will be important for practitioners to look into the assets and bank accounts of those potentially involved, including

- relatives, business associates, or close associates;
- intermediaries or "straw men"—individuals who are duped or willingly participate in shielding the corrupt official by holding an asset or opening and managing an account, often for a small fee; and
- corporate vehicles, including corporations, trusts, limited liability partnerships, and foundations. For a list and description of some corporate vehicles, see appendix B.[62]

---

61. In this regard, it is important that jurisdictions have broad definitions of "assets" or "property" and of the "proceeds of crime" included in their legislation. See United Nations Convention against Corruption (UNCAC), art. 2(d); and see section 6.2.1 of chapter 6 for a discussion of commingled assets.

62. The Stolen Asset Recovery (StAR) Initiative is conducting a study into the misuse of corporate vehicles in grand corruption cases (both in the perpetration of the corruption and the laundering of the proceeds)

In the case of assets held by financial institutions, some financial institutions will be able to provide the name of the *natural person* who beneficially owns the account.[63] However, not all banks will obtain this information, especially when a chain of legal persons is used to disguise the ultimate beneficial owner. They may identify shareholders or other parties involved; but these may not be the ultimate beneficial owner. Even when a beneficial owner is identified by the person opening the account, this may have been a false statement intended to hide the corrupt official. Given these limits—and the fact that many other assets do not list beneficial ownership information—practitioners will need to ensure that the investigation takes steps to determine the actual assets and companies that are beneficially owned by the targets.

Finally, practitioners should continually assess whether it is possible and practical to institute provisional measures to seize or restrain assets discovered in the course of their tracing efforts. In some cases, they may decide to keep the account open and monitor the activity to discover new leads. However, where there is a risk that the target will be tipped off and subsequently dissipate or move assets, the implementation of provisional measures should be considered. For a discussion of provisional measures, see chapter 4.

3.2 Creating a Subject Profile

In all investigations it is essential that practitioners collect and record all basic information related to the investigation targets. Practitioners should collect and record information that fully identifies the targets and notes any aliases used by those targets. For easy reference, all of the information should be maintained in an orderly fashion within the case folder. Box 3.1 provides a checklist of pertinent information that the practitioner should try to gather in the early stages of the investigation.

3.3 Obtaining Financial Data and Other Evidence

As targets are identified, practitioners will need to obtain information and financial data, and to ensure that reliable and admissible evidence is secured for trial. Depending on the investigation plan, the financial data may include all assets and liabilities and all income and expenses of the targets and their businesses. Documents and other leads will need to be gathered from a range of sources, including the Internet and other publicly available sources; government agencies; financial institutions, including e-banking facilities;

---

to assist policy makers in designing relevant national policies. The expected publication date is early 2011. The study will be available at http://www.worldbank.org/star.

63. The international community has adopted standards requiring financial institutions to conduct customer due diligence to identify their customers and beneficial owners, obtain information on the nature of the business relationships, and use enhanced due diligence in relationships with politically exposed persons (PEPs)—senior public officials, their families, and their close associates. See UNCAC, art. 52; and recommendations 5 and 6 of the Financial Action Task Force (FATF) 40+9 Recommendations. Unfortunately, these standards are not always in place. See Theodore S. Greenberg, Larissa Gray, Delphine Schantz, Carolin Gardner, and Michael Lathem, *Politically Exposed Persons: Preventive Measures for the Banking Sector* (Washington, DC: World Bank, 2010), 7, 13.

Checklist for Collection of Basic Information

Practitioners should collect and maintain the following information during the early stages of an investigation:

- Date and place of birth (include aliases); copies of birth certificates, passports, and national identity cards.
- Names and birth dates of spouses, children, both parents (and new partners, if divorced, separated, or widowed), siblings, spouses of siblings, immediate relatives (uncles, aunts, cousins, grandparents, grandchildren).
- Relevant telephone numbers (business, home, mobile), e-mail address, and contact details of any other Internet or social network communication. In some jurisdictions, it may be possible to obtain subscriber information from the service provider.
- Recent photographs of all targets and associates (preferably government-issued identification).
- A fingerprint card.
- Results of a criminal record search.
- Results of public-source searches on targets and associates, using Internet search engines, social networking sites, local media reports, and libraries.
- Information from other government agencies (see section 3.3.2 of this chapter), especially
  ○ land, vehicle, and utility information;
  ○ business records;
  ○ court records;
  ○ tax records;
  ○ border crossings and customs declarations;
  ○ immigration records;
  ○ salary statements (from a relevant government employer, if applicable); and
  ○ asset and income declarations.
- Real estate records, including purchase agreements, mortgages, loan applications, and appraisals.
- Information identifying banks or bank accounts and other entities that may hold business records. Consider retention orders (see also box 3.6).

money service providers; law and accounting firms; trust and company service providers; real estate agents; art dealers; business competitors; travel and other reward programs; businesses, relatives, employees, and associates of the targets; and the targets themselves.

Various investigative techniques (described below) are used to assist practitioners in these efforts.[64] The techniques provided are examples of those used around the world,

---

64. This section is not meant to be an exhaustive how-to manual for each technique. More detailed how-to guides may be available online and through such public sources as libraries and bookstores. In addition, many agencies—both domestic and foreign—have customized guides that they are willing to share.

but not all techniques are available or permitted in every jurisdiction. Furthermore, jurisdictions will differ in which techniques require judicial authorization or the application of a special procedure (typically for coercive measures, such as search warrants, bank account information, and electronic surveillance) and which do not (typically noncoercive measures, such as obtaining publicly available information and intelligence from other government agencies).

It is imperative that practitioners determine which techniques are authorized by law and that all legal requirements, policies, and procedures are followed. Respect for the rule of law and the due process rights of the accused will also be essential, particularly if international cooperation is being sought. Deviating from legal requirements, policies and procedures or infringing on the rights of the accused can be catastrophic to a case: it may lead to the invalidation and inadmissibility of evidence discovered through the use of that technique—and possibly the entire investigation. In cases requiring international cooperation, many jurisdictions will refuse to provide mutual legal assistance (MLA), if they perceive that the rights of the accused have not been respected (see section 7.4.4 in chapter 7). For information on these basic rights, see the United Nations International Covenant on Civil and Political Rights and the Universal Declaration of Human Rights.

With regard to the selection of a particular technique, this should be assessed as part of the overall investigative plan or framework. Typically, the practitioner should use the most basic investigative and non-intrusive techniques (for example, simple data checks) before implementing more complex techniques (such as wiretaps). In addition, practitioners should use covert techniques (surveillance, public information searches, information from other government agencies, and trash runs) before moving to overt techniques (search warrants) to avoid tipping off the targets. Practitioners must also keep in mind that the use of one technique may provide leads or information that will become grounds to take additional measures. A trash run or a search of a business or residence may reveal documents that link the targets to bank accounts; and these facts can be used to support a subsequent order to obtain bank account documentation because they demonstrate a nexus between the targets and the bank accounts. Physical surveillance may reveal a potential gatekeeper to be investigated; and documents obtained through a production order on a bank may reveal the names of bank officials or individuals involved in a transaction who may be able to provide additional leads if interviewed. For an example of how investigative techniques can be used in practice, see box 3.2.

3.3.1 A Return to the Basics

A technique to use at the outset will be the traditional five-question maxim: who, what, where, when, and how (see figure 3.1.). Even though asset recovery cases may be complicated paper cases that differ from traditional law enforcement investigations, the techniques used to resolve a fraud case can help unravel a complex stolen asset recovery case.

BOX 3.2   Tracing and Recovering Assets—Efforts in the United Kingdom

Law enforcement officers in the United Kingdom became aware of allegations of corruption and misappropriation of assets by former Plateau State (Nigeria) Governor Joshua Dariye, and they suspected that assets could be located in the United Kingdom. Through the following investigative techniques, they were able to trace and link the assets to the offense:

1. **Technique.** Investigators conducted public record searches for information on Dariye in the United Kingdom (through property, vehicle, and corporate registries); and sought intelligence on Dariye from other governmental agencies, including the FIU.

   Result. No link to Dariye was found.

2. **Technique.** Investigators identified Dariye's family and associates and checked for a nexus to the United Kingdom.

   Result. Investigators discovered that Dariye's children were attending private school in the United Kingdom.

3. **Technique.** Investigators made inquiries to the relevant bank (a permitted authority of financial investigators).

   Result. Investigations revealed that Dariye operated a Barclaycard account, and that the account was being paid off each month through the bank account of Joyce Oyebanjo. Oyebanjo was effectively Dariye's banker in the United Kingdom who paid off fees and utilities on behalf of Dariye, including the fees paid to a private school for his two children.

4. **Technique.** Investigators obtained a production order to access the school files.

   Result. Investigators confirmed that school fees were paid by Joyce Oyebanjo.

5. **Technique.** Investigators searched publicly available information and other governmental agencies for information on Oyebanjo. They also obtained a production order for her bank accounts.

   Result. Oyebanjo, employed as a housing officer in the United Kingdom, was found to have 15 bank accounts with funds totaling roughly £1.5 million (approximately $2.3 million), and £2 million (approximately $3.1 million) worth of real property. Furthermore, she was managing one of Dariye's properties in Regents Park Plaza, a property purchased in the name of "Joseph Dagwan" and paid for by the Plateau State Ecological Fund through various companies.

(continued next page)

BOX 3.2 *(continued)*

6. **Technique.** Investigators made credit reference checks, and those revealed bank accounts operated by the targets. Assets were traced from the bank account to other bank accounts, property, and vehicles. Production and search orders were used to obtain additional information and to trace assets.

   Result. Investigators discovered that Dariye had one bank account registered to a particular address in London. Examination of Dariye's and Oyebanjo's bank accounts revealed large electronic credits from various banks in Nigeria.

7. **Technique.** Investigators used a production order to obtain the conveyancing solicitor's file for the London address.

   Result. The file revealed that property had been purchased using a false name, and had been paid for from a Nigerian company's London-based bank account.

8. **Technique.** An MLA letter of request was sent to Nigeria to determine the origins of the funds received.

   Result. It was established that an ecological grant obtained by Dariye had been diverted and concealed in his own company bank account, with the assistance of bank staff. The funds were diverted to a company and associated bank account set up by Dariye in Nigeria and subsequently transferred to London for his use. The Nigerian company that purchased the London property was also linked to the ecological grant theft because the company had received £100 million (approximately $157 million) of the stolen funds. The company had paid £400,000 (approximately $626,800) for the London property after Dariye had authorized a Plateau State government contract for the installation of £37 million (approximately $58 million) worth of television equipment in the Plateau State.

This example illustrates that it is imperative for practitioners to "know their subjects" and to identify all close relatives, business associates, and other persons who could assist a target in stealing funds and moving them into foreign jurisdictions. Practitioners must use all techniques available (for example, other government agencies, public sources, and coercive measures), for they never know the origins of the next lead.

FIGURE 3.1   Five Effective Questions to Use in an Investigation

WHO?	WHAT?	WHERE?
Who stole the money? Who was involved (co-conspirators)?	What was stolen?	Where was it stolen? Where did it go?

WHEN?	HOW?
When did the event occur?	How much was stolen? How were the assets stolen? How were the assets moved? How do we get them back?

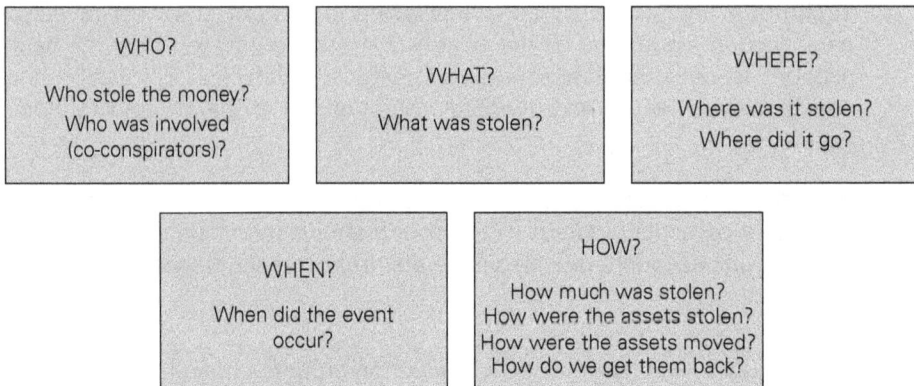

Source: Authors' illustration.

3.3.2 Information from Public Sources and Other Government Agencies

Information from public sources and other government agencies can provide useful background information on targets, their family members, associates, and companies; and can assist in identifying assets and potential witnesses, and in compiling the subject profile (see section 3.2) and financial profile (see section 3.5).

Public information can be accessed on the Internet, using search engines and social networking sites (including archived information), and from subscription Web sites or databases, media sources, libraries, and some government agencies. See appendix J for a list of some Web sites. Practitioners may consider subscribing to commercial database providers who hold relevant information.

Data from other government agencies (figure 3.2) also should be explored, including the following agencies:

- **Financial intelligence unit (FIU).** The FIU is an important source of financial intelligence because of its role as the national center for the collection, analysis, and dissemination of information regarding money laundering and the financing of terrorism. See box 2.1 in chapter 2 for a description of how FIUs can be important sources for initiating and investigating an asset recovery case.[65] FIUs typically collect suspicious transaction or activity reports (STRs) from reporting financial institutions, and it is often useful to review these reports. Some FIUs also collect and maintain currency transaction reports (CTRs), sometimes

---

65. For more information on FIUs, see International Monetary Fund/World Bank Group, *Financial Intelligence Units: An Overview* (Washington, DC, 2004).

Immigration and border-crossing information

Utility information

Customs declaration forms(s)

Government audit results

Financial intelligence unit reports

Information from government agencies

Asset and income declarations

Tax records

Land and vehicle ownership

Business information and records

Court records

Civil records

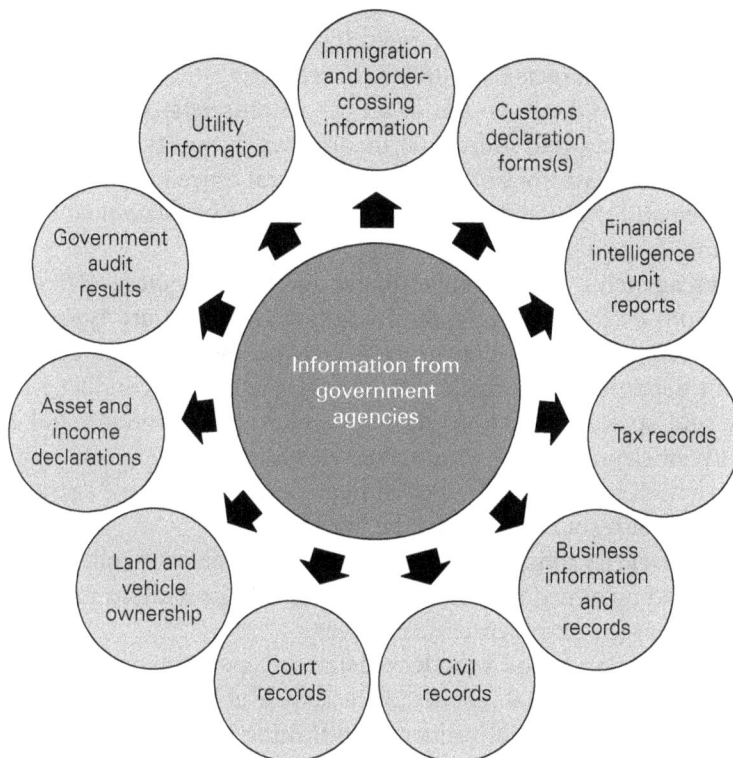

Source: Authors' illustration.

referred to as "reports on transactions above a specified amount." Most FIUs will conduct an analysis of all STRs that are submitted (referred to as an "intelligence report"), a process that can include a thorough assessment of the individuals and/ or businesses linked to the STR. See the sample FIU report in appendix C. Intelligence is also shared among FIUs through the Egmont Group. These are all sources of data that may yield intelligence that is helpful in reconstructing the money trail. Where permitted,[66] practitioners submitting a request to the FIU should include the following:

– any STR or CTR filed in relation to targets of the investigation;
– any STR or CTR filed in relation to businesses linked to the targets;
– any STR or CTR filed in relation to associates/relatives of the targets;
– any related intelligence reports of possible criminal conduct (some FIUs are not permitted to provide information in the absence of an STR).

---

66. In some jurisdictions, the FIU is not permitted to provide a copy of the STR or CTR to law enforcement. In these circumstances, the intelligence report (if drafted) is usually available on request and contains much of the same information.

- **Immigration and border-crossing authorities.** Obtain copies of forms or any other relevant documents that indicate targets' border crossings.
- **Customs.** Obtain copies of any customs declarations forms that indicate the cross-border movements of the targets. If there is a cash declaration requirement, check to see if the targets have declared currency.
- **Tax authorities.** Obtain copies of all tax records related to the targets of the investigation, including individual income tax, property tax, and business tax records. The tax assessor's office or the cadastral office may also provide ownership information, a legal description of the property, a statement of the property value, and the purchase history of the property.
- **Auditing agencies.** State or government auditing agencies (referred to in some jurisdictions as the "Office of the Inspector General") are typically mandated with providing an independent and objective review of the operations of the government department to which they are assigned. They conduct investigations, audits, and special projects to detect fraud and misconduct; and to promote integrity, efficiency, economy, and effectiveness in the department operations. If the corruption has involved a government department, these agencies may have information or resources to assist the investigation.
- **Ethics or integrity office.** The office that is responsible for collecting and analyzing asset and income declarations may be able to provide copies of declarations filed by the targets and their close relatives.[67]
- **Real property (land) and vehicle registries.** Depending on the jurisdiction, the city, county, or provincial records office may be able to provide data confirming ownership (deeds) for real property (indicating buyer and seller), liens on the property, mortgage(s), property tax, tax assessments, recent sales, and building permits. Vehicle records offices may provide title information and summary data on the vehicle at transfer or sale dates.
- **Corporate or business registries and licensing boards.** Business registries and regulatory boards can provide information that helps identify the assets of targets and their associates. Records may also identify possible co-conspirators. Some registries will provide the practitioner with ownership information; names of agent of record (typically a lawyer or accountant), shareholders, directors, and beneficial owners; and company financial statements. This search should be conducted for all types of businesses—sole proprietorships, partnerships, limited liability partnerships, and corporations.
- **Civil records repositories.** Civil registries can provide information about current and previous spouses (marriage and divorce records), siblings, parents, grandparents, and other relatives.
- **Court records repositories.** A check of court records can reveal if any of the targets have been involved in prior court matters. If so, review any plea agreements and the transcripts of any testimony, decision, or sentencing hearing for information on assets or for other relevant information. Also, check courts that

---

67. For more information on asset and income declarations, see Ruxandra Burdescu, Gary J. Reid, Stuart Gilman, and Stephanie Trapnell, *Stolen Asset Recovery—Income and Asset Declarations: Tools and Trade-offs* (Washington, DC: StAR Initiative, conference edition released November 2009).

may not be linked to law enforcement databases, including bankruptcy, civil, or family courts.

- **Utilities.** Examine the utility bills for all residences and businesses identified (including electric, water, telephone, cable or satellite, sewerage, and garbage) to determine the recipient of the utility bill, method of payment, the person or entity that executes the payments, and subscriber information. Request a general search of targets and associates to identify links to other addresses.

3.3.3 Physical Surveillance

Physical surveillance is the covert observation of investigation targets to gather information about them. Recording the movements of targets of an investigation can be useful for identifying the following: possible witnesses; co-conspirators; real property or other assets; lawyers, bankers, or accountants possibly involved in facilitating the laundering of corrupt proceeds; businesses; patterns of conduct; and other forms of intelligence that could be vital to the investigation. However, physical surveillance is not without risk. A target might realize that he or she is under surveillance, regardless of the quality and expertise of the surveillance team. The lead practitioner, in consultation with the team, must determine if the rewards outweigh the risks.

A successful surveillance operation requires adequate human resources and equipment. For example, radios or mobile phones are important for notifying other team members of the location and actions of a target; and recording devices can be used to record events or keep notes of movements or of other individuals contacted. In addition, an experienced lead practitioner should be assigned to assemble, coordinate, and supervise the surveillance. Team leaders will determine the size of the team and the format and locations of the surveillance; and they will prepare presurveillance briefings to explain the assignment to the team members, provide continuity at shift changes, and advise of any personal security issues. They will be responsible for making strategic decisions, such as choosing the type of surveillance (for example, stationary, mobile vehicle, or mobile foot), deciding whether to follow other targets encountered during the surveillance, and drafting a report of the significant events that occurred during the operation. Although surveillance is a useful technique, cost considerations may favor an intermittent approach because the cost of a 24-hours/7-days-a-week surveillance is usually prohibitive.

3.3.4 Trash Runs

Conducting trash runs involves looking through a target's garbage for relevant information, such as discarded bank statements, names of business associates, correspondence, bills, travel receipts, and so forth. In turn, this evidence can be used to support applications for search warrants by showing a nexus between a target and other individuals or assets.

As with other investigative techniques, practitioners will first need to determine whether this is permissible at law and identify any limitations because jurisdictions have different standards of "rights to privacy" as they relate to trash.[68] Where permitted, the trash run should be conducted at all the residences and businesses of the targets. Practitioners may focus on banking information; bills; any documents related to financial assets; or any documents related to businesses, other persons, companies, lawyers, accountants, or credit cards; and they should be sure to document the evidence collected (for example, date, time, officers involved, document number). Trash inspections should be conducted routinely on all other family, spouses, former spouses, associates, lawyers, accountants, and other businesspeople linked to the targets.

3.3.5 Mail Cover

Mail cover is the process by which a record is made of any data appearing on the outside cover of sealed or unsealed mail (for example, the return address and the cancellation date and country of the postage stamp) or of the contents of any unsealed mail. Mail covers can be excellent sources of leads to the location of assets. Mail received from a bank, law firm, company, or accounting firm, for example, alerts practitioners to potential sources of information on the assets owned by a target.

Where permitted, jurisdictions often allow mail covers without a warrant because the recipient of the letter has little to no reasonable expectation of privacy for the contents on the outside of the letter or parcel. Most jurisdictions require a search warrant or some other form of legal authority to open and read sealed letters and parcels. Operationally, it will be important for practitioners to consider the nexus between the target and the sender of each letter, record accurately all data on the outside of an envelope or package, log the date and time when the mail cover was conducted, and maintain a copy of the record in the case file.

3.3.6 Interviews

Interviews are an essential element of any investigation and tremendously important in an asset recovery case.[69] Statements can corroborate or clarify the information derived from documentary evidence, reveal new leads, or identify new financial documents. Important sources may include any complainants; the business associates, relatives, neighbors, employees, or other associates of the targets; business competitors; financial institution employees and other sources that have been in contact with the targets; and the targets themselves. It will be important to identify and interview any straw men involved in the case. These individuals have taken substantial risk with little reward,

---

68. In the United States, for example, there is no expectation of privacy over trash that has been set on the curb outside a house for pickup by sanitation engineers, so practitioners may collect and inspect it. However, there is an expectation of privacy if the trash is in a bin adjacent to the house, and a search warrant will be required. On the other hand, trash runs are not permitted in Ukraine.

69. Some jurisdictions make distinctions between interviews and interrogations, defining an interview as questioning of non-targets of the investigation and an interrogation as the questioning of investigation targets. In this section, we will use the term "interview" to include both forms of questioning. Practitioners must ensure that proper protections are afforded witnesses, experts, victims, whistle-blowers, and cooperating targets. See, for example, UNCAC art. 32, 33, and 37.

and they may prefer to inform authorities about the people they are hiding rather than be implicated in a scheme. Practitioners will need to be familiar with the laws related to conducting interviews with targets and non-targets, especially when working with authorities in foreign jurisdictions.[70] Some jurisdictions, for example, require that all statements be taken through a formal hearing. Others permit a range of interview options, such as routine questioning of witnesses by law enforcement (no formal or verbatim record), written statements, video or audio recordings of statements with warning to the interviewee, or recorded statements under oath.

Thorough preparation is essential to conduct a successful interview, including having a complete understanding of all the evidence, the targets, associates, timeline of events, and information already gathered in the investigation. A practitioner may prepare questions to cover the information desired; during the interview, however, the practitioner must be flexible and focus on the responses of the targets, not on the preplanned questions.[71] Because targets may attempt to communicate with one another and agree on a common version of events or influence the testimony of a witness, practitioners may take (or request from competent judicial authorities) appropriate measures to ensure that the targets are discouraged, prohibited, or prevented from communicating with one another or with witnesses prior to the interviews. In addition, the interview location selected should be one that offers the fewest distractions, provides discretion, and is most likely to solicit open responses (for example, a residence, police station, or place of business). The number of interviewers present should be limited to two, if possible.

3.3.7 Account Monitoring Orders

An account monitoring order is an *ex parte* order by the court (or the investigating magistrate in some jurisdictions) specifying that a particular financial institution must provide account information covering a specified period of time for the account identified in the order. The information must be given to an appropriate officer in the manner and at or by specified times stated in the order.[72] The order allows for real-time financial surveillance of the ongoing transactions in an account that practitioners can use to establish typologies of activity and identify new accounts. It can also be a means to establish sufficient grounds to ask for an order to disclose, restrain, or search and seize assets.[73] In cases of large cash withdrawals, it may also present opportunities for cash seizure because the withdrawal locations will be revealed.

---

70. Practitioners must ensure that interview requirements (for example, required warning to interviewee) are conveyed to foreign counterparts, and should inquire whether it is possible to participate in those interviews. For a discussion of cooperating with foreign practitioners or participating in the execution of the request, see section 7.4.6 of chapter 7.

71. In this regard, practitioners may find it more helpful to prepare themes rather than specific questions to guide the interview.

72. In the United Kingdom, the order can be in place for up to 90 days at a time.

73. Typically, the standard of proof or other requirements for account monitoring orders are less stringent than for disclosure, freezing, or seizure orders.

3.3.8 Search and Seizure Warrant

The execution of a search warrant on a house and business is a tremendous opportunity to gather evidence of criminal activity, discover information about assets, identify co-conspirators, and develop other leads that support the investigation.[74] In some cases or jurisdictions, this will be the primary technique used to obtain bank documents. See section 3.3.9 on orders for disclosure or production of documents.

Given the coercive nature of a search, laws typically require that searches be requested by an authorized individual—often a law enforcement officer or prosecutor—and be judicially authorized by a judge or investigating magistrate (barring exigent circumstances). Practitioners must be aware that civil and common law jurisdictions differ in their requirements for authorization, specifically in the standards of proof needed to obtain the warrant, the specificity required for the evidence to be seized, and the location of the evidence. In general, greater specificity is required in common law jurisdictions.

Preparing and Obtaining the Search Warrant

Common law jurisdictions will require a written application (except in exigent circumstances, where it can be made orally or by telephone). The application will comprise two documents: the warrant and the supporting affidavit (for information on drafting affidavits, see box 4.1 in chapter 4). The warrant itself sets out the details of the search, including who is authorized to conduct the search, its location, the hours or days when the search may be carried out (for example, day or night), its duration, what is to be searched, the inventory of items taken; and the subsequent report to the court. The supporting affidavit must articulate reasonable grounds to believe or "probable cause" that (1) a crime has been committed, (2) items sought are connected to the crime, and (3) items sought are likely to be on the premises to be searched (see box 3.3 for tips on elaborating these grounds).

Civil law jurisdictions will require similar information, but without the formality and with a standard of proof that may differ from "reasonable grounds to believe." An affidavit is not required, and law enforcement officers may be authorized by a prosecutor or investigating magistrate to conduct "all necessary searches to establish the truth."[75]

The applicant will also need to specify the items to be seized and locations to be searched. In civil law jurisdictions, it may be possible simply to refer to "all articles that may have connection to the crime committed." In common law jurisdictions, the applicant must be more specific. He or she must articulate why an article should be seized, and be sufficiently precise so that all important articles are covered (see box 3.4).

---

74. In addition to houses and businesses, items to be searched may include banks, people, cars, planes, ships, computers and other electronic media (such as compact discs and encryption keys), and packages or boxes.
75. In France and other civil law jurisdictions, this authorization is often called "commission rogatoire."

Planning and Executing the Search and Seizure

Except under exigent circumstances, practitioners will have the opportunity to plan the execution of the search warrant. They should consider the possibility of searching several businesses or houses at the same time, even in different jurisdictions, to avoid the destruction or disappearance of evidence. Although the degree of planning and coordination is very demanding, the results can be impressive. Practitioners will also need to consider the type of expertise required for the search. For example, a search may demand a computer forensic specialist who can gather electronic and computer data in a manner that avoids its loss, destruction, or damage; can present it in a manageable form; and can ensure that the necessary steps are taken to preserve its admissibility at trial (perhaps by taking a "mirror image" of the data to avoid claims of postsearch manipulation).[76]

Because the search will likely tip off the target, it will be important to take measures to secure assets that may not be at the search locations, such as bank accounts, whether in advance or simultaneous with the search. For the seizure of assets that will be subject to confiscation, it is critical to coordinate preseizure planning with prosecutors and asset managers (see section 4.2 in chapter 4, on pre-restraint planning). Appendix D provides a checklist of some additional considerations for planning the execution of the search.

---

76. Note that computer users will implement various mechanisms to protect or hide data or deem the system inaccessible if access is attempted by an unauthorized user. Computer forensic specialists will have tools for preserving systems, recovering lost information, monitoring cloud computing use, and so forth. Proper gathering of information will also ensure that information is managed.

The list below highlights some of the main items that practitioners will want to seize to assist with the investigation. Because common law jurisdictions require greater specificity in the warrants, examples of various forms of these items are also described.

- **Financial documentation.** Books, records, receipts, notes, ledgers, and other papers relating to assets, business interests, business transactions, real estate, letters of credit, money orders, checks, traveler's checks, bank drafts, banking correspondence, cashier's checks, wire transfers, bank checks, mortgage information, credit card information, safe deposit box information and keys, and other related items supporting the existence, concealment, or transfer of assets or the expenditure of funds. For documentation to be requested from financial institutions, see box 3.5 concerning orders for disclosure or production of documents.
- **Computers and computer storage devices.** Computers, electronic equipment, cell phones, answering machines, personal organizers, CD-ROMs, and other data storage devices. Seizure of computers should include the actual computer hardware, not simply a mirror or copy of the contents of the hard drive.
- **Items to identify associates or other leads.** Photographs, videos, address books, calendars, and trash.
- **Proceeds or instrumentalities of crime.** Currency, precious metals, jewelry, financial instruments such as stocks and bonds, and other valuable items such as artwork and other collectibles.
- **Shredded paper.** Shredded materials must be reconstructed.

Preserving the Evidence and Adhering to Postexecution Requirements

Once the warrant has been executed and evidence has been seized, the evidence should be taken to a secure location to be properly logged and examined, and the event should be documented in the case file.[77] If an interview of the target or associates occurred during the execution of the warrant, a report of the interview should be made as soon as possible and incorporated into the case file. The lead investigator will be responsible for preserving the chain of custody and the integrity of the evidence throughout the review period, and he or she must ensure that all evidence is detailed in the inventory. The lead investigator may also be responsible for reporting the results to a judge or prosecutor.

Practitioners should review all the documentary evidence seized; identify potential leads for tracing assets or possible co-conspirators; and, where necessary, take immediate action to restrain assets to avoid their dissipation or movement. If the practitioner has engaged the assistance of foreign authorities during the course of the investigation,

---

77. Some jurisdictions may require details on the location of each item at all times to fulfill chain of custody requirements.

it is often beneficial to apprise these authorities of the results of the search warrant in a timely manner so that they may respond favorably to the results.

3.3.9 Orders for Disclosure or Production of Documents

Obtaining business documents will be essential to an asset recovery case. Documents that are likely to require judicial authorization will include those held by banks, accounting and law firms, insurance companies, Web-based e-mail services, Internet service providers, and sometimes utility companies. The process for obtaining a disclosure or production order is similar to that for obtaining a search warrant (see section 3.3.8 for additional information on search and seizure warrants).

Similar to search warrants, jurisdictions will vary on the specificity required for disclosure orders. Common law jurisdictions will require a more specific list; civil law jurisdictions may be satisfied with a general phrase, such as "all documents that may have connection to the crime committed." In practice, many practitioners find it most helpful to combine these two approaches—providing a precise list of documents requested and concluding the list with the general phrase because many disclosing entities will want to limit the documents they offer for disclosure. If practitioners submit a request that is too narrow in scope, they risk being denied relevant information. Box 3.5 lists items to be included in requests to financial institutions.

Although the request should be broad enough to ensure that relevant documentation is captured, it will be important to avoid being inundated by boxes and boxes of irrelevant information—particularly if the tracing or investigative team does not have the capacity to review vast amounts of financial information in a timely manner. Requesting an excessive amount of documentation may also delay its delivery because it may take longer for the disclosing entity to produce the documentation. Or the disclosing entity may challenge the order on the basis of relevance and undue burden.[78] Where data retention laws, retention orders, or do-not-destroy orders are in place such that the records that might be relevant in later stages of the investigation will be maintained by the disclosing entity (see box 3.6), practitioners should develop their cases (particularly the large cases) in stages, using the documentary evidence as building blocks. They should first request what is considered imperative, and then submit subsequent requests to follow relevant leads or when capacity is increased. As a precaution against routine inadvertent destruction, it is a good idea to request that the financial institution preserve other relevant records. Adopting this building-blocks approach enables practitioners to focus efforts on smaller amounts of information and then follow the relevant leads, thus avoiding loss of time in reviewing boxes of documents and large electronic data sets that may not be relevant.

Where permitted by law, the requesting authority should consider asking that the application be heard *ex parte* (that is, without notice) to avoid tipping off the targets. Even

---

78. Another common ground for challenge by the disclosing entity is privilege (such as solicitor-client privilege).

Practitioners often need or opt to provide a specific list of items requested from financial institutions for accounts or targets, related persons, close associates, or related companies. In such cases, officials from FIUs or the central bank may be helpful resources in determining the types of documents that might be relevant. Examples of specific records to request include (but are not limited to) the following:

- All account-opening documentation, including forms that identify the beneficial owner (for example, "Form A" is used in Switzerland), powers of attorney signature cards, articles of incorporation or partnership agreements, and copies of identity documents provided when an account is opened. Include not only accounts under the names of the targets, but also those accounts that list any of the targets as a power of attorney or a signatory, or indicate some other pertinent relationship.
- Client profile, know-your-customer notes, account manager notes, teller or banker journal, cashier check log, any due diligence conducted by the financial institution, and any other data probing the economic background of the client, commercial activities, and transactions on the account (for example, copies of contracts, bills, letters of credit, list of partners, and affiliated companies).
- Loan documentation, to include mortgage information, copy of loan application, listing and/or description of any collateral (including liens against deposits), income, assets, and personal and/or business references.
- All bank account statements for the period under investigation.
- Any reports of suspicious activity that were submitted by an employee of the financial institution, to include those that might not have been forwarded to the FIU.
- Documents related to account transactions, including client orders, deposit and withdrawal slips, credit and debit memos, and checks (front and back).
- Wire transfer documentation, including the request form, advice statement, confirmation, and other relevant documents (see box 3.7).
- Correspondence files maintained by the financial institution, possibly including internal bank memos, records of client visits, phone order notes, e-mails, faxes, notes authored by account managers, and records or notes related to either or both instructions or transactions.
- Credit card information, including application, statements, payment history, transaction logs covering any interaction with credit card staff, and other cards under the umbrella of a target's account but in another person's name.
- Safe deposit information, including contracts, visiting records, and video surveillance of relevant areas (not usually box-contents viewing areas).
- All documents that may have connection to the crime committed.

Also see appendix E for an example of a draft production order to a financial institution.

BOX 3.6   Retention Orders

Most jurisdictions have laws that require businesses (such as banks, accountants, lawyers, Internet service providers, and telephone companies) to retain customer data and records for a prescribed period of time. The period of time will vary, depending on the type of business: it may be as short as a period of months (telephone companies and Internet service providers) or as long as several years (banks, lawyers, accountants). On the investigation side, practitioners are unlikely to have sufficient evidence for a disclosure or production order at the outset—an issue that becomes particularly problematic the shorter the retention period.

Fortunately, many jurisdictions address this issue by permitting retention orders or do-not-destroy orders. Such orders require that the document holder retain documents related to the targets past the period of time prescribed by statute, thus avoiding the loss of potentially relevant data or evidence. The requirements for obtaining such an order are typically less onerous than for a production or disclosure order and therefore should be considered in the early stages of an investigation. Practitioners should assess where documents may be held; determine the corresponding periods of retention; and, where permitted and necessary, obtain retention orders. Such actions will help preserve potentially relevant data for a future disclosure or production order.

where the order is made *ex parte* and there are provisions that prohibit those served with the production order from disclosing the request to the targets, practitioners must assess the risk that the targets will be informed, and they must take necessary action to restrain or seize the assets.[79]

3.3.10 Electronic Surveillance

The surreptitious interception of any wire, oral, telephone, computer, or other electronic communication used by the targets—referred to in this handbook as "electronic surveillance"—can be very useful to law enforcement officers in providing investigatory leads similar to those addressed in the discussion of physical surveillance (section 3.3.3). At the same time, electronic surveillance is labor intensive, can be cost prohibitive, and is a highly intrusive technique; therefore, many jurisdictions require judicial oversight and perhaps special authorization to ensure protection of privacy and due process rights of the accused. Some jurisdictions will permit consensual monitoring of communications with prior consent of one of the parties (for example, a cooperating witness, informant, or undercover agent), and this does not require a warrant.[80] In all

---

79. In cases requiring mutual legal assistance (MLA), practitioners should be aware of potential disclosure obligations of the requested jurisdiction, and they should address this issue prior to sending of the request. See section 7.1 of chapter 7 for additional information.

80. Consensual monitoring is permitted in some states in the United States. See Department of Justice, Office of the Inspector General, "Federal Bureau of Investigation's Compliance with the Attorney General's Investigative Guidelines (Redacted)," special report, (Washington, DC, September 2005), ch. 6, http://

cases, electronic surveillance must be done in a manner that adheres to domestic laws and internal policies and procedures.

Practitioners involved in electronic surveillance should be diligent in recording the subject(s), time, date, length of conversation, and other pertinent information for every communication intercepted. They should ensure that original recordings are secured as evidence—properly sealed and maintained in a secure and safe environment—and that working copies are made for practitioners. Translation services may be necessary for conversations in foreign languages. Intercepts should be monitored 24 hours a day, 7 days a week to ensure that time-sensitive information is quickly addressed and any follow-up actions are properly coordinated. Practitioners should also consider introducing a physical surveillance team that will closely coordinate with the electronic surveillance team because this will generate both visual and voice evidence.

3.3.11 Undercover Operations

Undercover operations are another investigative technique that can be used to infiltrate targets and uncover evidence and information about assets. In asset recovery cases, this might include the controlled delivery of funds through an undercover agent. However, such operations are legally and procedurally complicated, risky, and resource intensive. As with other techniques, legal requirements and procedures must be strictly followed to ensure admissibility of the evidence obtained. Officers must be skilled, trained, and suited to the investigation. Proper equipment to record and monitor meetings between undercover officers or informants and the targets or associates of targets must be secured and constantly monitored to protect the safety of the informants and undercover agents involved.[81]

Use of informants can be difficult, so undercover officers are usually preferred. When use of an informant is the only option, it is advisable to register the informant, provide the informant with clear and concise written instructions, and have the informant sign a written acknowledgment that instructions are understood. In addition, informants, vehicles, and other relevant belongings may need to be searched for contraband immediately before the undercover meeting to avoid accusations of evidence planting. Finally, because officer or informant safety is a priority, it will be important to control where meetings occur and to choose environments that are most conducive to the success and safety of the operation.

---

www.justice.gov/oig/special/0509/chapter6.htm. Section 3.3.11, "Undercover Operations," provides tips that can be applied in consensual monitoring. Where such monitoring is not permitted, a court order would be required (for example, in Ukraine).

81. For example, informants, officers, or consenting parties should wear a body wire or other concealed transmitting device (perhaps a device concealed in a pen, cell phone, cigarette package, briefcase, or laptop computer) as well as a separate recording device to ensure a clear recording (because transmitter signals can be disrupted and voice quality is often poor). In practice, it is helpful to record a preamble to the tape recording, stating practitioner's name, the date and time, and a brief description of events.

3.4 Identifying Relevant Data: Examples from Commonly Sourced Documents

Various documents will surface throughout an investigation, including bank account records, financial statements, contracts, invoices, deeds, shareholder agreements, articles of incorporation, receipts, and the like. They will reveal information on assets, movement of funds, individuals and companies linked to a target, and other relevant data. To assist practitioners, some examples of relevant data from commonly sourced documents are outlined here.

3.4.1 Suspicious Transaction Reports

Where disclosure to law enforcement is permitted, STRs and related documents may be excellent sources of data for practitioners because they typically include data on the transaction, a narrative on the reasons for the suspicion, and an analysis by financial analysts.[82] The amount of information provided and the quality of the narrative may vary, depending on the requirements of the jurisdiction or the person filing the STR. In general, however, there are many important points of information on the STR, including

- source and destination of funds;
- narrative explanation by the bank employee about the nature of the suspicion and know-your-customer (KYC) information;
- frequency of the use of wire transfers, checks, and so forth; and
- information on other assets or products held by the target at the bank.

From this information, practitioners can obtain information on the financial flow that will enable them to trace the money backward to confirm its illegal source or forward to follow where it has gone. The information will provide additional leads, such as bank accounts to subpoena and individuals or companies to interview. With regard to interviews, it may be helpful to speak directly with the compliance officer to discuss the STR and other background information on the target. For an example of the information that can be drawn from an FIU report, see appendix C.

3.4.2 Account-Opening Documents and Know-Your-Customer or Customer Due Diligence Records

Practitioners should carefully review all account-opening information and any KYC or customer due diligence efforts conducted by the financial institution. In the case of politically exposed persons (PEPs), financial institutions should have additional due diligence on the economic background and transactions in the file. This documentation will likely provide the practitioners with a lot of useful information and potential leads. For example,

---

82. In some jurisdictions, the FIU is not permitted to provide a copy of the STR or the CTR to law enforcement officers. In these circumstances, the intelligence report (if drafted) usually may be requested, and it contains much of the same information.

- the account manager and any persons named as power of attorney may be worth interviewing;
- the documents provided by the bank account holder to justify the source of funds (for example, contracts, letters, and real estate sales) may help
  a. identify the beneficial owner (look at addresses, companies, and individuals involved),
  b. provide a better understanding of the alleged economic background of the funds,
  c. reveal contradictions with the figures or with other evidence already gathered,
  d. identify potential witnesses, and
  e. prepare for interviews with targets;
- in the case of bank accounts in the name of a corporate vehicle, the documents incorporating the company, the names of the board members, and the names of the persons entitled to conduct business on behalf of the company may reveal persons worth interviewing.[83]

3.4.3 Bank Account Statements

As a first step, practitioners should focus on determining the origin of the funds entering the account and where the funds have been transferred. This includes debit and credit flows in the accounts through cash deposits and withdrawals, wire transfers, bonds, checks, loans, and so forth. In reviewing these flows, different techniques need to be used for assessing the origin and destination of the funds. Here are a few suggestions:

- **Cash.** Cash movements can be difficult to trace because of the lack of origin or destination information. Practitioners should obtain the cash deposit or withdrawal receipt from the bank, and this document should indicate the identity of the person initiating the transactions. In addition, practitioners will need to use traditional investigative techniques to follow the link to the cash deposits through e-mails, letters, and wire transfers; and by looking at activity in other accounts and safe deposit visiting records.
- **Bonds.** Bond deposits can be arranged from bank to bank, so practitioners will have to ask the banks for all information regarding the bonds and the method by which they were deposited into the account.
- **Checks.** If it is a deposit by check, practitioners may have to go to the bank account on which the check was drawn to identify the originator. If the check is endorsed— that is, signed on the back so as to cash, deposit, or sign it over to someone else— it should be treated similar to a cash deposit, requiring that the practitioner identify the person who endorsed the check. Practitioners should also review the "memo" line of the check because this may indicate suspicious activities. For example, checks to related companies for "management" or "consulting services" may reveal that the company is laundering proceeds through a series of companies that it owns.

---

83. In some cases, board members and employees of a gatekeeper or service provider responsible for creating shell companies may have little information to assist the investigation.

| FIGURE 3.3 | Basic Cross-Border Wire Transfer Process |

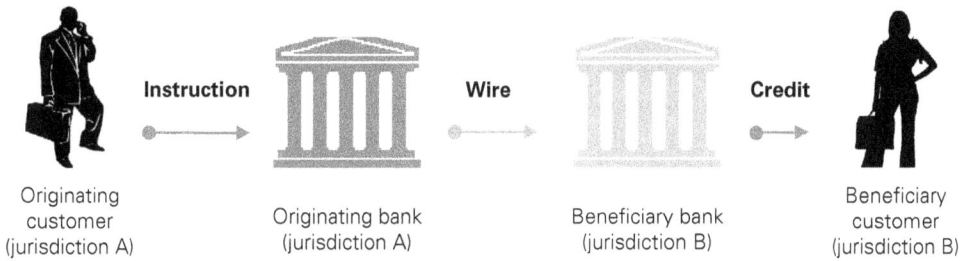

Instruction → Wire → Credit

| Originating customer (jurisdiction A) | Originating bank (jurisdiction A) | Beneficiary bank (jurisdiction B) | Beneficiary customer (jurisdiction B) |

Source: Authors' illustration.

3.4.4 Wire Transfers

Previous corruption cases have shown that large amounts of corruption proceeds are placed in financial institutions and then moved around the world through wire transfers (also referred to as "electronic funds transfers") in an effort to break the audit trail and secure funds in bank secrecy havens. A wire transfer is initiated with a request by a customer (financial institution, legal entity, or individual) to direct funds elsewhere, either domestically or across borders.[84] The request gives instructions through a system of messages by telephone, e-mail, fax, and/or cell phone (see figure 3.3).[85] Before the proceeds reach their final hiding place, such wire transfers are used to launder the funds through several financial institutions and transit jurisdictions using correspondent bank accounts, serial wires, cover payments, shell companies, and offshore jurisdictions. Some financial institutions have even been complicit in helping corrupt politicians, their relatives, and close associates launder funds through complex transactions using corporate vehicles and establishing special private wealth account privileges.[86]

A wire transfer comprises two components: (1) the instruction, which includes information on both the originator and the beneficiary institutions, and (2) the actual movement

---

84. This can include a chain of wire transfers that has at least one cross-border element (for example, a correspondent bank in another jurisdiction). See also FATF, Interpretative Note to Special Recommendation VII.

85. According to the FATF Special Recommendation VII on Wire Transfers, promulgated in 2001, the terms "wire transfer" and "funds transfer" refer to "…any transaction carried out on behalf of an originator person (both natural and legal) through a financial institution by electronic means with a view to making an amount of money available to a beneficiary person at another financial institution."

86. See United States Senate, Minority Staff of the Permanent Subcommittee on Investigations, "Money Laundering and Foreign Corruption: Enforcement and Effectiveness of the Patriot Act. Case Study Involving Riggs Bank" (Washington, DC, July 15, 2004), http://hsgac.senate.gov/public/_files/ACF5F8.pdf. Furthermore, a large international bank had a training manual for its employees so they would know how to "strip" (remove) information from a wire transfer to hide the fact that the transfer was for or on behalf of a sanctioned jurisdiction. See information at http://www.justice.gov/opa/pr/2009/December/09-ag-1358.html.

or funds transfer. There are many ways for financial institutions to send instructions, including electronic networks available through various interbank payment systems, e-mail, fax, telephone, and telex. By far the most common way for banks to communicate transfer instructions to each other is by accessing a special financial telecommunications system known as the Society for Worldwide Interbank Financial Telecommunications (SWIFT). Where the actual movement of money is concerned, the two major wholesale interbank payment systems available are the Clearing House Interbank Payments System (CHIPS) and Fedwire Funds Service (Fedwire). In addition, direct bank-to-bank and other intermediary payment systems are frequently used by banks to move customer funds between institutions.

CHIPS and Fedwire may be used for U.S. dollar transfers or as part of a U.S. dollar component of an international transaction. However, CHIPS has been used primarily to facilitate dollar-denominated international transfers. Unlike these payment systems, SWIFT is a messaging system only, and it does not hold or transfer funds or manage accounts on behalf of its members.

An actual funds transfer takes place through a "book transfer," and it may involve a correspondent bank. A book transfer is essentially an accounting process that physically moves funds from one account to another. If both the originating customer and the beneficiary customer have an account at the same financial institution, then an internal book transfer can take place between the two customer accounts. When funds are transferred between two unrelated financial institutions, a book transfer occurs through a correspondent or intermediary bank employed to bridge the relationship.[87] Many banks maintain correspondent accounts primarily for the purpose of processing and clearing wire transfer transactions with institutions that are members of and have access to CHIPS or Fedwire; doing so enables them to carry out wire transfers on behalf of their customers, even though they are not member institutions themselves. Correspondent banking relationships are also common between domestic and foreign banks because they can facilitate business and provide services to clients in foreign jurisdictions without the expense and burden of a bank having to establish a foreign presence.[88]

Gathering Relevant Documents and Information for Analyzing Wire Transfers

Practitioners will need to ensure that wire transfer documentation is requested from financial institutions because this will be critical to asset tracing efforts. This will include a copy of the wire transfer message itself, as well as other documents that financial institutions generate in the process of originating or receiving the transfer of funds. Box 3.7 outlines some of the forms and documents that may be produced in

---

87. In this case, if the originating bank maintains a correspondent account with a beneficiary bank, it may instruct the beneficiary bank to transfer funds out of the originating bank's correspondent account to the account of the beneficiary customer. U.S. Department of Treasury, Financial Crimes Enforcement Network, *Key Electronic Funds Transfer Systems: Fedwire, CHIPS, SWIFT*, Report OSA92/CB0012 (Vienna, VA, September 1992).

88. Additional information on correspondent banking communications and the use of serial and cover payment methods, including new cover payment practices developed by SWIFT, is discussed in appendix F.

Originating institution:

- Funds transfer request form
- Wire transfer copy
- Advice statement or confirmation of wire transfer
- Debit memo to originating customer
- Customer monthly account statement
- Internal log of outgoing wires (correspondent bank logs, payment and processing logs)
- Journal entry

Beneficiary (or correspondent) institution:

- Funds transfer request form
- Wire transfer copy
- Credit memo to beneficiary customer (if deposited)
- Customer monthly account statement
- Journal entry
- Cashier's check
- Interbank book transfer information that banks keep for the purpose of clearing transactions

connection with a wire transfer. A review of these documents and forms will reveal key information, such as the originator and beneficiary financial institution, customer parties, amount, date, and customer-to-customer or financial institution-to-institution information.

A practitioner seeking information should request wire transfer information in both spreadsheet format and advice statement form, if available. Because banks use different formats that are not standardized, a spreadsheet may contain information that makes it easier to understand the transaction, whereas the advice statement format could contain more comprehensive data.

Depending on the circumstances of the investigation, it will be important to obtain additional documents or apply scrutiny in different areas, such as those addressed here:

- **Underlying payment documents.** Invoices, shipping documents, receipts, consultant contracts, and other documents associated with a transfer will reveal key information about funds in question.
- **KYC information.** At the transaction level, the bank may not have identified the ultimate beneficiary when funds exited the account. KYC information may also be helpful in this regard.

- **PEP customers.** In cases involving PEPs, wire transfers may be found in the private banking business operations of a financial institution. PEPs-related inquiries should include a review of all accounts that have a power of attorney attached to them and those accounts maintained by law firms because these are common methods used by PEPs to move money.
- **Book transfers between personal and corporate accounts.** Such transfers may be useful in detecting a layering scheme.
- **SWIFT private gateways and name variants used by the financial institution.** A review of the separate SWIFT gateways used only for private banking clients within the bank and its various branches may uncover a separate and potentially special permission transaction originating through these gateways. SWIFT name variants used by the financial institution may reveal transfers through different avenues. A bank may have different wire transfer departments, addresses, or internal ways of identifying itself.[89] To ensure that the gateways and name variants are listed in the order to produce bank records, practitioners should consider gathering this information through interviews with bank officials (for example, compliance officials).
- **Suspicious transaction reports.** Where available, STRs or intelligence reports may reveal valuable wire transfer information and originator details.
- **Federal Reserve Bank inquiries.** For wire transfers submitted through Fedwire, the U.S. Federal Reserve Bank may be a useful source because it retains wire transfer records for 180 days. When requesting information, it is important to be very specific about the transaction by referencing as many details as possible (for example, date, transaction amount, originating party, beneficiary customer, receiving institution, account numbers, purpose of the transaction (if known), and so forth).
- **Transaction patterns at specific institutions.** When reviewing information obtained from smaller banks, practitioners may look for patterns of very large transfers relative to the bank's size (for example, a book transfer that amounts to 80 percent of the total money transferred for a particular bank over the course of a month).
- **Repaired, returned, and resent wires.** Monitoring systems will create a "repair item" for messages containing errors (such as incomplete originator information). Those messages are then set aside and alerted for manual review. Such documents will often be maintained by the originating and beneficiary banks, and may reveal patterns of activity by a target or bank.[90]

Interpreting Wire Transfer Documentation

In most cases, advice statements confirming a wire transfer and the debit and credit memos sent by banks to their originating or beneficiary customers will be easy-to-read

---

89. One bank was found to have 43 separate identifiers based on variations of its name and address.

90. These records may also be helpful when looking for a pattern of behavior by a financial institution that may demonstrate it has knowingly laundered the proceeds of crime. In addition, practitioners should ask for all rejected wires from a bank in question within, for example, the last 30 days; and they should be particularly alert to information that was supplemented or changed when the wire was resent.

documents containing information needed to trace the movements of funds, including account numbers and the identity of the originating and beneficiary customers. Where such documents are unavailable, the process of identifying and tracing funds will necessitate an understanding of how to read and interpret the various messaging systems used to effect wire transfers.

Payment systems such as CHIPS and Fedwire use a separate messaging format for wire transfer communication between member institutions; however, SWIFT offers a standardized messaging platform for the largest number of financial institutions globally. With regard to SWIFT messages, there are industrywide protocols for messaging formats, special codes for differentiating between information and direction, and encryption to prevent security breaches during data transmission. To identify the different types of SWIFT messages, there are numbers assigned to each of them. For a message identified as "MT 103," as an example, the "MT" prefix stands for "message type," and the three-digit number that follows represents a specific SWIFT message type (in this case, "103" means a single customer/credit transfer). Within a message type, specific field codes are used to demarcate important information. For example, field 50 (ordering customer) is a key field to focus on for tracing laundered funds because it may include more than just the customer name and address.[91] Figure 3.4 provides a sample of some of the relevant SWIFT messaging fields that practitioners will want to review.

SWIFT bank identifier codes (BICs) are another source for practitioners because these provide the name of the financial institution, jurisdiction, location, and/or branch. BICs are generally eight characters in length and consist of a bank code (unique to the financial institution), a country code (to identify the jurisdiction where the financial institution is located), and a location code (that provides a geographic distinction within a jurisdiction). Sometimes, an additional three characters are used for a branch code (to identify the physical branch of a financial institution).[92]

3.4.5 Accounting Records

In business accounting, financial transactions are supported by documentation and are recorded through journal entries that identify account names and amounts. These are summarized in the business's financial statements, which include income statements and balance sheets.[93] Corrupt officials and those involved in fraudulent schemes will often manipulate these records to conceal their illegal activities. Practitioners may find

91. There are three options for displaying information in field 50 (ordering customer) that may be useful to a practitioner: (1) account plus identifier, (2) identifier plus name and address, and (3) account plus name and address.

92. For more information on BICs, see http://www.swift.com. The Web site allows searches by institution name or by BIC, and search parameters may be narrowed by country, city, or both.

93. A *journal* is a record that keeps accounting transactions in chronological order. Most commonly used are cash receipts, disbursements, sales, purchases, and general journals. A *ledger* records transactions by type of account. An *income statement* lists revenue and expenses, and a *balance sheet* lists assets and liabilities.

FIGURE 3.4 Sample SWIFT Message Format and Code Interpretation

:20: PAYREF-XT78305

:32A: 091010EUR#1010000#

:50: [CUSTOMER NAME AND ADDRESS]

:59: [BENEFICIARY NAME AND ADDRESS]

Code Interpretation

20	Transaction reference number (coded number assigned by the originating institution to identify the transaction)
32A	Value date, currency code, and amount of the transaction
50	Ordering customer (party ordering the SWIFT transaction)
59	Beneficiary (party designated as the ultimate recipient of the funds)

In addition to the above codes, other codes may include

52D	Ordering bank (financial institution initiating the SWIFT)
53D	Sender's correspondent bank
54D	Receiver's correspondent bank
57D	The financial institution at which the ordering customer requests the beneficiary be paid
70	Details of payment
71A	Details of charges for the transaction
72	Instructions from the sending bank to the receiving bank

Source: Authors' illustration.

illicit transactions by analyzing and comparing accounting entries, actual payments, and the documents used to justify them.

In cases where bribery and/or other inappropriate payments to third parties are suspected, it is common that fictitious invoices are submitted by the bribe recipient (agent, intermediary, or third party) to the paying party (usually the company seeking to win a contract). Inappropriate payments masked by fictitious invoices are a pervasive problem, and they facilitate paying business consultants, agents, intermediaries, and other third parties for questionable purposes. One reason for using fictitious invoices is to provide a false "audit trail" in the records of the bribe-paying company, thereby concealing the true purpose of the underlying payment. In addition, they are difficult to identify because they appear to be plausible, legitimate documents.

If the use of fictitious invoices is suspected, practitioners should focus primarily on identifying discrepancies between invoiced amounts and the actual value (or the nonexistence) of purchased goods or services. The various documents recording the transaction—the contract, the documentation to the paying agent (for example, invoices or e-mails), payment records, bills of lading, and the process for the payment itself—may reveal red-flag indicators (see box 3.8). When such discrepancies are

BOX 3.8 **Red Flags in Contracts, Payment Documentation, Payment Records, and Payment Mechanisms**

Contracts:

- Invoices for significant payments to third parties in the absence of a formal contract
- Lack of specificity in the contract or agreement on the services to be performed
- Absence of written evidence confirming that due diligence was performed to confirm the identity and legitimacy of the contracting party
- Back-dated contracts or contracts in which services have been supplied and billed prior to the date the contract came into existence
- Multiple contracts with different parties for performance of the same services in the same location (that is, paying multiple contractors for the same service)
- Existence of annexes or side agreements (including oral agreements) that unreasonably expand or alter the scope of the original contract
- Success-fee commissions to be paid to the "agent" if the paying party wins a key contract, particularly where the activities of the agent are not specified
- A commission rate that exceeds the expected market rate for the jurisdiction

Payment documentation (invoices, receipts, e-mails to justify payment, minutes, and other documentation provided by third parties to justify payments as a vendor of goods or services):

- Failure to provide supporting information to confirm that services were provided
- Deliverables or reports provided by third parties that are the same as, similar to, or not commensurate with the commission payable (for example, a search of report phrases on the Internet may reveal that the contract has been plagiarized)
- Invoices that contain generic add-on fees or surcharges
- Invoices missing expected information, such as tax identification or corporate registration numbers
- Value of services rendered that is not commensurate with the amount paid
- Recipient bank details that differ from the jurisdiction or location where services were performed
- A third-party name that appears to be a shell company or to be managed by shell companies
- A recipient name that differs from the name of the contractual third party
- Multiple third parties who share the same business address
- Multiple consultants who have the same generic invoice format or addresses

(continued next page)

BOX 3.8 *(continued)*

Payment records and entries in accounting records:

- Significant invoices or invoice amounts recorded in generic general ledger accounts, such as miscellaneous expenses or consulting
- Use of suspense or transitory accounts that eventually are written off as bad debt
- Payments processed outside of the normal accounts payable process (for example, one-off manual payments, cash payments)
- Failure to follow payment procedures (for example, obtaining one signature when two are required)
- Reluctance of company personnel to approve invoices for payment through normal channels, such as online or directly on the invoice
- Pressure from a third party or company personnel to process payment urgently
- Unusual interest by company personnel in the processing of payments to specific third parties
- Unusual responses or hostility from company personnel or third parties in response to a search for additional supporting documentation
- Payments to third parties for which risk management processes were not followed

Payment mechanisms by which funds are remitted from the company:

- Request for payments to be remitted through tax-haven jurisdictions
- Requests by employees to hand-deliver payment
- Requests to split payment across multiple company bank accounts and/or country offices
- Requests by employees that payments be made in cash or cash equivalents
- Requests by employees for purchase of high-value "gifts" (such as watches or jewelry)

found, it will be possible to filter the population of suspicious transactions and focus the investigation on the issuer of the fictitious invoice (the suspected bribe recipient).

In the absence of more specific leads, attention should be paid to large, unusual, or one-off items recorded under expenditure accounts—consultancy, commissions, entertainment, travel, and miscellaneous expenses. In addition, practitioners should consider account receivables that are not repaid and are written off as bad debts.

3.4.6 Insurance Policies

Some life insurance policies may be of great value and may be purchased with a single downpayment, making them attractive to would-be money launderers. Practitioners should determine if the targets have cash-value insurance policies. In addition, insurance policies may reveal other assets owned by the targets (perhaps jewelry or cars). Typically, such information can be gathered through the various investigative techniques.

3.4.7 Purchase and Sale Documents

Documents related to the purchase and sale of assets—whether real property, shares, vehicles, jewelry, or artwork—will include land registry documents, purchase and sale agreements, loans, mortgages, financial statements, tax returns, and credit card statements. Practitioners should focus on documenting the values at and dates of purchase and sale, the name of the buyer or seller, the method of payment (cash, check, currency), and the source of funds. With assets purchased with cash, it may be difficult to trace the date of purchase or the value, particularly when there are numerous potential sellers or dealers (as is true for artwork, jewelry, and vehicles). Travel data (gathered from border-crossing information, credit card information, or travel reward programs), insurance policies, jewelry repair bills, vehicle identification numbers, dealer stickers or decals on the vehicles, and art dealers may provide assistance in determining the seller of these items and the dates of purchase.

Practitioners also need to consider assets ostensibly owned by family members or close associates but effectively controlled, held, or gifted by a target (see section 4.3.1 in chapter 4 for a discussion of this issue in the context of provisional measures).

3.5 Organizing Data: Creating a Financial Profile

It will be important to organize the information gathered into an account profile for each bank account; and this information, in turn, can be combined with other financial data collected (such as other asset holdings, liabilities, income, and expenses) to build the financial profile of a target. A standard computer spreadsheet program could be used for this purpose (see appendix G for a sample financial profile form).

As an example, the account profile should include the following information:

- name of the bank and branch location;
- bank account number and type;
- names of bank account holder, beneficial owner, and those granted powers of attorney;
- dates of account opening and, if applicable, closing;
- currency;
- account balance at the time of the disclosure;
- annual credit turnover;
- annual debit turnover; and
- whether the assets have been restrained.

Practitioners may then consider entering into a spreadsheet program additional relevant data, such as the credit and debit activity that occurs within the bank account

FIGURE 3.5   Sample Flow Chart

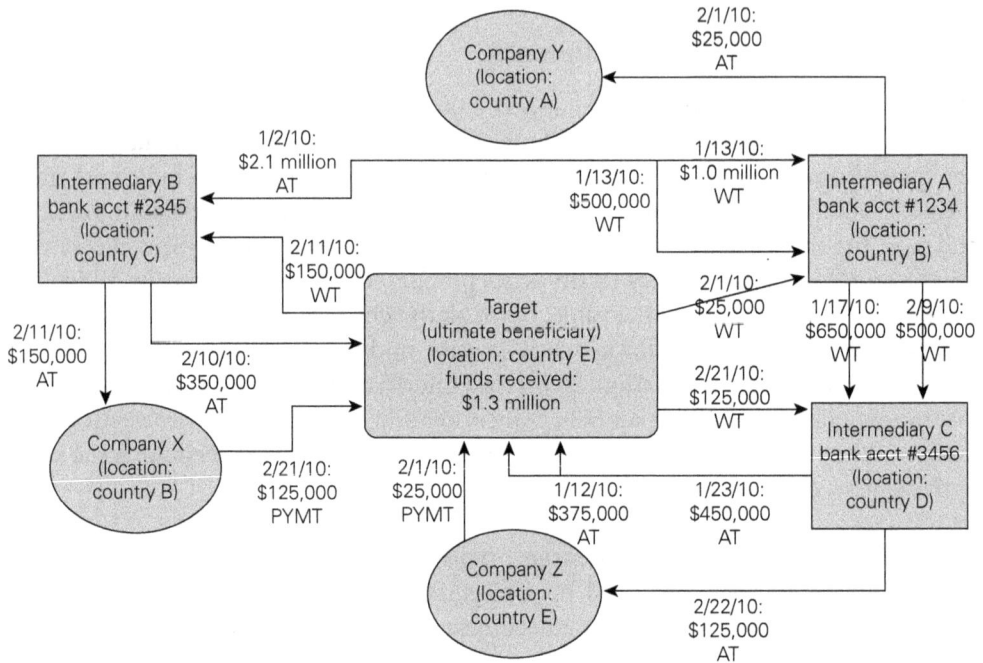

Source: Authors' illustration.
Note: AT = account transfer; PYMT = payment; WT = wire transfer.

during the relevant period under investigation, with the date, amount, and (when available) the source of funds or where the funds were sent (bank and bank account holder's name).

To assist with organizing and eventually presenting and explaining the data, practitioners should map out the flow of funds in a flow chart (see examples in figures 3.5 and 3.6). These flow charts provide a visual snapshot of the targets, associates, gatekeepers, and corporations involved; and of the assets, bank accounts, and corporate vehicles. Not only is this snapshot or "big picture" view helpful for practitioners as they try to understand and interpret the flows, but it also becomes essential when explaining the flow and associations developed during the course of the investigation to a prosecutor or judge.

In addition, practitioners should consider using a document management system, particularly in complicated cases and with large amounts of data.

3.6 Analyzing Data: Comparing the Flows with the Financial Profile

In this critical phase, analysts will compare and contrast dates, origins, destinations, bank account holders, banks, and sources of information so they may group and

FIGURE 3.6 Sample Chart of Relationships and Assets

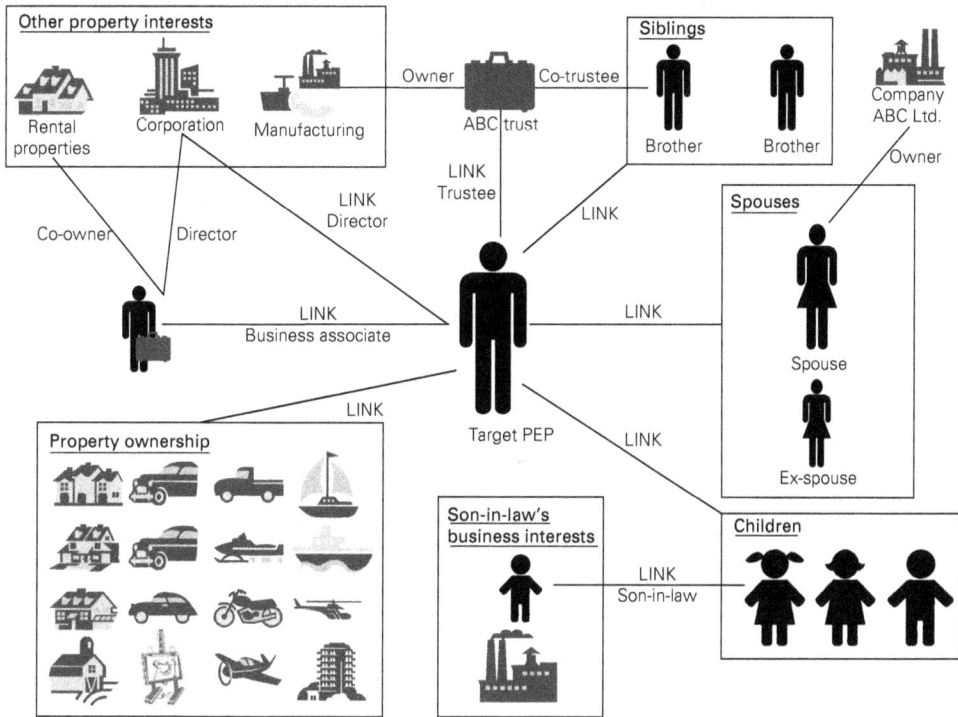

Other property interests

Rental properties · Corporation · Manufacturing

Co-owner · Director

LINK Director

LINK Business associate

LINK

Property ownership

Owner · ABC trust · Co-trustee

LINK Trustee

Siblings

Brother · Brother

LINK

Company ABC Ltd.

Owner

LINK

Spouses

Spouse

LINK

Target PEP

Ex-spouse

Son-in-law's business interests

LINK Son-in-law

Children

Source: Authors' illustration.

reconcile transactions and identify gaps in data. For example, one account may show the withdrawal of a large sum of cash, leaving the analyst without destination information; another may show a subsequent deposit. Or perhaps physical surveillance records reveal that a target traveled to a foreign jurisdiction in the days following the withdrawal. Payments to contractors may be linked to subsequent deposits. In one case, for example, several deposits by a corrupt official were found to be the same percentage as the payments to the contractor. This analysis will help in better understanding the asset flow and in developing new leads.

Another technique used by practitioners is a net worth analysis—a comparison of the value of the assets held by a target with his or her reported income. Any unreported income is likely to have illicit origins, and practitioners will subsequently need to direct efforts to show a link between the asset and the offense. In jurisdictions that prosecute illicit enrichment, the net worth analysis is a necessary step in the investigation.

To assist in identifying corruption and money laundering schemes, it may be helpful to review information or research on the various typologies and red flags for identifying criminal activity. Many agencies and international organizations publish such reports, and they are available online. They include

- Financial Action Task Force (FATF) typology reports (for example, FATF typologies on money laundering and terrorist financing in the real estate sector);
- FIU annual reports on STRs; and
- reports by the FIU, financial sector supervisor, or banking association on typologies and red flags for identifying criminal activity and money laundering.

3.7 Garnering International Cooperation

Asset recovery in corruption cases frequently crosses borders and involves many different jurisdictions; therefore, information on assets and bank accounts located abroad will have to be requested. Some information (such as land, vehicle, and corporate information; and financial intelligence) may be obtained through informal channels (perhaps counterpart practitioners, liaison magistrates or regional attachés, or practitioner networks such as the Egmont Group), rather than through an MLA request. However, if a requesting jurisdiction is seeking documentation to be used as evidence in domestic court proceedings, an MLA request will be required. In all cases, it may be possible for practitioners to participate in the activities undertaken in the foreign jurisdiction. Chapter 7, on international cooperation, provides further guidance on this process and discusses some of the challenges encountered in asset tracing.

4. Securing the Assets

Efforts toward asset confiscation are of little value if, at the end of the day, no asset is available for confiscation. Given that assets can be hidden or moved out of reach in a short period of time and that an investigation and confiscation can take years (offering a target ample time to move or dissipate assets), it is critical that measures be taken early on to secure the assets that may become subject to a confiscation judgment. These measures are referred to as provisional measures, and they include the seizure and restraint of assets. The measures should be taken as close to the beginning of the case as possible; and, where feasible, should secure the assets until the conclusion of the confiscation proceedings.[94]

The laws governing provisional measures in most jurisdictions involve the balancing of two opposing principles. The first principle is the public interest in ensuring that the proceeds and instrumentalities of crime are preserved and maintained until the end of the confiscation case; and the second principle is the right of the individual to enjoy the ownership and use of his or her property. A similar balancing occurs when a person is charged with a serious offense, and a determination must be made whether that person should be allowed to remain in the community on bail pending trial or be held on remand.

4.1 Terminology: Seizure and Restraint

In both common and civil law jurisdictions, two distinct mechanisms have been developed to control and preserve assets that may be subject to confiscation: seizure and restraint. *Seizure* involves taking physical possession of the targeted asset. Although court orders are generally required, some jurisdictions grant law enforcement agencies the right to seize assets. For example, bulk cash or other assets "reasonably suspected or believed" to be the proceeds or an instrumentality of crime may be seized in exigent circumstances. Such powers, often emanating from customs laws, are particularly useful for seizing suspicious cash that is transported across international boundaries in contravention of cash import or export reporting laws.

Restraint orders are a form of mandatory injunction issued by a judge or a court that restrains any person from dealing with or disposing of the assets named in the order,

---

94. Although some jurisdictions limit the duration of the provisional orders, generally the limitations may be extended. In Liechtenstein, for example, the court must limit the duration for which the order is issued, but the deadline may be extended upon application (Code of Criminal Procedure, sec. 97a[4]).

pending the determination of confiscation proceedings.[95] Unlike seizure orders, restraint orders do not result in the physical possession of the asset. Judicial authorization is usually required; however, some jurisdictions permit restraint to be ordered by prosecutors or other authorities.[96] At the same time, not all jurisdictions use the same terminology for seizure and restraint of assets. For example, one jurisdiction will "seize" bank accounts, whereas another will "restrain" them. Other jurisdictions have introduced such terms as "freezing" or "blocking."[97] Practitioners should be aware of the distinction between the terms when sending or receiving an order involving another jurisdiction, and they must ensure that requests use terminology that can be understood. Often it is a good idea to describe the purpose of the order rather than the name of the order to be requested because the terminology may confuse the recipient (see section 7.4 of chapter 7 for additional information on drafting mutual legal assistance [MLA] requests).

4.2 Provisional Order Requirements

Similar to search and seizure warrants and disclosure orders, laws typically require that provisional measures be judicially authorized by a judge or investigating magistrate. Many jurisdictions will also permit emergency or short-term provisional measures to be implemented administratively, through either the financial intelligence unit (FIU), law enforcement agency, or other authority under law (see section 7.3.4 of chapter 7 for a discussion of these avenues).

4.2.1 Evidentiary Requirements

The requirements for obtaining a seizure order (also see chapter 3) or a restraint order usually involve the following:

- either (1) a target has committed an offense from which a benefit has been derived (value-based confiscation), or (2) the assets being sought are linked to criminal activities (property-based confiscation) (see chapter 6 for a discussion of property-based and value-based confiscation);[98] and

---

95. Restraint orders are similar (not identical) to the common law Mareva injunctions. See chapter 8 for a discussion of restraint orders.

96. A prosecutor has the authority to restrain assets in Colombia and Mexico. For example, see Law 793.02, Colombia).

97. Some confiscation laws contain both restraint and freezing orders. Restraint orders, made by a judge, are high-level orders that can restrain any type of property; freezing orders, made administratively by law enforcement officers or public servants, are lower-level orders that can restrain limited classes of lesser-value property.

98. The exact formulation of the test will vary from jurisdiction to jurisdiction. For example, the High Court of Australia has defined reasonable belief as "an inclination of the mind towards assenting to, rather than rejecting, a proposition and the grounds which can reasonably induce that inclination of the mind may, depending on the circumstances, leave something to surmise or conjecture" (*George v. Rockett*, 170 CLR 104, High Court of Australia, 1990).

- proceedings have been instituted or are about to be instituted.[99]

In common law jurisdictions, these requirements are generally established on a "reasonable grounds to believe" or "probable cause" standard of proof. Similarly in civil law jurisdictions, the decision will rest with the prosecutor's or judge's belief in or knowledge of these requirements. Additional requirements may include grounds to believe that there is risk of dissipation or that the assets are subject to confiscation and an undertaking as to damages.[100]

4.2.2 Procedural Requirements

Applicable rules of procedure may be outlined in confiscation laws or may incorporate criminal or civil procedural laws by reference. Common law jurisdictions, for example, will require the application to be in writing; and the application or motion usually consists of two documents: (1) the seizure warrant or restraint order, and (2) the supporting affidavit (see box 4.1 for a description of affidavits and important evidence to include). Civil law jurisdictions, on the other hand, may simply require a recitation of the facts demonstrated by relevant documents or evidence contained in the case file before the judicial authority. In some other civil law jurisdictions, the prosecutor or investigating magistrate may restrain or seize assets based on the need to preserve evidence or avoid dissipation of assets subject to confiscation.

Provisional measures can be strongly contested or appealed by targets and their families or associates, particularly when substantial property interests are subject to restraint or seizure. The result is that the application process for provisional measures may be converted into a mini-trial in which allegations supporting the application are challenged. Mindful that provisional measures simply require a reasonable belief of certain facts, prosecutors should urge the court to avoid deliberating on the ultimate merits of the case, which will be determined at trial. This determination is most appropriately left to the court dealing with the related prosecution and confiscation.

Many jurisdictions permit the prosecutor to make applications for provisional measures *ex parte,* or without notice to the asset holder, on the notion that notice would tip him or her off and create an opportunity to move or hide assets. Under some laws, prosecutors or investigating magistrates will have an absolute right to proceed *ex parte* if they choose to; other legal systems permit such applications only if certain conditions are satisfied, such as showing a risk of dissipation.

---

99. Some restraining order provisions permit application to be made at any time, as long as an investigation (criminal or non-conviction based) is under way. This gives much more flexibility to apply for restraining orders at the earliest possible time, and is a development that should be encouraged.

100. In those jurisdictions where undertakings must be given, there is a limited scope of circumstances in which the prosecution is required to pay damages, particularly to criminal defendants. The ultimate discharge of the order does not result in the automatic imposition of a damages order, unless it can be shown that the prosecutor either acted in bad faith or was negligent in the discharge of his or her duties.

BOX 4.1   Drafting Affidavits

An affidavit is a sworn statement of fact based on the personal knowledge or belief of the affiant. Used mainly in common law jurisdictions, it is an important procedural aid that permits the admission of evidence through a written statement that is not subject to cross-examination. Without an affidavit, the applicant or prosecutor must call witnesses (vive voce evidence) who will then be subject to cross-examination—evidence cannot simply be recited or submitted by the prosecutor as is permitted in some civil law jurisdictions.[a] Affidavits are useful in asset recovery cases for all applications to the court, including search and seizure warrants, restraint orders, and disclosure or production orders; and may be permitted for certain types of evidence at trial.

In applications for seizure, restraint, or other investigative techniques, an affidavit is typically sworn to by law enforcement officers; they can introduce all relevant material, including hearsay evidence, even though it may have been derived from numerous sources. Practitioners will need to ensure affidavits are drafted in a manner prescribed by the rules of the court.[b] In addition,

- because an affidavit is essentially the evidence for the application, it must outline how the case meets the evidentiary requirements for granting a restraining order.
- hearsay evidence is permitted in affidavits and applications for court orders. Where the deponent relies on information obtained from another person, the affidavit should state the source of the information and that the deponent believes it to be true.
- any supporting documents relied on should be annexed to the affidavit.
- care should be taken to ensure that the facts in the affidavit are correct.
- if the requesting jurisdiction invokes a confidentiality provision in the mutual legal assistance (MLA) request, the requested jurisdiction must gain consent before any information obtained from the assistance request may be submitted to a court in the form of an affidavit.

a. In the United States, affidavits are not required when a complaint is filed in a non-conviction based confiscation case. A short recitation of the facts giving rise to the confiscation in the complaint is sufficient. b. Many jurisdictions have forms available to guide practitioners.

If there is any risk that notice of an application for a restraint order will result in dissipation or if the assets subject to the restraint are inherently movable—such as funds in a bank account, jewelry, cash, vehicles—good practice dictates that the application proceed on an *ex parte* basis.

An *ex parte* order may be effective for a limited time, during which the applicant must either (1) provide notice to the asset holder and an opportunity for a hearing; or (2) apply to the court for an extension of time in which to do so. Some jurisdictions will require that the asset holder be provided with details of the proceedings, such as a transcript.

4.2.3 Provisional Restraint or Seizure of Assets in Foreign Jurisdictions

There are various avenues to achieve seizure or restraint of assets located in foreign jurisdictions.[101] On receipt of a request from the requesting jurisdiction, the authorities in the foreign requested jurisdiction may enforce the restraint or seizure order that is in place in the requesting jurisdiction.[102] Alternatively, the authorities in the requested jurisdiction may apply for a domestic restraint or seizure order, based on the facts provided by the requesting jurisdiction. There may also be informal or administrative avenues to achieve seizure or restraint of assets (see chapter 7 for additional details on these avenues).

4.3 Pre-restraint or Pre-seizure Planning

Proper planning is essential for effective restraint or seizure. Outlined below are a number of important considerations for practitioners to take into account.

4.3.1 Identification of Assets Subject to Provisional Measures

The assets subject to provisional measures will be those needed to satisfy the eventual confiscation order. Applications for provisional measures should be carefully crafted to correspond to the confiscation sanction or sanctions (because more than one can be pursued) that might operate against restrained or seized assets.

Ensuring that the appropriate assets are subject to provisional measures will depend on the confiscation system in place (that is, whether it is a property-based or value-based system). For example, if the only available sanction against a target is a property-based confiscation order, no purpose would be served in seizing a house that cannot be characterized as the proceeds or an instrumentality of corruption. However, if an available sanction is a value-based confiscation order or if substitute asset provisions exist, there may be very good reason to seize such an asset, provided that there is some evidence that the target has derived a benefit from the alleged offense.

In cases where rebuttable presumptions or reverse onus provisions apply, the scope of the order can be expanded to include the assets that would be confiscated by operation of the presumption. For example, if the offense invokes a presumption that some or all assets are proceeds of corruption, these assets can be subject to provisional measures (see section 6.3.1 of chapter 6 for a discussion on rebuttable presumptions).

---

101. See United Nations Convention against Corruption, art. 54(2)(a) and 54(2)(b), for lists of these mechanisms.

102. This avenue requires that the requesting jurisdiction have extraterritorial jurisdiction over the assets located in the foreign jurisdiction and that these assets must be listed in the restraint order. Laws permitting direct enforcement in the requested jurisdiction often have provisions that prohibit the requested jurisdiction courts from considering issues and challenges that are available to the target and his family or associates in the confiscation proceeding pending in the requesting jurisdiction. Such provisions prevent the adjudication of similar challenges in two different jurisdictions.

Assets Controlled, Held, or Gifted by a Target

Although some jurisdictions will permit the seizure of assets without consideration of the identity of their owner or holder, other jurisdictions—particularly value-based systems—will limit confiscation to assets "owned" by the target. A strict interpretation of ownership can be problematic, especially given that corrupt officials are likely to hold assets in ways that disguise ownership. For example, assets might be:

- owned by a family member or associate of the target, but held by them for the benefit of the target;
- owned by a corporate entity or trust, either owned or indirectly controlled by the target; or
- gifted by the target to the family member, associate or company.

The capacity to "pierce the corporate veil"—to reach corporate assets that are essentially controlled by the target—and to include assets in the hands of third parties is particularly important if an order for provisional measures is to work effectively. Fortunately, most jurisdictions broadly define "ownership" to include assets that are effectively controlled, held, or gifted by the target. Such laws go beyond what the person might own to include assets owned by a trust, corporation, or individual that is controlled by the target. Some jurisdictions use other procedural aids, such as presumptions, that effectively shift the burden of proving ownership to the third party.[103] Such provisions assist with the restraint or seizure of assets that a target has sold to a third party for less than market value or under simulated legal transactions (for example, payment of professional fees or debts that do not exist).

Other jurisdictions permit only the restraint or seizure of assets that are held by a target; and they define "held" broadly to include ownership and assets owned by others, but in which the target holds a beneficial interest.

With regard to assets that are gifted, some jurisdictions permit the restraint or seizure of assets that have been gifted within a reasonable time, such as a five- or six-year period.[104] These provisions are similar to the "claw back" provisions used to recover assets disposed of by a bankrupt person or entity in the period leading up to the bankruptcy.

In linking a target to an asset or account held in the name of an associate, close relative, or company, it is helpful to look into the transactional activity surrounding the asset and to consider a number of factors, including:

- the amount paid for the asset (market value), including whether the mortgage responsibility was transferred with the title;
- the source of funds used to purchase the asset;

---

103. In Colombia, if assets have been transferred or sold to a third party, those assets can be restrained; the third party then has the burden of proving that it is not involved with the criminal enterprise.
104. Colombia permits confiscation of gifted items at any time (Law 793.02). In the United Kingdom, legislation permits going beyond the six-year period if the asset can be linked to the offense.

- the person paying the expenses and outgoings associated with the asset;
- the capacity or resources of the owner of the asset to purchase or maintain the asset; and
- the person occupying, possessing, or controlling the asset.

These questions can lead to the accumulation of evidence, circumstantial or otherwise, that will permit a court to draw the inference that assets owned by a third party are actually beneficially owned or controlled by the target and therefore (if the law permits) subject to restraint or seizure and eventual confiscation.

Partial Interests in Assets

A target will often hold a partial interest in or a share of an asset, business entity, or investment. Unless it is alleged that the remaining interests are beneficially owned or controlled by the target, it is important to ensure that restraint is limited to the target's interest in the asset (for additional information and guidance, see section 4.7 of chapter 4 on third-party interests).

4.3.2 Asset Management Considerations

In addition to determining which assets are subject to provisional measures, it is essential that consideration be given to what, if any, asset management requirements will be generated by the proposed restraint or seizure (see chapter 5 for a discussion of asset management issues). This will involve the investigation team (including any investigators tasked specifically with tracing the assets) and the prosecution team (including the prosecutor tasked with obtaining the order). When it is determined that a restraint or seizure will take place, the team should consider involving the agency responsible for asset management (if one exists). The manager can provide valuable advice about whether assets should be restrained or seized and the particular powers and conditions that should be included in the order to facilitate management of the asset. In addition, early involvement will allow the manager the opportunity to consider whether logistical arrangements will be needed to achieve physical control of the assets.

Although all bank accounts, share certificates, cash, and other intangible assets that hold value will be included in the restraint or seizure order, some form of cost-benefit analysis should be undertaken for assets that will require management because it is an expensive activity that has the potential to cost more than the value of the assets being managed. Just because assets *can* be restrained or seized does not necessarily mean that they *should* be. As a general rule, assets should not be seized or restrained if the likely costs of maintaining, storing, or managing them will exceed or substantially diminish the return on confiscation. Some jurisdictions have set thresholds to avoid restraint or seizure of low-value assets or they refuse to restrain or seize certain types of assets (such as livestock). Others will appoint a depository holder, escrow agent, or custodian for assets that are too risky or expensive to administer or they will permit the seizure and sale of certain items.

This general rule should not be applied inflexibly. There may be reasons in an individual case where restraint or seizure is in the public interest, such as an abandoned house used for illegal activity. Likewise, even if there is value in an asset, there may be reasons for restraining but permitting continued use of it—for example, the family home and contents or cars.[105] Clear policies in relation to these matters should be developed and communicated to practitioners and asset managers.[106]

Another consideration in the planning stage is whether the asset can be preserved without requiring management services, such as by registering a lien on the real property in the public records. Box 4.2 is an example of how planning can result in small changes to a proposed order that eliminate the need for the appointment of an asset manager, with consequential savings in expenditure, complexity, and administrative work; and without much loss in the value of the asset.

4.3.3 Partial Control or Limited Restraint

Some assets may be controlled at different levels, and advance consideration should be given to the degree of control that is required to preserve the assets for confiscation. For example, a target may be the proprietor of a business that is operated on land owned by the target; and it may be possible to restrain the land and buildings, as well as the business itself. Making and acting on such a determination will involve a number of considerations. Although land can be restrained without requiring the appointment of an asset manager, maintaining buildings and a business is likely to be costly and will require management. Businesses, in particular, may require specialized management skills involving marketing and sales, customer service, logistics and supply, asset management, and human resource management; failure in any of these areas can turn a profitable business into an unprofitable one. On the other hand, the profits generated from the buildings or business may not be subject to confiscation unless they are included in the restraint order. Table 4.1 defines some of the advantages and disadvantages of the different options.

4.3.4 Preparation for Taking Physical Possession

The only practical way to preserve assets is often to take physical possession of them. Before an asset manager can take physical possession, arrangements must be put in place to ensure safe seizure of the asset, safe storage facilities, and safe transfer to the storage facilities. In some cases, storage can be accomplished relatively easily: for example, jewelry or bullion may be stored safely in safe deposit boxes at a bank. Other types of assets—such as valuable artwork, motor vehicles, or yachts—require specialized storage facilities that may take time and substantial cost to arrange.

---

105. See, for example, section 4.5 of chapter 4 or sections 5.4.2 and 5.4.3 of chapter 5.
106. In the United States, the government is prohibited from seizing real property during the course of confiscation proceedings, unless the government demonstrates that the property is abandoned or is deteriorating in value. However, prosecutors will place a lis pendens (lien) on the public land records to give notice of the pending proceeding. The lien prevents any future purchaser from obtaining bona fide purchase for value status.

BOX 4.2 An Example of Pre-restraint Planning Decisions in Practice

In the course of an investigation into the corrupt activities of a government official, it was determined that asset confiscation proceedings would be brought against the official at, or shortly before, his arrest. The following is a list of the official's assets and the considerations and decisions made with respect to restraint and management:

- **Large residential dwelling occupied by official and family.** The property was included in the restraint order, and the existence of the order was noted on the title to warn prospective purchasers or secured lenders. An asset manager was not appointed; and the official and his family were permitted to remain in the dwelling on condition, as noted in the order, that the official maintain the property and pay rates, taxes, and mortgage payments.
- **Investment seaside house (rented out by agent).** Although initially thought to be an asset that would need to be managed, it was discovered that the ongoing management and profits generated were being managed by a property agent. It was decided that the asset could be adequately restrained without an asset manager by means of an appropriately drafted order requiring the property agent to pay accumulated rent into a restrained bank account. The property agent was authorized by the order to pay property outgoings and fees from rental receipts. The existence of the order was noted on the title.
- **Small plastic fabrication factory (located in an industrial unit owned by the official) operated by a company owned by the official.** It was determined that the factory was of little value: the current account balance was low and investigators suspected it was simply used as a vehicle to launder the proceeds of corruption. As a result, restraint was not sought and the business was left in the hands of the official. Within six months of the arrest, the plastic factory business folded.
- **Industrial unit.** It was discovered that the only "tenant" of the unit was the factory, and the factory had not been paying rent to the official. This property was included in the restraint order, which was noted on the title. It was determined that the factory could continue to occupy the unit without paying rent providing that it continued to maintain the buildings and pay rates and taxes. After the plastic factory business folded, the restraint order was varied by providing for the appointment of an asset manager to manage this property. He arranged to lease the property, paid the outgoings on the land and buildings from the rent, and invested the profits.
- **Personal bank accounts and share portfolio.** These were restrained, with the exception of one low-value account into which the official's salary was paid (used by the official to pay living expenses for himself and his family). Because the share portfolio was not very large and was held in blue-chip companies with a stable value, an asset manager was not appointed at the outset. After the asset manager was appointed to control the industrial unit, the share portfolio was also placed under his control.
- **Three high-value cars.** The cars were restrained and placed in the custody of law enforcement (provided for in legislation) with vehicle management procedures and facilities that enabled them to look after high-value cars properly.

TABLE 4.1	Considerations in Partial Control or Limited Restraint	
Option	Advantages	Disadvantages
Restrain the land only. (Leave hotel business and buildings in possession of target to manage and pay related fees.)	May not necessitate the appointment of an asset manager because the business is responsible for outgoings and taxes. In the event that confiscation is unsuccessful, there is a low risk that the authority will be liable for post-restraint losses of the business.	The profits from the land and the business will not be subject to confiscation. If the business is being used to launder money, this option will allow such activities to continue; therefore, it would be better to consider the third option.
Restrain the land and buildings only. (Lease or rent land to hotel business.)	Profits from the land in the form of rent (less outgoings) will be subject to confiscation. Management tasks involving only the land and buildings may not be particularly difficult or onerous.	Asset manager may need to be appointed. Profits from the business will not be subject to confiscation.
Restrain everything (land, buildings, hotel business).	The full value of the property, including the hotel business, will be restrained and subject to confiscation.	This is a major intervention and involves placing expert managers to oversee the operation of the business and to ensure that the profits of the business are properly restrained. In the event that confiscation is unsuccessful, the authority may be liable for post-restraint losses of the business.

Source: Authors' compilation.
Note: Assets = hotel business of target operated on land owned by target.

With regard to how an asset will be seized, the asset manager (or asset management authorities) should coordinate with practitioners investigating the criminal matter. If search warrants are to be executed on premises that have assets to be seized, the best time to take possession is during the execution of the warrants. When the officers have secured the premises and completed their preliminary searches for evidence, the premises can be checked easily by the asset manager for the presence of assets he or she has been authorized to seize.[107] The applicant for the seizure order will need to ensure that the asset manager has the necessary authority to enter the premises because he or she may not be covered under the authorities granted to law enforcement.

When assets must be seized independently of a criminal investigation (for example, to enforce a seizure order in a non-conviction based [NCB] confiscation proceeding), it may be necessary to obtain orders authorizing the asset manager to enter the premises to take possession of certain assets. Asset managers should liaise with law enforcement on security issues, and law enforcement officials should be prepared to provide agents for this purpose.

4.4 Timing of Provisional Measures

Proper timing of provisional measures is one of the most challenging parts of asset confiscation work. If they are imposed too early, a target may be tipped off and cease activities (thereby making it difficult to gather evidence and identify other accounts, targets, or the typologies used). However, if the measures are imposed after a target is aware of the investigation, the likely result is that assets will be dissipated or hidden. As a result, practitioners investigating offenses must coordinate with practitioners seeking recovery of the assets. They must be attentive to the risk that a target may become aware of the investigation, and they should remain sufficiently agile to obtain provisional measures when needed. A target may be tipped off at any of the following stages:

- When certain investigative techniques are used in the course of an investigation— techniques such as search of residences or businesses, interviewing witnesses, production orders, or issuance of a MLA request. It will be important to ensure that assets are secured before (or simultaneously with) the use of these techniques.
- At the time a target is charged with a criminal offense.
- At the time an application for confiscation is made.

The consequence of bad timing is the loss of assets and additional evidence. Practitioners should begin consultations in the early stages of an investigation and before any overt action is taken against a target. They should develop a strategy that will permit criminal investigation objectives to be achieved together with the restraint or seizure of a target's assets at the optimal time.

Provisional measures are less effective in jurisdictions that permit the implementation of measures only after a target has been charged. Most investigations and tracing efforts

---

107. Sometimes practitioners are empowered by confiscation legislation to seize assets that are covered in the restraining order or that they believe are the proceeds or instrumentalities of crime. This may remove the need for the asset manager to be present during the search; however, procedures for dealing with the assets should be worked out in advance between the asset manager and the practitioners.

can take months, if not years—thereby increasing the opportunity for a target to hide or dissipate assets or to flee the jurisdiction. It is fortunate that some jurisdictions have addressed this issue by permitting provisional measures at any time during an investigation into an offense. The existence of NCB confiscation laws can also provide an opportunity to restrain or seize assets much earlier because the power to do so is not dependent on criminal charges.

4.5 Exceptions to Restraint Orders for Payment of Expenses

Some jurisdictions will permit exceptions to be made to a restraint order to pay for certain categories of expenses, including the living expenses of a target and his or her dependents, legal expenses arising from the confiscation proceedings and any related criminal prosecution, and the bona fide debts and business expenses of a target.

Such exceptions are a controversial topic.[108] Applications for exceptions to the restraint order have the potential to entirely strip out the value of a restraint order. Those people with assets under restraint orders have an obvious incentive to try to use restrained assets under threat of confiscation rather than unrestrained assets—the existence of which may not be known. On the other hand, there are issues of due process and the right to counsel that must be considered.[109]

In jurisdictions that permit the drawing down of restrained assets, practitioners should ensure that there are no other unrestrained assets with which to pay the expenses.[110] Using investigative techniques (such as production or disclosure orders, interviews, search orders, and previous statements made under oath), practitioners may be able to locate evidence of unrestrained assets in or outside the jurisdiction and then use that information to argue before the court that the exception should not be made while other assets are available. In this regard, statements made in disclosure or examinations under oath that reveal lies or contradictions are useful to prosecutors because they damage the credibility of the applicant (see section 4.6 of chapter 4 on ancillary orders).

When it is established that no unrestrained assets are available, the applicant will likely have to submit a bill of costs for consideration by the court. Some jurisdictions will place a statutory cap on the fee that lawyers may charge, often an amount comparable with legal aid rates.[111]

---

108. Theodore S. Greenberg, Linda M. Samuel, Wingate Grant, and Larissa Gray, *Stolen Asset Recovery—A Good Practices Guide to Non-Conviction Based Asset Forfeiture* (Washington, DC: World Bank, 2009), 74.

109. Jurisdictions that do not allow such exceptions typically rely on the legal aid system or appoint a curator ad litem.

110. In some jurisdictions, it will be the responsibility of the applicant (target) of the restraint order to demonstrate to the court through sworn testimony that he or she has no untainted assets with which to pay expenses.

111. In Ontario, Canada, legislation permits the claimant to apply to the court for the release of reasonable legal expenses in NCB confiscation cases. The payments are subject to limits in the Civil Remedies Act. The

4.6 Ancillary Orders

Ancillary orders are subsidiary orders to a restraint or seizure order. Their purpose is to increase the effectiveness of the primary order. Examples are orders

- requiring a target or persons associated with a target to disclose details of the nature and location of the target's assets;
- placing restrained or seized assets under the control of an asset manager (see chapter 5);
- requiring a target to be examined under oath before an official of a court or other appropriate authority regarding his or her assets; and
- requiring third parties to produce documents relating to the assets of a target.

Disclosure and examination powers can be useful ways to probe complex asset holdings and obtain evidence useful in defending against applications to fund expenses from restrained funds. A prosecutor should not conduct examinations unless he or she is familiar with all available information on the assets and is in a position to test and challenge evidence given by the examinee. Information from a financial institution, for example, may be used to show that a target is failing to disclose assets, and it may lead to charges of contempt or failure to comply.

To protect a target's privilege or right against self-incrimination, evidence obtained under an ancillary order may not be used in related criminal proceedings.[112] The examiner should identify potential targets of criminal proceedings and be aware of the ramifications of eliciting incriminating evidence. Close consultation with the criminal prosecutors is necessary.

4.7 Third-Party Interests

Third-party claims will inevitably arise in cases of asset restraint or seizure. Targets often will have complicated holdings that involve third parties with legitimate interests—for example, business partners and investors. A third party may have an interest in or own an instrumentality that was used in the commission of an offense but be unaware of the illegal uses to which it was put. Or the legitimacy of the third party's interest may be at issue: On paper, the third party may own an asset that is alleged to be controlled by a target or it may be alleged that the third-party owner was not a bona fide purchaser.

Where a third party holds an interest or share in a business or investment venture with a target, practitioners will want to ensure that the interest is held bona fide and that the

---

maximum amount of funds available for legal expenses is calculated as a percentage of the total funds, and there are limits on the legal rates.

112. These protections are usually set out in legislation or enshrined as constitutional rights. Some jurisdictions also require an undertaking by the prosecution.

interest concerned is not beneficially owned or controlled by a target. If confirmed, it is important to draft the order in such a way that the third-party interests are not restrained or seized. In such cases, a restraint order can require that the business continue under normal processes, but with strict reporting requirements to the court and oversight by the asset manager—thus permitting uninvolved third parties to participate in and benefit from the business, but escrowing any benefits due to the target and preventing any involvement by the target in the running of the business.

If assets are jointly owned by a target and an innocent third-party investor who has used legitimate funds to invest in the assets and was not complicit in any way with the illegal activity, it may not be appropriate to obtain a restraint order over the entire asset. Instead, it may be sufficient to restrain "the interest of [target] in asset *x*." In practice, such an order will block dealings in the entire asset because it will be difficult for the third party to deal independently with his or her interest. However, this way of constructing the order will make it clear to the third party that it is not intended to confiscate his or her interest—thereby avoiding unnecessary disputes with the third party.

The asset subject to confiscation is often encumbered by a lien or other security held by a person or entity that had no involvement in or knowledge of the illegal use of the asset (for example, a bank that has issued a loan). Where satisfied that the creditor was not complicit in the illegal activity, a number of jurisdictions have streamlined the process for recognizing such creditors as innocent owners. Some jurisdictions require that a lienholder, like any other party in interest, file a timely claim in the confiscation proceeding; and if such a claim is not filed, the lien will be extinguished in the confiscation proceeding. When the confiscation proceedings are complete and the asset is confiscated and sold, the creditor is paid from the proceeds.

In all cases, practitioners should be open to submissions from third parties and, where permitted, should consent to vary the restraint order or release assets or instrumentalities held legitimately.[113] However, where no satisfactory or verifiable explanations can be given or there is a compelling public interest to seize the asset (for example, a drug house), third-party claims should be left to the court to determine in accordance with the criteria set out in the legislation for the protection or exclusion of third-party interests from restraint and confiscation (see section 6.4 of chapter 6 for a discussion of third-party interests in the confiscation phase).[114]

---

113. When making such releases of property, practitioners should ensure that the third parties execute release documents, holding harmless and waiving any future claims against any government officials and their contractors who were involved in the seizure or restraint.
114. Depending on the laws of the jurisdiction and the circumstances of the case, there may be a risk that the government will have to pay damages if the confiscation order is unsuccessful, if it is determined that a loss was incurred (in the property value or income) and the property manager should have released the assets to the third party.

4.8 Alternatives to Provisional Measures

Although provisional measures are the preferred mechanism for securing assets, there may be cases where evidence is insufficient to obtain the relevant order. In such cases, practitioners should consider alternative means of achieving the same result. In many jurisdictions, anti-money laundering legislation—in particular, requirements to report suspicious activity or transactions—can provide these alternative tools to secure assets: FIUs may have administrative authority to restrain or refuse consent to release funds on receipt of a suspicious transaction or activity report (STR); and financial institutions may decide independently to restrain accounts to avoid being implicated in a money laundering scheme. As a result, if the practitioner advises a financial institution that a corrupt official has been indicted or that other suspicious activity has taken place, this may raise sufficient suspicion for the bank to issue an STR, and may prompt the FIU or bank to implement one of these alternative means to secure the funds.

5. Managing Assets Subject to Confiscation

Once assets have been secured through provisional measures, authorities will need to ensure the safety and value of the assets until they are eventually confiscated (or released)—potentially, a period of years. These control mechanisms are sometimes capable of working effectively over assets without any need for ongoing supervision and management. For example, once an order to restrain or seize a bank account has been served on the bank, the bank can usually be relied on to ensure that the account is blocked effectively. Other assets may require more-targeted approaches to ongoing maintenance, control, and management—assets such as unique investment vehicles, exotic or valuable livestock, or luxury real estate. It is essential for any asset confiscation system to have both the flexibility to control and manage such assets pending confiscation and the ability to realize them and pay the proceeds to the state, the government, or other authorized recipients after confiscation.[115]

The starting point for establishing a functional asset management system is appropriate legislation and accompanying regulations that enable the preservation of the economic value of assets in an efficient, transparent, and flexible manner. Sufficient and appropriate resources must be allocated, including the identification of a centralized competent authority to manage and control the assets and the appointment of senior personnel with management and administrative skills to oversee the program. It cannot be assumed that existing law enforcement structures already have the skills and resources required to manage assets. Although there may be some basic capacity in this area—for example, a law enforcement agency seizes and stores property that is evidence of criminal offenses—the systems are insufficient to deal with the seizure or restraint and confiscation of a wide range of assets. Without carefully drafted legislation, regulations, and funding for asset management, even the most successful confiscation system may be rendered ineffective by the inability to manage the assets seized.

---

115. The importance of the management of seized assets has been recognized by the international community. See United Nations Convention against Corruption, art. 31(3). Guidance also has been issued on the topic in G8 Lyon/Roma Group, Criminal Legal Affairs Subgroup, "G8 Best Practices for the Administration of Seized Assets" (April 27, 2005), http://www.coe.int/t/dghl/monitoring/moneyval/web_resources/ G8_BPAssetManagement.pdf; and the General Secretariat, Organization of American States, "Model Regulations Concerning Laundering Offences Connected to Illicit Drug Trafficking and Related Offences," art. 7 (Washington, DC, 1992).

5.1 Key Players in Asset Management

As demonstrated in this handbook, asset confiscation requires the coordinated efforts of individuals and agencies with different skill sets working together, including law enforcement officers, financial analysts, prosecutors, investigating magistrates, and the asset manager or asset management agency. Although one group might have more involvement than another at any given time, it is important that all groups are aware of what is happening in the case, from the beginning to the end.

Asset managers must have the skills, resources, and legal authority to (1) preserve the security and value of assets pending confiscation (including the sale of rapidly depreciating assets); (2) if necessary, hire contractors with specialized skills to accomplish management tasks; (3) liquidate assets for a fair price after confiscation; and (4) distribute the proceeds in accordance with applicable legislation following payment of all necessary expenses. Such skills are unlikely to be found among law enforcement officers, prosecutors, or the courts; instead, authorities should seek to obtain the needed expertise in other ways, including

- **Creating a separate specialized asset management office.** Set up an agency with responsibility to manage seized or restrained assets, hire qualified asset managers, conduct pre-restraint planning and analysis, and coordinate post-confiscation realization or liquidation.[116]
- **Creating an asset management unit within an existing agency.** In some cases, a new unit dedicated solely to the duties of managing assets subject to confiscation is established within an existing government agency.[117] Logically, this is often an agency with ready expertise in asset management.[118]
- **Outsourcing asset management.** In those jurisdictions where establishing an asset management office or co-opting an existing agency is not an option, engage private, locally available property trustees.[119]

---

116. Examples of specialized asset management offices include the Canadian Seized Property Management Directorate and the Haitian Bureau d'Administration du Fond Special de lutte contre la drogue. The Financial Action Task Force (FATF) has recommended asset management offices in "Best Practices: Confiscation (Recommendations 3 and 38)," adopted by the plenary of the FATF in February 2010. The Camden Asset Recovery Inter-Agency Network also recommended the creation of asset management offices at its 2008 annual general meeting.

117. In Colombia, the antinarcotics agency has a specialized asset management unit responsible for managing seized or restrained assets pursuant to Colombia's anti-drug trafficking laws. In the United States, the U.S. Marshal's Service, a generalist law enforcement agency, has been performing asset management functions in the U.S. Asset Forfeiture Program since 1984.

118. An example is the Insolvency and Trustee Service Australia, the government office responsible for administering bankruptcy and insolvency laws. In addition to performing its primary role as the administrator of the bankrupt estates and to managing the assets of bankrupt individuals or insolvent companies, the office also provides specialized asset management services in support of Australian federal confiscation laws.

119. South Africa is an example of a jurisdiction that makes use of private trustees, or curators bonis, to provide asset management services in support of the enforcement of the Prevention of Organised Crime Act, 1998. This legislation permits the court appointment of people to manage assets seized or restrained

5.2 Powers of the Asset Manager

Asset managers derive their authority through existing laws or rules of court, which often include important information-gathering powers to assist managers with their duties.

5.2.1 Legal Powers

When an asset management office is placed in control of assets by a court, pursuant to a restraint or seizure order, the office (or manager) must be given legal powers to carry out the various requisite functions. Typically, these powers will be granted through confiscation laws, asset management laws, anti-money laundering laws, and rules of the court. The powers should include the following:

- authority to pay all necessary costs, expenses, and disbursements connected with the restraint or seizure and the management of the assets;
- authority to buy and sell seized or restrained assets that are in the form of shares, securities, or other investments;
- authority to insure assets under control;
- in the case of a business, authority to operate the business, including to employ or terminate the employment of people in the business, hire a business manager if required, and make decisions necessary to manage the business prudently;
- in the case of assets that represent shares in a company, authority to exercise rights in respect of those shares as if the asset manager were the registered holder of those shares; and
- authority to pay salaries of the asset manager and people involved in asset management, in accordance with a defined scale or regulation, or in accordance with an order of the court that is subject to full disclosure and mandatory audit (see section 5.8 of chapter 5 for a discussion of fees payable to asset managers).[120]

Asset managers are sometimes given powers to deal with depreciating or perishable assets—particularly, the power of an interlocutory sale prior to entry of a final confiscation order (see section 5.4.7 of chapter 5 for further information). If not given authority to deal with perishable assets, or if confronted by any other management issue for which no specific guidance or powers are given in the legislation, the asset manager may have to apply to the court that made the restraint order to seek guidance and authority. The drawback with this process is that it is time-consuming and costly.

---

under the act and to realize property in satisfaction of confiscation orders. The Asset Forfeiture Unit of the South African National Prosecution Authority has created a manual to guide people appointed as curator bonis under the act.

120. In some jurisdictions, salaries of asset managers are paid from confiscated assets. It is not recommended that the salaries of practitioners responsible for the investigatory or litigation decisions leading to confiscation be paid directly from such funds because doing so creates the appearance that assets are being seized for monetary reward.

5.2.2 Information-Gathering Powers

Asset confiscation laws often contain information-gathering powers. In many cases, these powers may be used only by law enforcement officers, prosecutors, or investigating magistrates. However, sometimes they are available to asset managers who have been directed to take control of assets of which the exact nature and location are unknown, or to enforce value-based money judgments or benefits orders. These powers may include production orders, search warrants for documents relevant to tracing assets, compulsory statements by targets disclosing assets, and examinations.

Exercising the power to order a target to disclose to the asset manager in a sworn statement the nature and location of his or her assets is a useful tactic that can be employed in both civil and common law jurisdictions.[121] Even if a target does not disclose the existence or location of a previously unknown asset, the existence of such a statement—or even the refusal to make a statement—can be helpful in defending against a target's subsequent applications to have access to restrained assets to pay for legal fees or living expenses.[122] Also, discovery of false information or refusal to make such disclosures may often be prosecuted as contempt or failure to comply with the disclosure order. In addition, the power to examine under oath a target, people associated with the target, or a target's professional advisers (for example, accountants, real estate agents, and lawyers) can be useful in tracing assets.

5.3 Recording Inventory and Reporting

When an asset manager takes control of restrained assets, it is essential to maintain detailed records of the assets and any transactions involving them. The manager makes a detailed inventory and description of the assets and their condition, and provides subsequent updates.[123] These records should be supplemented with photographs or video recordings that show the condition of the asset at the time of seizure or restraint. Appraisals should be obtained and included in the records. These records can protect the asset manager and the applicant for the restraint order from subsequent claims that assets were damaged by staff or agents of the asset manager.

Managers should also be careful to record any management issues or defects identified at the time of seizure or restraint—for example, a leaky roof in a warehouse containing goods. Managers should give this information to the court, the prosecutor, or both so that appropriate measures may be taken and so that the asset manager is not blamed for pre-existing conditions.

---

121. Authorities in Brazil and the United Kingdom are able to request such disclosure orders.

122. These examination powers sometimes infringe the target's right or privilege against self-incrimination. Where this happens, authorities are usually prevented from using any evidence derived from the examination in related criminal proceedings.

123. Technological support can be essential to maintaining an updated inventory list. Some jurisdictions have introduced computerized tracking systems specifically designed for these purposes.

A reporting component is also important to an effective asset management system. It increases the transparency of asset management activities and may raise awareness among the public about the purpose and achievements of the office. Reports on specific cases should be delivered to the applicant for the restraining order and, if mandated by legislation, to the court. The inventory and valuation should be annexed to this report. In addition, annual reports on the general activities of the unit and overall statistics may be required.

5.4 Common Types of Assets and Associated Problems

5.4.1 Seized Cash, Bank Accounts, and Financial Instruments

Money often is difficult to trace, but it is usually easier to manage. Seized cash, except cash to be used as evidence, is most often preserved in an interest-bearing account.[124] Similar policies will be in place in jurisdictions that restrain or seize bank accounts.[125] Financial instruments (such as cashier's checks, money orders, certificates of deposit, stocks, bonds, and brokerage accounts) will also need to be seized, with procedures taken to preserve or redeem their value. With stocks, bonds, and brokerage accounts, a professional (such as a stock broker) will have to be contacted for a valuation of the assets and a determination of how best to preserve their value. In some cases, the professional may require the authority to liquidate accounts or hold them in a different manner to preserve the value of the assets.

5.4.2 Real Property (Land)

As a general rule, real property and improvements are good assets to seize for confiscation purposes, particularly in jurisdictions with an efficient landownership system that records ownership and encumbrance details at a central land registry or land titles office.[126] Under such systems, recording a lien or other notice of encumbrance in the public land records is quite simple and will give notice that the land is subject to confiscation proceedings to any potential arm's-length purchaser to whom a target wants to sell his or her land (in contravention of the restraint order). Failure to record notice on a title may impede or defeat the efforts of the authorities to confiscate: even with a restraint order in place, a target could transfer land to a bona fide purchaser for value, and that purchaser could subsequently claim bona fide ownership.

In the absence of complications, land often can be restrained effectively without appointing an asset manager. However, there are several problems:

---

124. In Colombia, U.S. dollar deposits are transferred to the U.S. Federal Reserve Bank for verification of authenticity and then invested in securities issued by the Colombian government.

125. In Switzerland, the Swiss Bankers Association and law enforcement agencies have worked together on a system for managing bank accounts subject to confiscation.

126. Older systems are generally indexed in books accessible to the public, and newer systems may be found electronically indexed and often available through online databases.

- **Rates, taxes, and secured loans.** Land is usually the subject of government rates and taxes, and it may be encumbered to banks as security for mortgages or loans. Where land is restrained, the order should provide that the target or other occupant of the land is required by court order to maintain current payment of taxes and other debts that have the potential to encumber the land with a lien. In the event the owner stops paying rates, taxes, and loan payments, the court should be alerted. Alternatively, the manager may reach an agreement with the target or other occupant that grants the right to continued occupancy, conditional on the payment of these expenses; and that grants the manager the immediate right to take possession and evict the occupants if the conditions are not met. If required to evict the occupants, the asset manager may seek to lease the asset at a rate that is sufficient to meet expenses or to sell the asset and use the proceeds to pay outstanding debts. Ultimately, taxes and liens will usually take priority over the confiscation order.
- **Expenses, outgoings, and capital improvements.** The restraint of land may be complicated by heavy, property-related expenses and utility bills, some of which may be urgent. Some types of land require significant and expensive maintenance to retain their value—for example, a golf course or farm. If funds are available from the target's assets, a designated confiscation fund, or some other contingency fund, they should be used to maintain the overall value. If funds are not available or the value cannot be maintained, leasing or selling the land (where permitted, with or without consent of the owner) may be the better option.

5.4.3 Motor Vehicles, Boats, and Airplanes

Vehicles indisputably pose significant management challenges. They are difficult and costly to store and maintain between seizure and confiscation—potentially, a period of years. The market value of seized vehicles may be debatable, and they typically depreciate at a rapid rate.

Frequently, vehicles seized by practitioners are simply left outside in a yard (see figure 5.1). This is not an appropriate asset management strategy because it exposes the seizing agency to claims for compensation and substantially reduces the recovery of any sales proceeds if the vehicles are eventually confiscated.

Proper maintenance of motor vehicles, boats, and airplanes requires a secure, appropriate storage facility where proper maintenance may be provided and people with expertise in maintaining and meeting any regulatory requirements for the type of vehicle seized. This storage and expertise can be expensive, and financing will need to be provided by the agency responsible for the seizure (for example, a law enforcement agency or asset manager if pursuant to seizure order) or other source (including the target or a confiscation fund).

Given these expenses and the depreciating nature of vehicles, it may not be worth seizing vehicles that are old or in poor condition because their realizable value may not cover the cost of maintaining them. Where authorized by law, consideration should be given to selling such vehicles while they are relatively new and in good condition (with

FIGURE 5.1 Seized Motor Vehicles Left Outdoors

Source: Courtesy of Clive Scott.

or without the consent of the owner). Because it is often in the interests of all parties to convert a depreciating vehicle into an asset that holds its value or appreciates, it may be possible to make such an agreement by the consent of all parties—including the target. One final option would be to permit a target to retain use of the vehicle or other conveyance during the course of the confiscation proceeding and to post a bond guaranteeing the payment of an amount equivalent to its value at the time the case was initiated.

5.4.4 Businesses

Generally, it is not possible to restrain or seize a business effectively without placing it under the control of an asset manager; and the risks and expense of this course of action may be considerable. Given that a business may hold little value (for example, it may not own its inventory or the premises on which it operates), an equity valuation of the business should be undertaken before any restraint or seizure is requested to accurately determine its debt load and equity. If such a valuation cannot be made before requesting a restraint or seizure order, it should be done shortly after the provisional action. For a business with little value, it may be best to include it for confiscation but not undertake the financial risks associated with its continued operation; instead, close operations or sell the business. There is also the possibility that identifying the business as a target for confiscation will damage its goodwill value. One way to prevent this is to permit the current manager to continue its operation, but under the control of a business manager contracted by the asset manager or appointed by the court.

Pre-restraint planning will be critical to any restraint or seizure of a business. Restraint orders should be made *ex parte* to avoid the removal of business assets and cash. Individuals with the necessary skills to manage the business should be sourced and available to assume control immediately at the time of restraint.

The asset manager or appointed manager or contractor should take immediate control of bank accounts, accounting systems and records, important business data (such as customer records), valuable stock, and valuable plant and equipment. If the business will continue in operation, all books and accounting records must be made available and should be assessed by the manager. In addition, managers will need to engage with staff and key personnel to prepare themselves for eventual decisions about the reliability of those employees. Removal of staff may prove costly and can result in loss of corporate knowledge, customer dissatisfaction, and loss of business; however, retaining staff whose loyalty lies with a target may be hazardous to the business as well.

Regular reports on the performance of the business should be sent to the prosecution agency responsible for the restraint order. Any problems with the business should be raised immediately.

5.4.5 Livestock and Farms

This category of assets is often a subset of a business because cattle, sheep, or game animals are usually part of an agricultural business; or horses are kept for breeding or racing purposes. They may also be hobby farms. Whatever the form, managing animals can be quite problematic for asset managers.

When these assets are of very high value to certain markets (for example, race horses can be worth hundreds of thousands or even millions of dollars), practitioners are more inclined to include them in restraint orders. However, maintaining animals can be very expensive, with costs for stock-feed, veterinary procedures, yard and pasture maintenance, and staffing costs. Given these expenses and the fact that sufficient revenue streams to fund them are unlikely, some jurisdictions refuse to seize livestock and farms. Others may be authorized to restrain the farm, then seize and sell the livestock (with or without consent of the owner). Again, a bond could be posted if a target or associates desire to continue the operation during confiscation proceedings.

5.4.6 Precious Metals, Jewels, and Artwork

In addition to ensuring compliance with procedures and safeguards for the inventory of such items, asset managers will need to retain expertise for inspection, verification, and valuation. A secure and appropriate storage facility must be arranged or set out in legislation or regulations.[127]

5.4.7 Perishable and Depreciating Assets

This category of assets generally includes

- highly perishable assets, such as a boatload of fresh fish or a consignment of cut flowers that will lose all value if not sold within a few days;

---

127. In Azerbaijan, seized diamonds must be secured at a financial institution.

- moderately perishable assets, such as a field crop or farm animals that will lose value if they are not harvested or sold at an appropriate time (possibly within weeks or months);
- depreciating assets, such as cars, boats, and electronic equipment that lose 15–30 percent of their value each year.

In an ideal situation, confiscation laws have provisions that empower an asset manager to sell perishable or rapidly depreciating assets and place the proceeds in an interest-bearing account supervised by either the asset manager or the court. Where such powers are not available or do not apply, it may be possible to request that a court exercise general discretionary powers to make appropriate orders relating to restrained assets. Consent of all parties is preferable, but the court should have authority to enter such orders even if contested.

5.4.8 Assets Located in Foreign Jurisdictions

Assets may be restrained and seized by foreign jurisdictions through informal assistance (for example, through administrative avenues) and pursuant to a mutual legal assistance request (see section 4.2.3 of chapter 4 and chapter 7). When a restraint order is registered, enforcing it will be the responsibility of the authorities in the foreign jurisdiction. An asset manager may be appointed by the court in the foreign jurisdiction to achieve this.

Generally, the asset managers in both jurisdictions will work together to maintain the assets. At the same time, it is wise to ensure that the asset manager in the requesting jurisdiction has additional powers to help enforce the foreign restraint order and manage the assets. Such powers would not grant the asset manager physical control over the assets in the requested jurisdiction; but they would permit the asset manager to hire contractors, lawyers, and other agents in the requested jurisdiction for the purpose of obtaining orders from the courts of the requested jurisdiction.

There may be additional problems when dealing with foreign jurisdictions. The requested jurisdiction may not have the domestic authority or the operational ability to restrain or seize certain types of assets. For example, some jurisdictions refuse to seize or restrain live animals. Or the requested jurisdiction may not have an asset manager or funds dedicated to asset management. These issues can be resolved through discussions with the requested jurisdiction, although ultimately the requesting jurisdiction may have to provide funds to hire a manager to manage the assets in the requested jurisdiction.

5.5 Ongoing Management Issues

5.5.1 Expenses

In optimal circumstances, an asset manager will have a reasonable mix of assets—income-generating, cash, capital, and depreciating assets—so that expenses can be paid from income, thereby maintaining the overall value of the portfolio and preserving it pending the outcome of confiscation proceedings. However, sometimes no cash or income will be available to fund the preservation or maintenance of assets. In these cases, the asset manager will need to either sell the assets or generate sufficient funds to pay for maintenance—perhaps from the target or from a confiscation or confiscation fund (see section 5.9).

5.5.2 Heavy Debts

In some cases, an asset manager is placed in control of the assets of a target who also has massive debts. The asset manager may apply to the court for the release or sale of other restrained assets to pay those debts. Creditors often compete with the confiscating authority's case by attempting to collect judgment liens or force the target into bankruptcy proceedings.

In these circumstances, the asset manager should have a good understanding of how the provisions of the confiscation legislation relate to bankruptcy or company liquidation legislation. In some jurisdictions, the bankruptcy or liquidation legislation takes priority when the individual or company is declared bankrupt. The confiscating authority simply joins the queue with other unsecured creditors. In other jurisdictions, confiscation laws are immune from the operation of bankruptcy and company liquidation law, which effectively gives the confiscating authority and its application priority over all other creditors.

5.5.3 Living, Legal, and Business Expenses

An asset manager will often be given responsibility by a court for the disbursement of funds from restrained assets for the living, legal, and business expenses of a target and his or her dependants (see chapter 6 for additional background on this issue). In most cases, the expenses will be determined by law or fixed by the court, although the asset manager may occasionally be involved in determining what is "reasonable" for certain purposes—an assessment that the target can dispute on application to the court.

As the payment of these expenses is frequently disputed before the court, it is important for the asset manager to make decisions carefully and to record and document these decisions and any transactions connected with them.

5.5.4 Use of Assets Subject to Confiscation

The use of assets that have been seized, but not ordered confiscated, presents major ethical and financial implications that militate against the practice. The primary ethical issue is this: if prosecutors, magistrates, law enforcement officials, or military personnel are permitted immediately to use any vehicle or conveyance seized in the preliminary stages of a case, they may have little incentive to pursue the confiscation proceeding to its conclusion, thus effectively perpetually depriving the owner of his or her assets without a court judgment. Also, such provisional-use practices create an unwanted incentive for law enforcement to seize assets without necessarily developing the requisite evidentiary showing. Financially, there are cost issues—particularly in the event of a court order requiring the return of the asset: because the use of the asset diminishes its value, restitution from the general treasury funds of the jurisdiction will be necessary.

5.6 Consultations

As discussed above, the asset manager must be involved in consulting with other practitioners in relation to proposed restraint and asset management decisions. Consultation can also be beneficial when a management proposal or decision may affect the value of the restrained assets. Such consultations may militate against claims for losses due to mismanagement, particularly if these consultations include the target, the practitioner who obtained the restraint order, and any third party with interest. Advice by all parties consulted should be recorded in writing and considered seriously. Ultimately, however, the asset manager has the final decision, subject to the direction of the court.

5.7 Liquidation (Sale) of Assets

When appointed to take control of assets pursuant to a restraint order, the asset manager's role is usually expressed in terms of preservation, maintenance, and management. In most cases, sale of restrained assets is contemplated only in relation to perishable and depreciating assets or after a confiscation order has been made. In addition, the authority to sell the assets varies: in some jurisdictions, the asset manager is given the authority under statute; in other jurisdictions, the court must make an order conferring realization powers on the asset manager.

When selling assets pursuant to realization powers, an asset manager usually has considerable discretion in how to go about the process. The most transparent procedures should be used because they will prevent or minimize allegations of mismanagement. For this reason, it is generally best to arrange to sell assets at well-advertised and professionally run public auctions. Occasionally, specialized or exotic types of assets will be restrained. They can be sold using methods (such as sales to specialized markets) to attract the maximum price. Decisions to sell assets in this way should be the subject of expert advice and well documented. Many jurisdictions are accomplishing these objectives with online auctions or other Web listings of assets for sale with preset minimum bids.

5.8 Fees Payable to Asset Managers

In some jurisdictions, fee structures for the payment of the asset manager are clearly defined in the confiscation laws or by reference in some other law (for example, property trustee or company liquidation laws). Sometimes these fees are left to the discretion of the court and are subject to full disclosure and mandatory audit.

Asset confiscation legislation usually envisages that the asset manager's fees will be deducted from the proceeds of confiscation, either as a fixed percentage or on a fee-for-service basis, perhaps calculated on an hourly rate or in accordance with a scale of fees. Because the manager may be required to manage assets over a lengthy period of time, it is good practice for the manager to prepare regular updates of the fees incurred under his or her appointment and to provide them to the prosecutor. The accumulation of fees may alert the prosecutor to the fact that the order is becoming uneconomical, and may suggest that other methods or configurations of order should be considered.

There will be circumstances where the asset manager performs extensive work but fees cannot be deducted (for example, where confiscation proceedings are discontinued or unsuccessful). Under such circumstances, the manager's fees must be paid by the confiscating authority. An existing confiscation fund can be a useful tool to pay asset management costs. Good practice suggests that these issues be considered and made the subject of agreement by prosecutors, asset managers, and the courts at the earliest possible time to avoid misunderstandings and potentially costly disputes at a later stage.

5.9 Funding Asset Management

Resources are required for all phases of asset confiscation, including tracing, restraining, managing, and liquidating. As discussed above, asset management can be expensive; and it requires mechanisms that ensure predictable, continued, and adequate financing. In some cases, management may be financed from the general budget; in other cases, it is financed through a confiscation fund. The issue has been addressed in other Stolen Asset Recovery Initiative publications.[128]

---

128. Theodore S. Greenberg, Linda M. Samuel, Wingate Grant, and Larissa Gray, *Stolen Asset Recovery—A Good Practices Guide to Non-Conviction Based Asset Forfeiture* (Washington, DC: World Bank, 2009), 90; and Stolen Asset Recovery Secretariat, "Management of Confiscated Assets" (Washington, DC, 2009).

6. Mechanisms for Confiscation

An asset confiscation regime is a prerequisite for any jurisdiction that wishes to provide the full panoply of methods for recovering the proceeds of corruption and money laundering. Confiscation involves the permanent deprivation of assets by order of a court or other competent authority.[129] Title is acquired by the state or government without compensation to the asset holder. International instruments and standards emphasize the importance of confiscation systems by requiring, at a minimum, that parties have criminal confiscation systems in place as a means to combat and deter corruption, money laundering, and other serious offenses.[130] Non-conviction based (NCB) confiscation is encouraged in the United Nations Convention against Corruption (UNCAC) and the Financial Action Task Force 40+9 Recommendations, and is being adopted more widely as jurisdictions continue to expand their confiscation programs.[131]

The rationale for confiscation is clear: First, in crimes involving corruption and other financial predatory crime, there are victims (either a state, a government, or private individuals) who should be compensated with any recoverable funds. Second, because greed is a primary motive behind corruption and financial crime, confiscation provides deterrence by removing the possibility of enjoying the illegal gains. In other words, confiscation sends a message that "crime does not pay."

Like all legislation, confiscation laws have not been without legal challenge in many jurisdictions and before international courts. The challenges have included debates over property rights and whether targets of confiscation are afforded the constitutional rights of those involved in criminal matters, including the presumption of innocence; the right to be heard before a criminal court; and rights against self-incrimination, double punishment, and retrospective punishment. Many of these debates have centered on the issue of whether confiscation should be considered a punishment or a remedial measure: if it is a punishment, the proceedings would attract the safeguards of the criminal process; if a remedial measure, the scope of application expands and may include hearings before administrative agencies or civil courts, use of a different standard of proof, use of rebuttable presumptions (although many jurisdictions permit rebuttable

---

129. United Nations Convention against Corruption (UNCAC), art. 2; United Nations Convention against Transnational Organized Crime (UNTOC), art. 2; United Nations Convention against Narcotic Drugs and Psychotropic Substances, art. 1.

130. UNCAC, art. 2, 31, 54, 55; UNTOC, art. 2, 6, 12, 13; United Nations Convention against Narcotic Drugs and Psychotropic Substances, art. 1, 5; and recommendations 3 and 38 of the Financial Action Task Force (FATF) 40+9 Recommendations.

131. UNCAC, art. 54(1)(c); recommendation 3, FATF 40+9 Recommendations.

BOX 6.1   Historical Background and Recent Developments in Confiscation

The concept of asset confiscation has been around for a very long time. Examples of ancient confiscation laws have been found in texts that are thousands of years old. Confiscation laws, descended from these ancient precedents, developed as part of both English common law and early civil law. Beginning with strengthened efforts in the 1980s to combat drug trafficking and organized crime, some jurisdictions implemented both a criminal confiscation regime and an NCB system. More recently, jurisdictions have redoubled their efforts to obtain confiscation, often motivated by the relatively low levels of recovery of criminal profits, compared with the enormous figures estimated to compose the criminal economy. This reevaluation has led to the following broad trends in confiscation legislation:

- introduction of (NCB) confiscation provisions;
- reduced standards of proof;
- reversal of the burden of proof in some circumstances;
- an increased use of rebuttable presumptions; and
- greater use of administrative confiscation authority and abandonment procedures in relation to cash and instrumentalities of crime.

presumptions with certain criminal offenses), and retrospective application. Ultimately, many courts have adopted an approach that permits a broader scope of application.[132]

A confiscation regime must provide for the identification, seizure or restraint, management, confiscation, liquidation, and sharing or return of the proceeds and instrumentalities. And because most large-scale corruption and money laundering cases cross international borders, the confiscation regime must be capable of having domestic orders enforced in foreign jurisdictions. This chapter addresses specific steps for obtaining a confiscation order and the procedural aids or enhancements that some jurisdictions apply. For information on the other aspects of confiscation, see chapters 3, 4, 5, and 7. Some of the historical background and recent developments related to confiscation are provided in box 6.1.

Prosecutors may have a number of confiscation methods available under their domestic regime; and they should try to keep all options available, particularly in cases where challenges to the confiscation are extremely likely and where evolving events may

---

132. The European Court of Human Rights (ECHR) has held that where the amount is limited to the benefit obtained, and could not be substituted by imprisonment but rather by other measures of economic value, confiscation of the proceeds of crime will have a remedial character. *Welch v. United Kingdom,* No. 17440/90 (ECHR, February 9, 1995); *Philips v. United Kingdom,* No. 41087/98 (ECHR, July 5, 2001); *Butler v. United Kingdom,* No. 41661/98 (ECHR, June 27, 2002). For examples from specific jurisdictions, see Theodore S. Greenberg, Linda M. Samuel, Wingate Grant, and Larissa Gray, *Stolen Asset Recovery—A Good Practices Guide to Non-Conviction Based Asset Forfeiture* (Washington, DC: World Bank, 2009), 19–21.

eliminate one method. For example, if a prosecution collapses because of inadmissible evidence or death of the defendant, the existence of a parallel NCB application preserves the opportunity to confiscate. The availability of multiple options may also enable the authorities to use one method to seize or restrain assets and then switch to another method to confiscate.[133]

Strategically, it may often be prudent to obtain multiple confiscation orders over the same asset, such as a property-based confiscation order and a value-based order. In such a case, if any charge is dismissed, an acquittal is obtained, or a conviction is reversed on appeal, then the other confiscation order may still stand. In some jurisdictions with NCB confiscation, the NCB confiscation proceeding may be stayed until the criminal case has been concluded and appeals exhausted. If confiscation legislation does not require an election to be made one way or another, practitioners should not abandon a potentially available sanction.

6.1 Confiscation Systems

Generally, there are three types of confiscation used to recover the proceeds and instrumentalities of corruption: criminal confiscation; NCB confiscation; and, in some jurisdictions, administrative confiscation.

6.1.1 Criminal Confiscation

Criminal confiscation requires a criminal conviction by trial or following a guilty plea by the defendant. Once a conviction is obtained, the court can make a final order of confiscation—often as part of the sentence. In some jurisdictions, confiscation is a mandatory order; in others, the court (or jury) has discretion in imposing it.[134] Criminal confiscation systems may be property-based or value-based systems (described further in section 6.2).

In some jurisdictions, different standards of proof may be applied in the two phases of the case (that is, during the adjudication of the conviction and during the confiscation proceedings). During the adjudication of the conviction, the prosecutor's primary

---

133. The United States often *seizes* or *restrains* assets using NCB confiscation before an indictment is obtained, but switches to criminal confiscation to *confiscate* these same assets after a conviction is entered: *United States v. Candelaria-Silva,* 166 F.3d 19, 43 (1st Cir., 1999). A reason for doing this is that the practitioner will often want to seize or restrain before the evidence will support the obtaining of a formal charge. Generally, however, if a conviction is eventually obtained, it is easier at that point to have the confiscation ordered as part of the sentence in the criminal case. Similarly, under Colombia's *extinción de dominio* system, the NCB confiscation proceeding may go forward independently and parallel to the criminal case. But if the defendant is convicted, the *de comiso* (criminal) confiscation is often easier to obtain than is completing the NCB confiscation process.
134. In Cameroon, for example, confiscation is mandatory in some corruption cases. Section 184(4) of the Cameroon Criminal Code on misappropriation of public funds states that confiscation "shall be ordered in every case."

burden is to convict the defendant for the offense at the required criminal standard of proof, whether "beyond a reasonable doubt" or by "intimate conviction." This standard of proof must be met to prove the crime before confiscation can be ordered. Subsequent or secondary burdens may be imposed during the court's consideration of confiscation. In some jurisdictions, this secondary burden may be established on the lower "balance of probabilities" standard of proof; other jurisdictions apply the same standard used in criminal cases.

Because of the need for a conviction, there may be difficulty in using this procedure to confiscate assets when the offender has died, fled the jurisdiction, or is absent. Some jurisdictions have incorporated absconding provisions that declare the offender "convicted" for confiscation purposes once it is established that he or she has fled the jurisdiction.

6.1.2 NCB Confiscation

NCB confiscation—sometimes referred to as "objective confiscation" or "*extinción de dominio*"—authorizes the confiscation of assets without the requirement of a conviction.[135] Because it is often a property-based action against the asset itself, not against the person with possession or ownership, NCB confiscation generally requires proof that the asset is the proceeds or an instrumentality of crime.[136] In addition, NCB confiscation is not linked to the obtaining of a conviction.

This type of confiscation most often takes place in one of two ways: The first is confiscation within the context of criminal proceedings, but without the need for a final conviction or finding of guilt.[137] In such situations, NCB confiscation laws are incorporated into existing criminal codes, anti-money laundering acts, or other criminal legislation; and are regarded as "criminal" proceedings to which the criminal procedural laws apply. The second way is confiscation through an independent statute that introduces a separate proceeding that can occur independently of or parallel to related criminal proceedings, and is often governed by the rules of civil procedure (rather than criminal procedure laws).[138] In jurisdictions applying civil procedure, a lower balance of probabilities or "preponderance of the evidence" standard of proof is required for confiscation—thus easing the burden for the prosecution.

Some jurisdictions pursue NCB confiscation only after criminal proceedings have been exhausted or unsuccessful. In other jurisdictions, a stay of the NCB confiscation proceedings is ordered until the criminal investigation is completed.[139]

---

135. For a list of jurisdictions that have NCB confiscation, see footnote 20.

136. In Brazil and the Philippines, the system is not purely property-based because the authorities may obtain a personal judgment against an individual, not against the asset. Antigua and Barbuda and Australia apply value-based NCB provisions in addition to property-based NCB confiscation.

137. Examples of jurisdictions include Liechtenstein, Slovenia, Switzerland, and Thailand.

138. Examples of jurisdictions include Colombia, South Africa, the United Kingdom, and the United States. "Civil confiscation" or "civil forfeiture" systems would fit into this category.

139. Civil rules permitting pretrial discovery (such as depositions of witnesses, interrogatories, and document production or disclosure orders) may adversely impact an ongoing criminal investigation.

NCB confiscation is useful in a variety of contexts, particularly when criminal confiscation is impossible or unavailable, such as when (1) the offender has died, fled the jurisdiction, or is immune from prosecution; (2) an asset is found and the owner is unknown; or (3) there is insufficient evidence to seek a criminal conviction, or criminal proceedings have resulted in an acquittal (applies in jurisdictions that apply a lower standard of proof). This type of confiscation may also be useful in large and complex cases where a criminal investigation is in progress and there is a need to restrain and confiscate the assets before a formal criminal charge is brought.[140]

NCB confiscation systems are not intended to replace criminal confiscation. In cases where it is possible to prosecute and obtain a conviction, the conviction should be obtained and powerful and relatively economical criminal confiscation should be available to prosecutors.

6.1.3 Administrative Confiscation

Administrative confiscation occurs without the need for a judicial determination. It is often used to confiscate assets when a seizure is not contested and certain requirements are met (for example, notice to parties and by publication; no objection is filed). In addition, there may be statutory limits to administrative confiscation, such as a maximum value of the asset or certain types of assets that can be confiscated.[141] Laws establishing an administrative confiscation often require that decisions be subject to subsequent court approval.

Administrative confiscation is commonly associated with—and often evolves from— the enforcement of customs laws, laws combating drug trafficking, and laws requiring the reporting of cross-border transportation of currency. For example, it may be employed to confiscate a vehicle used to transport prohibited goods or cash found in the hands of a courier. In such cases, the statutory authority is typically granted to police and customs officers. This process can result in a speedy and economical confiscation of such assets.

6.2 How Confiscation Works

As indicated above, a confiscation judgment may be either (1) a property-based judgment (naming a specific asset) or (2) a value-based judgment (naming an amount of money owed by a specific person). Some jurisdictions will employ both systems, permitting confiscation of identified assets and a judgment that can be satisfied from the legitimate assets of a person. In these situations, a property-based system may be the

---

140. Many civil law jurisdictions permit a restraint order in such instances; but many common law jurisdictions either do not permit a restraint order or do require that a formal charge be brought within a specified time frame after the restraint order.

141. In the United States, currency of any amount and personal property valued at less than $500,000 may be confiscated administratively; but real estate, regardless of value, must always be confiscated judicially.

first choice; but a value-based confiscation would be available when the proceeds have been dissipated or hidden.

Both approaches target proceeds of crime, and there is a large overlap between the operational reach of the laws. However, they differ in the procedures used and the evidentiary requirements for obtaining these proceeds. This section attempts to highlight some of these differences.

6.2.1 Property-Based Confiscation

The property-based system (also referred to as "in rem" confiscation or a tainted property system) is aimed at assets connected to or found to be the proceeds or instrumentalities of crime. This requires that a link be established between the identified assets and an offense.

Property-based confiscation is most useful when identified assets can be linked with evidence of an offense—for example, money seized from a person who has taken a bribe (proceeds) or the vehicle used to transport a substantial cash bribe to the recipient of the bribe (instrumentality). However, when assets cannot be linked to an offense because the target has not directly participated in criminal activity or the benefits are distanced from the crime through money laundering, this type of confiscation becomes more difficult. Some jurisdictions have adopted legal enhancements to overcome these barriers, such as substitute asset provisions and extended confiscation (see section 6.3).

The legislative definition of proceeds and instrumentalities subject to confiscation—and interpretation by courts—will be an important consideration for practitioners when determining the assets to be included in the confiscation request. Below are some issues that have been raised and some examples of how definitions have been interpreted to capture (or not capture) proceeds or instrumentalities.

Proceeds Obtained Directly or Indirectly

Generally, proceeds are defined as anything of value obtained directly or indirectly as the result of the offense.[142] "Direct proceeds" would include funds paid for a bribe or amounts stolen by an official from a national treasury or government program. "Indirect proceeds" would include an appreciation in the value of the bribe payments or a stock portfolio purchased with the stolen treasury fund.

Indirect proceeds do not accrue directly from the commission of the offense; rather, they are ancillary benefits that would not have accrued were it not for the commission of an offense.

---

142. Many jurisdictions have adopted the "proceeds of crime" definition used in United Nations Conventions, including UNCAC, art. 2; UNTOC, art. 2; and United Nations Convention against Narcotic Drugs and Psychotropic Substances, art. 1. These conventions define "proceeds of crime" to mean "any property derived from or obtained, directly or indirectly, through the commission of an offense."

The task of valuing the proceeds (or, in the case of value-based confiscation, valuing the "benefits") derived from an offense can be difficult. For example, if a corporation pays a bribe to ensure that its bid for a military contract is accepted, there are a number of possible options for quantifying the proceeds or benefit, such as the following[143]:

- **Gross value of the defense contract.** If the contract was to supply two patrol boats for $50 million each, the value of the benefit would be $100 million. This method assumes that the contract would not have been received by the offender were it not for the payment of the bribe—an assumption that may or may not be correct.
- **Net profits derived from the contract.** In the example above, if the company had $60 million of expenses in supplying the boats, the net profits would be $40 million.
- **Value of increased profits derived by eliminating competition from the contract.** This may be extraordinarily difficult to measure.

It is important to note that including appreciation in the value of the asset does not mean that losses in the value can be deducted. The value of the proceeds or benefit is usually assessed or "crystallized" at the moment the benefit was derived, and subsequent losses are ignored.

Commingled Proceeds

As proceeds are laundered, they may be mixed with other assets that may not be proceeds of crime, and they may be converted into other forms of assets (see the example in box 6.2). As a result, these assets are technically not the direct proceeds of crime, but rather the assets obtained from the original proceeds.[144] Some examples of statutory wording that define what can be confiscated in commingled situations include the following:

- **"Any asset or part of an asset"** allows the court to separate out the relevant proceeds that have been mingled with non-proceeds.
- **Assets "derived, obtained, or realized from an offense"** or assets **"substantially derived or realized from an offense"** can ensure that proceeds of crime mingled with non-proceeds will not lose their status as proceeds. "Substantially derived" may limit recovery to a portion of the proceeds derived from the offense. For example, the court may not be prepared to find that the investment bank account was "substantially derived" from the corruption offense if only 10 percent of the account represents proceeds.
- **"Any asset with which proceeds have been mingled,"** the most far-reaching approach, subjects all commingled assets to confiscation.[145] Under such language,

---

143. The Stolen Asset Recovery Initiative is currently working on a paper with the Organisation for Economic Co-operation and Development that will grapple with the quantification of the proceeds of crime (expected to be released in spring 2011).

144. International agreements oblige states parties to allow for confiscation of transformed and intermingled assets. UNCAC, art. 31(4) and (5); UNTOC, art. 12(3) and (4); United Nations Convention against Narcotic Drugs and Psychotropic Substances, art. 5(6)(a) and (b).

145. An example of this type of provision is the definition of "proceeds of unlawful activities" in the Prevention of Organised Crime Act, 1998 (South Africa), which includes property "that is mingled with property that is proceeds of unlawful activity."

theoretically, one dollar in proceeds deposited in an account with a balance of $999 will taint the whole account and result in its confiscation.
- **Any instrumentality with which proceeds have been mingled.** Some jurisdictions permit the confiscation of the entire bank account that was used to launder funds as an instrumentality of an offense.

Proceeds Derived from Foreign Offenses

Because corruption cases often involve situations in which the criminal conduct occurs in one jurisdiction and the proceeds are invested in another, confiscation laws often provide jurisdiction to permit recovery of assets that have been obtained through offenses committed abroad. A number of jurisdictions have legislation authorizing the confiscation of proceeds of crime if the conduct is unlawful in both jurisdictions.[146] Others list specific serious crimes, such as foreign corruption, drug trafficking, and crimes of violence as providing a basis for confiscation.

Instrumentalities of an Offense

Instrumentalities are generally assets used or intended for use in any manner or part to commit or facilitate the commission of an offense—for example, a vehicle used to transport a substantial cash bribe to the recipient of the bribe. Assets may become instrumentalities, notwithstanding the fact that they have been acquired legitimately with lawfully obtained funds. It is the illegal use to which the object has been put that makes it an instrumentality.

An issue that practitioners will need to consider is the definition of "use"—whether defined by statute or in case law. For example, if a corrupt official *uses* a telephone in a house to accept a bribe and arrange for delivery of funds, it may be debatable whether the house was sufficiently or substantially "used" to commit the offense. Another example could be a yacht on which a corrupt official has been lavishly entertained. Courts in some jurisdictions require that there be more than an accidental or incidental connection between the asset and the offense: the offense must be related to, dependent on, could not have been committed without, or resulted directly from the use of the asset.[147] Courts in other jurisdictions have found that any use of asset, no matter how peripheral, is a "use" for the purposes of confiscation. In such cases, an asset that has been indirectly used as an instrumentality of an offense is subject to confiscation where legislation provides that "use" means "in connection with" an offense.

6.2.2 Value-Based Confiscation

Unlike property-based confiscation orders that are directed at specific assets, value-based confiscation is focused on the value of benefits derived from criminal conduct and often imposes a monetary penalty equal to that value. In this system, there is a quantification of benefits which flowed to the defendant from the offense (direct benefits) and most often any increase in value due to appreciation of the assets (indirect benefits). At sentencing, the court will impose a liability equal to that benefit on the defendant. This judgment may be enforceable as a judgment debt or fine against any asset of the defendant, whether or not it has any link to the offense.

The absence of a requirement to link the specific assets to an offense often facilitates the practitioner's ability to obtain a confiscation judgment. However, the benefits must be linked to the offenses that form the basis of the defendant's conviction, and that may be problematic in cases where the prosecutor proceeds or succeeds on only some of the offenses. In addition, the assets are limited to those owned by the defendant, although this issue is often resolved through presumptions and broad definitions of "ownership" to include assets that are held, controlled, or gifted by the defendant (see section 4.2.1

---

146. See, for example, the Proceeds of Crime Act, 2002 (United Kingdom), sec. 241; and Criminal Code (Liechtenstein), sec. 20b(2).
147. See *Re an Application Pursuant to Drugs Misuse Act,* 1986 [1988] 2 Qd. R. 506 (Australia).

of chapter 4). Value-based confiscation laws may also be paired with property-based confiscation laws to achieve maximum coverage.

Similar to property-based confiscation, the legislative definition and interpretation of key terms will be important. Some of the issues raised in litigation are set out below.

Assessing Benefits

The term "benefits" is usually defined broadly to include the full value of cash or non-cash benefits received directly or indirectly by a defendant (or a third party, at the defendant's direction) as a result of the offense (see section 6.2.1 for a description of direct and indirect). Benefits will usually cover more than the rewards of a financial nature.[148] Some examples include:

- the value of money or assets (including "illegal" assets)[149] actually received as the result of committing an offense;
- the value of assets derived or realized (by either the defendant or a third party at the direction of the defendant) directly or indirectly from the offense;
- the value of benefits, services, or advantages accrued (to the defendant or a third party at the direction of the defendant) directly or indirectly as a result of the offense (for example, the value of the lavish entertainment in a bribery case[150]; or of forced manual, household, or other labor in a human trafficking or smuggling case); and
- the value of benefits derived directly or indirectly from related or prior criminal activity.

In some jurisdictions, the existence of benefits may be inferred from increases in the value of assets held by a person before and after the commission of an offense.[151]

As stated above, a potential drawback to value-based confiscation is that the benefits are linked to the offenses that form the basis of a defendant's conviction. This is problematic in jurisdictions where prosecutors do not always proceed on each offense (unless they are obliged to); instead, they may proceed on a selection of charges that are representative of the overall criminality of the defendant and that achieve an appropriate range of

---

148. Some jurisdictions will provide guidance in legislation. See, for example, the Proceeds of Crime Act, 2002 (Australia), sec. 122.

149. Benefits may include legitimate assets, as well as assets that are illegitimate or illegal—for example, proceeds generated from criminal enterprises. The value of illegitimate benefits is difficult to assess and must be estimated based upon the evidence available. Most helpful to practitioners are value-based confiscation systems that have flexible benefit assessment procedures, such as those that permit the assessment based on the black-market value and inferences over the period of the crime based on receipts from a finite period.

150. Recent cases have revealed bribes in the form of high-priced entertainment—for example, a $90,000 dinner for six people, travel expenses and trips to theme parks, and use of assets.

151. This inference of benefits takes place in jurisdictions that have laws against illicit enrichment or unjust resources, such as Argentina and Colombia.

sentencing options.[152] Several methods have evolved to address this potential issue, such as:

- **Representative charges that capture a continuing course of criminal conduct over a period of time.** Where permitted, charges for a corruption offense committed between [date] and [date] will eventually permit an order of confiscation for all the benefits derived from this "course of conduct" over the entire period.
- **Rebuttable presumptions and extended confiscation.** A rebuttable presumption, raised on conviction for a single offense, could allow the inference that benefits derived over an extended, specific period of time are benefits of that offense. Such a presumption would permit the confiscation of assets that may have been derived from other offenses for which the offender was not charged or convicted. Similarly, provisions that allow the court to confiscate assets for "related criminal activities" will permit the court to include any related or similar criminal activity in calculating benefits (see sections 6.3.1 and 6.3.3 for additional information).

If the relevant legal system permits a value-based confiscation order only for the conduct on which the defendant is convicted, a practitioner must take care in choosing the charges on which to prosecute the defendant (that is, choose the offense according to the desired confiscation). In addition, any decision to drop or amend charges must be considered carefully because such decisions can have drastic effects on the calculation of benefits.

Gross or Net Benefits

In most jurisdictions, the term "benefits" is specifically defined as "gross benefits"—not "net benefits" or "profit"—after deduction of any expenses incurred in deriving the benefit. A calculation based on "net benefits" would enable the corrupt official to deduct legal, banking, transportation, and other fees paid in the process of laundering funds and would enable him or her to retain parts of the proceeds. The computation of gross benefits should not be mitigated by any loss in value or dissipation of an asset because the value of the criminal benefit is "crystallized" at the moment the benefit is generated.

Joint and Several Liability

In some jurisdictions, defendants can be held jointly and severally liable for value-based confiscation orders. The result is that the full value of the benefit is recoverable from each of the convicted defendants. For example, in the case of a crime committed by five people that generated a total benefit of $500,000, the entire amount is recoverable from each individual, rather than $100,000 from each of the five offenders. This is useful if four of the defendants are found to be impecunious, but the fifth has assets of $1 million.

---

152. This would not be an issue if proceeding on the offense of illicit enrichment or unjust resources because all benefits would be linked to the one offense.

6.2.3 Discretion to Confiscate

The court's authority to enter a confiscation order is often discretionary.[153] Some confiscation laws provide specific factors that the court must consider in exercising its discretion to grant or refuse confiscation. These factors include

- the hardship that will be endured by any person as a result of the entering of the order;
- the ordinary use to which the asset subject to confiscation is put; and
- the proportionality between the offense and the amount to be confiscated.[154]

6.2.4 Use of Expert and Summary Testimony to Present Confiscation Evidence in Court

Evidence establishing the link between the asset and the offense or the value of benefits can be complex and difficult for the judge (or jury) to follow. Such evidence is often best presented using flow charts and spreadsheets that present the financial material in a more easily comprehensible way (see figures 3.5 and 3.6 in chapter 3 for sample flow charts). A forensic accountant or financial investigator with training and experience in presenting evidence can be helpful in this regard. If permitted, the witness could introduce summary evidence in the form of spreadsheets or charts that, when prepared properly, can clearly show how benefits were derived and how complex schemes were operated. Care must be taken to ensure that presentation aids are accurate and precisely reflect the evidence in source documents: a factual or methodological error may impeach the credibility of the evidence, leaving a big hole in the prosecution's case.

6.3 Confiscation Enhancements

Most jurisdictions provide for procedural aids or enhancements designed to improve the effectiveness of the confiscation law or to capture an extended range of assets.[155] With the exception of substitute asset provisions, which are needed only in property-based confiscation systems, most are applicable in both property-based and value-based systems.

6.3.1 Rebuttable Presumptions

A rebuttable presumption is an inference of the truth of a proposition or fact drawn by a process of probable reasoning in the absence of actual certainty from a defined set of

---

153. Such legislation would state that the court "may" order confiscation when requirements are met.

154. Hardship, ordinary use, and proportionality most often apply to cases involving instrumentalities, such as a lawfully acquired family residence that is also used as a base for illegal activity (both lawful and unlawful purposes). See, for example, *National Director of Public Prosecutions v. Prophet,* [2006] ZACC 17 (Constitutional Court of South Africa) (factors to consider upholding the confiscation of a residence as an "instrumentality" of a drug operation).

155. Enhancements are encouraged in international conventions and agreements. UNCAC, art. 48, 59; the European Council Framework Decision 2005/212/JHA of 24 February 2005 on Confiscation of Crime-Related Proceeds, Instrumentalities and Property, art. 3.

circumstances. Thus, if a practitioner establishes the defined set of circumstances sufficient to raise a presumption, the party against whom the presumption exists has the burden to overcome the presumption by presenting proof to rebut the presumption. If the party fails, the prima facie presumption is converted into an uncontroverted fact.

In criminal law, primacy is given to the presumption of innocence—the legal or constitutional right of the accused to be considered innocent until proven guilty. The burden of proof lies with the prosecution to establish guilt to the required standard, and failure to do so results in an acquittal. Rebuttable presumptions are used infrequently in criminal cases because they effectively reverse this burden[156]; however, they are more common in confiscation and civil proceedings or other proceedings in which the presumption of innocence does not apply because neither criminal liability nor individual liberties are at stake.[157]

Presumptions are enormously helpful in confiscation cases involving corrupt public officials because these officials—particularly those who have a long tenure in public service—have had extensive opportunity to embezzle and conceal funds and are often able to influence witnesses and thwart investigations into their assets. Relieving the prosecution of the burden to establish that unexplained wealth is linked to specific instances of illegal conduct or a benefit from crime greatly enhances the possibility of obtaining a confiscation judgment.

Presumptions are powerful tools, and practitioners must ensure they are used appropriately. Any chronic abuse of the tools available in a confiscation system can bring the entire system into disrepute.[158] For example, using presumptions to confiscate all the assets of a person who has committed a relatively minor crime could raise questions about the integrity of the confiscation system. Common bases for presumptions include the following:

- **Possession.** Under this presumption, assets found in the possession of a person at the time of the offense, or shortly before or after the commission of the offense, are considered to be either the proceeds or an instrumentality of the offense.
- **Associations.** This presumption has been applied in organized crime cases in which assets belonging to a person who has participated in or supported a criminal organization are presumed to be at the disposal of the organization and can be confiscated.[159] The inclusion of this enhancement helps attack the economic base of entrenched criminal groups.

---

156. For example, a person in possession of more than a prescribed amount of a drug may, in the absence of evidence to the contrary, be presumed to be a drug trafficker.

157. Note that criminal confiscation is adjudicated after the conviction has been obtained. Tax and customs legislation also apply such presumptions in their proceedings.

158. Some jurisdictions have reserved the application of some presumptions to serious offenses: the Confiscation Act, 1987 (Victoria, Australia) and the Proceeds of Crime Act, 2002 (Commonwealth of Australia). In the United Kingdom, presumptions in value-based confiscation cases are permitted only in "criminal lifestyle" cases: Proceeds of Crime Act, 2002, sec. 6 (United Kingdom).

159. In 2005, Switzerland's Federal Supreme Court ruled that Nigeria's former president Sani Abacha, his family, and associates constituted a criminal organization; and it ordered the confiscation and return of $458 million of Abacha-related assets, using these provisions. See also Criminal Code (Switzerland), art. 72.

- **Lifestyle.**[160] This presumption may be raised when the prosecutor can show that the offender does not have sufficient legitimate sources of income to justify the value of assets accumulated over a period of time.[161] Items that the offender can show were acquired lawfully may be excluded from the confiscation order. This presumption requires the offender to justify more assets than those related to the specific offense.
- **Transfers of assets.** The law can impose a presumption that transfers to family and close associates or any transfers for below-market value are not legitimate.[162] The titleholder would have to prove that the asset was the subject of an arm's-length transaction that involved payment of fair market value.[163] If not rebutted, the transfer will be invalidated.
- **Nature of the offense.** This presumption is usually linked to conviction for a class of particularly serious offenses, such as trafficking in substantial quantities of drugs, major forms of corruption or fraud, racketeering, or organized crime. When the person is convicted of such an offense, a rebuttable presumption is raised and the assets accumulated during the period of the crime are presumed to be the proceeds of crime and subject to confiscation.

Although the burden lies with the offender to rebut the presumption, the prosecutor will normally present some information to counter any rebuttal evidence an offender may choose to produce and to help the court draw the inference that the asset was acquired with illicit proceeds or was an instrumentality of crime. The presence of such material will make it much more difficult for an offender to rebut the presumption with a simple assertion as to the lawful source and use of the asset.

6.3.2 Substitute Asset Provisions

Substitute asset provisions help overcome obstacles often faced in property-based confiscation regimes—such as tracing or linking the assets to the offense—by permitting the confiscation of assets not connected to the offense. Such provisions may require proof that

- the original assets were derived as a benefit from an offense or a particular asset was used as an instrumentality of the offense; and
- the asset cannot be located or is otherwise unavailable.

---

160. A presumption based on lifestyle is separate and distinct from the offense of illicit enrichment or unjust resources. Although the definition is often the same, the procedures applied are different.

161. In South Africa, the presumption extends for a period of seven years prior to the initiation of proceedings. Prevention of Organised Crime Act, Second Amendment, 1999, sec. 22. In the United Kingdom, the period is six years for defendants determined to have a criminal lifestyle. Proceeds of Crime Act (United Kingdom), sec. 10(8); also see Criminal Code (France), art. 131-21.

162. In Thailand, transfers of property to family members are presumed to be dishonest: Anti-Money Laundering Act, 1999, sec. 51 and 52.

163. In Colombia, the party attempting to rebut the presumption must also prove that the transaction actually occurred (that is, the party had sufficient income to purchase and the selling party received the funds).

When it is established that the offender has dissipated the direct proceeds, the prosecutor may apply for confiscation of an equivalent value of the offender's untainted assets.

Value-based confiscation laws do not need substitute asset provisions because they impose a similar monetary liability on the person deriving the benefit that can be enforced against any of that person's assets.[164]

6.3.3 Extended Confiscation

Some jurisdictions permit courts to confiscate (or include in the benefit assessment) assets derived from similar or related criminal activities.[165] The offender need not be charged with an offense for these other related activities; however, the court must find the related activities are sufficiently connected to the offense (see example in box 6.3). In some other jurisdictions, courts may be allowed to confiscate all or part of the assets of a convicted person, without consideration of whether they were purchased before or after the commission of an offense.[166] Such provisions will often be limited to serious crimes—such as terrorism, organized crime, money laundering, or drug trafficking— and will apply only to assets belonging to the offender.

6.3.4 Mechanisms to Void Transfers of Assets

In addition to the use of presumptions to void certain transfers of assets (see section 6.3.1), some jurisdictions have enacted statutory provisions that hold that title to the confiscated assets vests in the state or government at the time of the unlawful act giving rise to the confiscation.[167] If the asset is subsequently transferred, it remains subject to confiscation—with the exception of transfers to bona fide purchasers without knowledge that the asset was subject to confiscation.

6.3.5 Automatic Confiscation on Conviction

This type of provision results not in the operation of a rebuttable presumption, but in actual confiscation by automatic operation of the statute. Such a provision eliminates the need for any judicial determination when certain conditions are satisfied.[168] The

---

164. In the United States, substitute assets may be confiscated in most criminal confiscation cases, but not through NCB confiscation.

165. Such extended powers of confiscation are required in European Union jurisdictions. Council of the European Union Framework Decision 2005/212/JHA of February 24, 2005, on Confiscation of Crime-Related Proceeds, Instrumentalities and Property, art. 3. In South Africa, the Prevention of Organised Crime Act, 1998, sec. 18(1)(c), permits value-based confiscation orders to be assessed on "related activities."

166. Criminal Code (France), art. 131-21.

167. This concept is used for some confiscations in the United States, and it is referred to as the "relation back doctrine." Title 21, United States Code, sec. 853(c) and 881(h); and Title 18, United States Code, sec. 1963(c). Such provisions may also be found in administrative confiscation laws.

168. Automatic confiscation is applied in Australia.

Over a two-month period, customs official Ms. X accepted three bribes from undercover agents. The bribes totaled $20,000. Evidence obtained showed that she was planning further dealings that would generate additional bribes, and that her wealth increased by $500,000 in excess of what she could have been expected to have saved from her government salary during the previous two years. Several suspicious transaction reports concerning Ms. X conducting unexplained transactions involving large amounts of cash were found as well.

Ms. X was convicted on three counts of corruption, based on the bribes from the undercover agents. The prosecutor applied for a confiscation order, based on the benefits derived from the commission of the three offenses and any "criminal activities related to the offense"—an option available under the jurisdiction's confiscation law. The prosecutor submitted evidence that Ms. X was engaged in a business of extracting bribes from importers, and that the $500,000 unexplained increase in her wealth was derived from her corrupt business practice that was "related to" the offenses for which she was convicted. The court ordered a judgment for $520,000—the amount of the three bribes plus the value of the wealth derived from the related offenses.[a]

a. Had the "related activities" clause not been included in the legislation, the prosecution would have only been able to seek an order for $20,000 (the amount of the three bribes).

person claiming an interest in an asset subject to automatic confiscation—either a defendant, innocent owner, or third party—may apply to exclude the asset from the operation of the law by proving the lawful derivation and use of the asset. The claimant bears the burden of proof.

6.4 Third-Party Interests

Third parties with a potential legal interest in assets subject to confiscation are entitled to notice of the proceedings and the opportunity to be heard.[169] Typically, appropriate notice is sent to individuals the authorities believe may have a legally recognized interest. This test should be applied liberally; and if a party indicates he or she has an interest, formal notice should be given. Because confiscation extinguishes all rights in the asset, some additional form of notice is generally given to the population-at-large through newspapers, legal gazettes, or the Internet. There should also be procedures for recognizing the legitimate interests of third parties in the restraint order (see section 4.5 in chapter 4 for a discussion of this issue).

Procedural steps for the assertion of third-party interests may vary, depending on whether the confiscation is criminal or NCB. Generally, for criminal confiscation, the

---

169. UNCAC, art. 31(9), 35, 55(3)(c), 57; UNTOC, art. 12(8), 13(8); United Nations Convention against Narcotic Drugs and Psychotropic Substances, art. 5(8).

criminal proceedings dealing with the underlying offense must be concluded and the defendant's interest ordered confiscated before third-party interests are heard by the court. Some jurisdictions permit prejudgment appearances by third parties who can assert limited defenses, such as that provisional restraint is causing severe hardship or that the asset is from a legitimate source and is needed for living expenses. Under NCB systems, third-party claims are generally considered during the course of the primary litigation. Typically, the party must prove that (1) he or she has a legally cognizable interest in the assets; and either (2) the interest was obtained prior to the commission of any criminal offense and the party did not have reason to believe the assets were involved in the underlying crime; or (3) the interest in the assets arose after the criminal activity was committed and the party was a bona fide purchaser for value of the assets.

6.5 Confiscation of Assets Located in Foreign Jurisdictions

It is quite common for corruption and money laundering investigations to move beyond domestic borders, thus requiring cooperation with foreign jurisdictions. The involvement of a foreign jurisdiction both complicates a case and opens up a whole new range of possibilities. For example, if a case involves domestic offenses for corruption and money laundering and foreign offenses for money laundering, several possibilities may arise:

- Domestic confiscation proceedings may be enforced in the foreign jurisdiction through a mutual legal assistance request and the assets returned to the requesting jurisdiction, pursuant to international agreements, treaties, or other agreements (see chapter 7 for a description of mutual legal assistance proceedings).[170]
- Foreign confiscation proceedings may return the proceeds of the confiscation to the jurisdiction harmed by corruption offenses by means of direct recovery or a sharing agreement (see chapter 9 for a description of these proceedings).
- Both domestic and foreign confiscation proceedings may be pursued in tandem.

Figure 6.1 illustrates these possibilities.

6.6 Recovery through Confiscation for the Victims of Crime

It is becoming increasingly common for jurisdictions to use confiscation mechanisms as a means to provide restitution to the victims of crime.[171] Legislation and regulations have been designed to give priority to victims over the general treasury or confiscation fund of the state or government. If sufficient assets exist to satisfy a confiscation judgment and restitution order, the confiscated assets could be deposited to benefit the state or government after the victims receive restitution.

---

170. For example, see the return provisions outlined in UNCAC, art. 57.
171. This practice is supported in international agreements. See UNCAC, art. 57(3)(c); and UNTOC, art. 14(2).

FIGURE 6.1 Confiscation of an Asset in a Foreign Jurisdiction

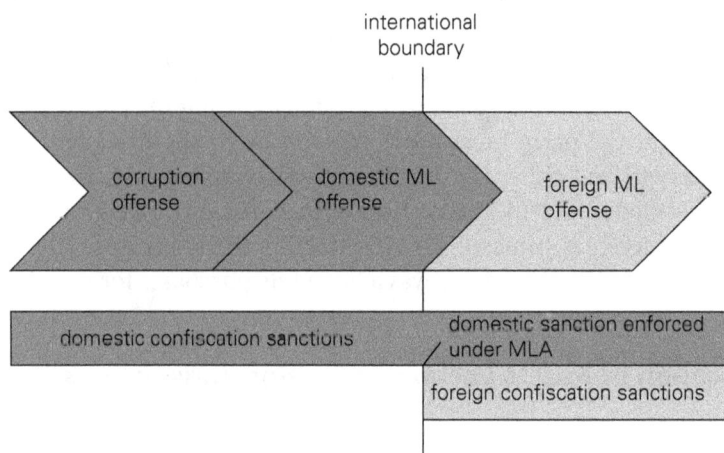

Source: Authors' illustration.
Note: ML = money laundering; MLA = mutual legal assistance.

Such mechanisms ensure that confiscation orders are not enforced at the expense of victims who are owed restitution as a result of the underlying criminal conduct. Another advantage lies in the general restraint provisions for confiscation that permit a more aggressive provisional restraint once formal charges are filed than is often available in a civil litigation action to obtain restitution or secure compensation. Finally, using confiscation to obtain restitution for victims may save them the significant fees or percentages of recovery that are usually required in a private law (civil) case.

6.7 Disposal of Confiscated Assets

Confiscation laws frequently require confiscated assets to be liquidated and the proceeds paid into a consolidated government account or general treasury. A number of jurisdictions have established asset confiscation funds into which realized assets must be paid.[172] These funds are used for designated law enforcement and confiscation program purposes, including the purchase of equipment, training, investigative expenses, and prosecutorial and asset management and liquidation costs[173] (for a discussion of issues related to the management of assets subject to confiscation, see chapter 5).

---

172. The jurisdictions include Australia, Canada, Italy, Luxembourg, Namibia, Spain, South Africa, and the United States. For a list of jurisdictions with confiscation funds, see Theodore S. Greenberg, Linda M. Samuel, Wingate Grant, and Larissa Gray, *Stolen Asset Recovery—A Good Practices Guide to Non-Conviction Based Asset Forfeiture* (Washington, DC: World Bank, 2009), 91.

173. For more information on these options, see Theodore S. Greenberg, Linda M. Samuel, Wingate Grant, and Larissa Gray, *Stolen Asset Recovery—A Good Practices Guide to Non-Conviction Based Asset Forfeiture* (Washington, DC: World Bank, 2009), 90–94; and Stolen Asset Recovery Initiative Secretariat, "Management of Confiscated Assets" (Washington, DC, 2009).

7. International Cooperation in Asset Recovery

Corruption cases and most complex money laundering cases generally require asset recovery efforts beyond domestic borders. Some parts of an offense may be committed in another jurisdiction: a company paying bribes for a contract may be headquartered in a jurisdiction outside the jurisdiction in which the bribes are paid, and the officials receiving the bribes may launder their ill-gotten gains in another jurisdiction. In addition, the international financial sector is a particularly attractive setting for people seeking to launder funds and impede asset tracing efforts. Intermediaries or gatekeepers, such as accountants, lawyers, or trust and company service providers, offer access to the financial sector and serve to disguise a corrupt official's involvement in a transaction or ownership of assets. Corrupt officials use complicated financial schemes often involving offshore centers, shell companies, and corporate vehicles to launder the proceeds of corruption. In addition, money can be moved quickly—often instantly—with the click of a keyboard key or a cell phone button, with the help of such tools as wire transfers, letters of credit, credit and debit cards, automated teller machines, and mobile devices.

In contrast, asset tracing and recovery by law enforcement officials and prosecutors may take months or years because the principle of sovereignty restricts domestic authorities' ability to take investigative, legal, and enforcement actions in foreign jurisdictions. Successful tracing and recovery efforts often depend on assistance from foreign jurisdictions, a process that may be slowed and complicated by differences in legal traditions, laws and procedures, languages, time zones, and capacities.

In this context, international cooperation is essential for the successful recovery of assets that have been stashed abroad. The international community has concluded a number of multilateral treaties or instruments requiring states parties to cooperate with one another on investigations, production of evidence, provisional measures and confiscation, and asset return (see box 1.1 in chapter 1). Figure 7.1 illustrates that international cooperation is integral to each phase of asset recovery.

Practitioners should take into account that international cooperation is "mutual": not only will the jurisdiction that has been plundered of its assets be requesting assistance from the foreign jurisdiction(s) where the assets are hidden, but it may need to provide information or evidence to these jurisdictions to obtain the most effective recovery of assets. In addition, practitioners must be proactive in seeking international cooperation, as well as in alerting their counterparts in foreign jurisdictions to potential corruption offenses. Examples of the primary forms of cooperation include informal

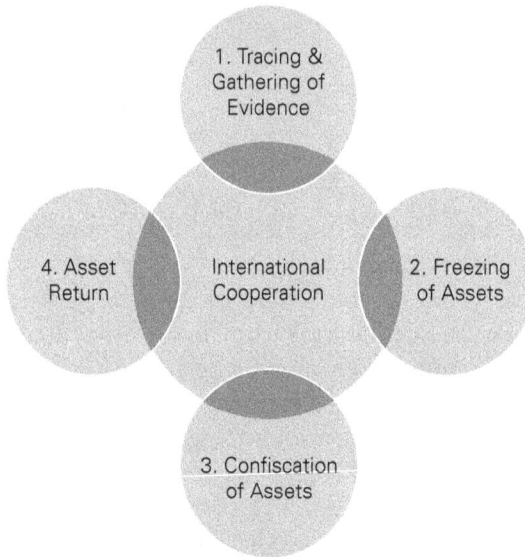

Source: Authors' illustration.

assistance,[174] spontaneous disclosures of information, joint investigation teams, mutual legal assistance (MLA) requests, transfer of proceedings to another jurisdiction, implementation of domestic laws that permit direct recovery, enforcement or registration of a provisional restraint or confiscation order from another jurisdiction, and extradition.[175]

The decision about the forms of cooperation and process will vary from case to case. This chapter highlights the strategic considerations, challenges, and characteristics of the various options that practitioners will encounter in international cooperation.

7.1 Key Principles

Practitioners in need of international cooperation should keep the following four key principles in mind from the outset of their efforts.

---

174. For the purposes of this handbook, "informal assistance" is used to include any type of assistance that does not require a *formal* mutual legal assistance (MLA) request. Legislation permitting this informal, practitioner-to-practitioner assistance may be outlined in MLA legislation and may involve "formal" authorities, agencies, or administrations. For a description of this type of assistance and comparison with the MLA request process, see section 7.2.

175. Extradition is the process through which a jurisdiction surrenders a suspected or convicted criminal. Whereas parts of the extradition process and requirements are similar to MLA, there are a number of additional issues—such as the extradition of nationals, specialty, and the doctrine of non-inquiry. An extensive review of these issues is beyond the scope of this handbook.

7.1.1 Incorporate International Cooperation into Each Phase of the Case

When the case reaches beyond domestic borders, it is important that practitioners immediately focus on international cooperation efforts and ensure they are maintained for the duration of the case. Some authorities have waited until a domestic conviction and a confiscation order were achieved before beginning the process of tracing and securing the assets abroad—often with frustrating and adverse results: the delay gave the corrupt official ample opportunity to transfer funds to bank secrecy or uncooperative jurisdictions. Therefore, it is imperative to involve authorities from other jurisdictions at the outset, at least through informal means. Establishing proactive contact early may aid practitioners in understanding the foreign legal system and potential challenges, in obtaining additional leads, and in forming a strategy. It also gives the foreign jurisdiction the opportunity to prepare for its role in providing cooperation.

7.1.2 Develop and Maintain Personal Connections

Forming personal connections with foreign counterparts is the hallmark of successful asset recovery cases. A telephone call, an e-mail, a videoconference, or a face-to-face meeting with foreign counterparts will go a long way to moving the case to completion. It is important in all phases: obtaining information and intelligence, making strategic decisions, understanding the foreign jurisdiction's requirements for assistance, drafting MLA requests, or following up requests for assistance. It helps reduce delays, particularly where differences in terminology and legal traditions lead to misunderstandings. And it can demonstrate that an administration is serious and committed to the case, thereby building trust among the parties and fostering increased attention and commitment to the case.

In larger cases, an early face-to-face meeting among practitioners in the various jurisdictions who will be involved in the investigation may facilitate the exchange of information. It also helps counterparts build trust, assess strategies, and learn about requirements for submitting MLA requests (see box 7.1 for an example). In some cases, particularly when faced with resource constraints or in cases that involve several jurisdictions, practitioners have invited representatives of the foreign jurisdictions to attend a case conference held domestically.[176] In other cases, practitioners have opted to visit the foreign jurisdictions involved in the case.

Establishing personal connections can be difficult. Many practitioners do not have easy access to the Internet to determine whom to contact, are not authorized to make long-distance phone calls, and lack resources to attend the international or regional meetings that help them develop personal networks. Even where a contact's name and telephone number are obtained, language differences may be an additional barrier.

Personal connections are so integral to a successful recovery, however, that every attempt must be made to ensure they happen. The time and effort spent making connections will be worth the results—whether in securing guidance on how best to

---

176. Practitioners from Brazil have used this case conference option.

In September 2000, televised videos showed Vladimiro Montesinos, chief of Peru's intelligence service under President Alberto Fujimori, bribing an elected congressman. Switzerland subsequently used a spontaneous disclosure to alert Peru to the presence of frozen funds in Switzerland, and invited Peru to file an MLA request. The Peruvian prosecutor personally contacted the Swiss investigating magistrate conducting the case—both by phone and eventually in person in Zurich. Making the personal connection resulted in the following important outcomes:

- **Enabled key strategic decisions.** Through discussions of the options for asset recovery, Peru ultimately decided to pursue the case domestically, and to use MLA and legislative waivers to recover the frozen funds in Switzerland.
- **Clarified requirements for MLA requests.** Contact gave the Peruvians a better understanding of the Swiss system and an idea of what they needed to prove and provide to be successful in a request to Switzerland.
- **Developed trust.** Personal contacts demonstrated the political will and commitment of both parties, and they helped promote trust between the parties.

These outcomes, enabled by personal connections, were central in the repatriation of $93 million in two years.

proceed, gathering leads for the case, or seeking drafting assistance with an MLA request. Box 7.2 provides a list of avenues for pursuing personal connections.

7.1.3 Engage in Informal Assistance Channels Before, During, and After Transmitting an MLA Request

Many practitioners immediately resort to drafting an MLA request when they determine that international cooperation is required. However, some important information can be obtained more quickly and with fewer formalities through direct contact with counterpart law enforcement agencies and financial intelligence units, or from liaison magistrates or law enforcement attachés posted locally or regionally. Such assistance may lead to a more rapid identification of assets; confirm the assistance needed; and, even more important, provide the proper foundation for an MLA request. Such contacts also offer an opportunity to learn about the procedures and system of the foreign jurisdiction and to assess strategic options. Such informal contacts often need to be cleared through the practitioner's domestic central authority to ensure that protocol with the other jurisdiction is not violated and that laws and regulations regarding foreign assistance are observed.[177]

---

177. Taking action without proper clearance could irreparably compromise the foreign aspect of the case.

BOX 7.2   Contact Points for International Cooperation

Personal contacts: Connections developed through previous cases, meetings, conferences, and so forth.

Referrals: Counterparts, personal contacts, liaison magistrates or law enforcement attachés, networks, and international organizations (for example, World Bank or the United Nations Office on Drugs and Crime) may have referrals based on their personal networks.

Counterparts in foreign jurisdictions:
- Law enforcement agencies (such as police and those involved in anticorruption, customs, drug law enforcement, and tax efforts)
- Financial intelligence units
- Regulatory authorities (banking, securities)
- Prosecutors
- Investigating magistrates
- Foreign counsel (Some jurisdictions will retain counsel who are more familiar with the procedures and requirements of the foreign jurisdiction.)

Liaison magistrates and regional law enforcement attachés: Many jurisdictions have resource persons based in their embassies or consulates abroad to facilitate international cooperation with foreign jurisdictions. These individuals have knowledge of the laws and procedures of both their own jurisdictions and the host jurisdiction, and that knowledge can help practitioners avoid the pitfalls of working with different legal systems. Their roles vary, but generally they will facilitate contact with counterparts, provide informal assistance, help with MLA request preparations (reviewing drafts), and help in following up an MLA request. Practitioners may wish to contact the foreign jurisdiction's local embassy, consulate, or ministry of foreign affairs to see if such a resource person exists.

Examples of jurisdictions with resource persons include Argentina, Chile, Colombia, France, the United Kingdom, and the United States (the Federal Bureau of Investigation and Immigration and Customs Enforcement).

Central authorities:
- *Domestic:* The domestic central authority may be able to refer practitioners to contacts abroad and provide information on jurisdictions with which there are multilateral or bilateral agreements.
- *In requested jurisdiction:* The office of the central authority in the requested jurisdiction should be able to provide guidance on how best to proceed in light of the needs of the requesting jurisdiction and the laws of the requested jurisdiction. Many offices also provide assistance with drafting requests.

(continued next page)

BOX 7.2 *(continued)*

Practitioner networks:

- *Stolen Asset Recovery/Interpol Focal Point List:* a 24/7 focal point contact list of national officials who can respond to emergency requests for international assistance, available at http://www.interpol.int/public/corruptionstar/default.asp
- *Egmont Group:* an international network of financial intelligence units
- *Interpol, Europol, Aseanpol, Ameripol:* International (and regional) police organizations that facilitate cross-border police cooperation
- *World Customs Organization* and its regional intelligence liaison offices
- *Camden Assets Recovery Inter-Agency Network (CARIN):* an informal network of police and judicial bodies working to confiscate the proceeds of crime
- *Asset Recovery Inter-Agency Network for Southern Africa:* a CARIN-style informal network of Southern African police and judicial bodies working to confiscate the proceeds of crime
- *Arab Anti-Corruption and Integrity Network*
- *Asociación Iberoamericana de Ministerios Públicos*
- *Red Iberoamericana de Cooperación Jurídica Internacional Hemispheric Information Exchange Network*
- *Organization of American States network:* vets and links practitioners through a secure software system
- *European Judicial Network:* representatives of national judicial and prosecution authorities designated as contact points for MLA
- *Eurojust:* judges and prosecutors from European Union member-states who assist national authorities in investigating and prosecuting serious cross-border criminal cases

7.1.4 Be Aware of Potential Barriers

Practitioners may encounter many barriers in trying to obtain international cooperation, so it is important that they recognize possible obstacles and take the necessary measures to overcome them.[178] Differences in legal traditions and confiscation systems, jurisdiction issues, procedural variations, legal obstacles, and delay are among the barriers that practitioners will need to consider and take steps to overcome (see section 2.6 of chapter 2 for a discussion of some of these obstacles). Practitioners should be mindful that information provided to a foreign jurisdiction—informally or through an MLA request—may result in the foreign jurisdiction initiating its own domestic investigation and subsequently refusing to provide assistance while there are local "ongoing proceedings." In addition, disclosure obligations may delay the assistance process significantly. Also, despite having a confidentiality obligation under an MLA treaty, leaks of information often occur.

---

178. The Stolen Asset Recovery (StAR) Initiative currently is undertaking a study of the barriers to asset recovery. The expected publication date is early-2011. The study will be available at http://www.worldbank.org/star.

To gauge risks, practitioners should use their personal contacts to learn about the other systems, confirm strategy, and discuss the implications of providing information prior to discussions of substance. To facilitate moving forward without breaching confidentiality or secrecy laws, practitioners often speak in hypothetical terms during the early phases of the case and strategy planning. For example, "Person x did action y. How would I achieve outcome z in the foreign jurisdiction?" Box 7.3 describes some ideas for overcoming the barrier of disclosure obligations.

7.2 Comparative Overview of Informal Assistance and MLA Requests

MLA is a process by which jurisdictions seek and provide assistance in gathering information, intelligence, and evidence for investigations; in implementing provisional measures; and in enforcing foreign orders and judgments. This handbook distinguishes between assistance that requires an MLA request and assistance that can be provided informally. An MLA request is typically submitted in writing and must adhere to specified procedures, protocols, and conditions set out in multilateral or bilateral agreements or domestic legislation. In the investigation stages, these requests generally ask for evidence, provisional measures, or the use of certain investigative techniques (such as the power to compel production of bank account documents, obtain search and seizure orders, take formal witness statements, and serve documents). An MLA request is generally required for the enforcement of confiscation orders.

Informal assistance typically consists of any official assistance rendered outside the context of an MLA request. Some jurisdictions consider informal assistance to be "formal" because the concept is authorized in MLA legislation and involves formal authorities, agencies, or administrations. The importance of such cooperation has been emphasized in international agreements.[179] In contrast to an MLA request, the information gathered through informal assistance may not be admissible in court; rather, it is more like intelligence or background information that can be used to develop the investigation and may lead to an MLA request.[180] This "informal" process may occur over the telephone between counterparts (that is, among law enforcement agencies, investigating magistrates, or prosecutors), through administrative cooperation (for example, financial intelligence units), or through face-to-face meetings between counterparts.[181] It may incorporate noncoercive investigative measures, such as gathering publicly available information, conducting visual surveillance, and obtaining information from financial intelligence units; and may extend to spontaneous disclosures of information, conducting a joint investigation, or asking the authorities in another jurisdiction to open a case. In some jurisdictions, emergency provisional measures can be achieved through informal assistance, although they must be followed with an MLA request. Table 7.1 elaborates on the differences between informal assistance and an MLA request.

7.2.1 The Process for International Cooperation

As described above, the process for asset recovery will use a combination of both informal requests for assistance and formal MLA requests to obtain information, intelligence, evidence, provisional measures, confiscation, and eventual return of assets. It is unfortunate that this is not a simple process in which one can request everything all at once by submitting an MLA request for information on bank accounts held, copies of any bank documents, and the restraint or seizure and confiscation of any funds that are found to be linked to the target or convicted criminal. Although it may seem easier to have everything in one request, such a request often lacks the evidentiary basis required—particularly for the latter phases of obtaining provisional measures and confiscation. Moreover, a request containing everything at once may become too complex to be processed in the requested jurisdiction, requiring the mobilization of multiple agencies and ultimately a lengthy delay in response.

---

179. United Nations Convention against Corruption (UNCAC), art. 48 and 50; United Nations Convention against Transnational Organized Crime (UNTOC), art. 26 and 27; United Nations Convention against Narcotic Drugs and Psychotropic Substances, art. 9; recommendation 40 of the Financial Action Task Force (FATF) 40+9 Recommendations.

180. In general, common law jurisdictions will not permit the results of informal assistance to be used as evidence in court. Civil law jurisdictions, on the other hand, may permit the judge to consider information gathered through informal assistance. Chile and Switzerland, for example, will permit the admission of such evidence.

181. UNCAC art. 46(9) requires a state party to render noncoercive assistance without requiring dual criminality, where consistent with the basic concepts of its legal system. Recommendation 37 of the FATF 40+9 Recommendations also requires that, to the extent possible, countries should render MLA, notwithstanding the absence of dual criminality—particularly for less-intrusive and noncoercive measures.

TABLE 7.1	Differences between Informal Assistance and MLA Requests	
Factor	Informal assistance	MLA requests
Purpose	• Obtain *intelligence* and *information* to assist investigation • Emergency provisional measures in some jurisdictions	• Obtain *evidence* for use in criminal trial and confiscation (in some cases, non-conviction based [NCB] confiscation) • Enforcement of restraint order or confiscation judgment
Type of assistance	Noncoercive investigative measures; proactive disclosure of information; joint investigation; opening of a foreign case	Coercive investigative measures (such as search orders) and other forms of judicial assistance (such as enforcement of provisional measures or confiscation judgment)
Contact process	Direct: law enforcement, prosecutor, or investigating magistrate directly to counterpart, among Financial Intelligence Units, between banking and securities regulators	Generally not direct: central authorities in each jurisdiction to proper contact point (law enforcement, magistrate, prosecutor, or judge)[a]; letters rogatory through the ministry of foreign affairs
Requirements	• Usually just agency-to-agency contact; sometimes a memorandum of understanding • Must be lawfully gathered in both jurisdictions	May include dual criminality, reciprocity, specialty, ongoing criminal investigation, or link between assets and offense
Advantages	• Information is obtained quickly; formality of an MLA request is not required (for example, dual criminality) • Useful for verifying facts and obtaining background information to improve an MLA request	Evidence is admissible in court; enables enforcement of orders
Limitations	Information cannot always be used as evidence; difficult to determine contacts; few resources allocated to networking; potential leaks	Time consuming; resource intensive; many requirements that are often difficult to meet; potential leaks

Source: Authors' compilation.
a. There may be bilateral or multilateral agreements that permit direct contact among practitioners.

Instead, the better method is a step-by-step process in which information or evidence obtained pursuant to one request is used to support the next (follow-up) request. For example, it may be possible through informal assistance to obtain bank account details that will help provide the necessary foundation and background information for an

MLA request to seize bank documents. The activity revealed in these documents will help practitioners trace the assets and determine additional accounts to restrain or seize. It will assist with gathering the evidence required for provisional measures, whether emergency provisional measures (through informal assistance where available) or an MLA request. Eventually, the accumulated information and evidence will provide the basis for domestic confiscation and enforcement.

Following a step-by-step process enables practitioners to make important strategic decisions at each stage. In addition, it leads to greater communication among counterparts, thereby building or fostering a relationship of trust between jurisdictions. Figure 7.2 provides a simple flow chart to illustrate this step-by-step process.

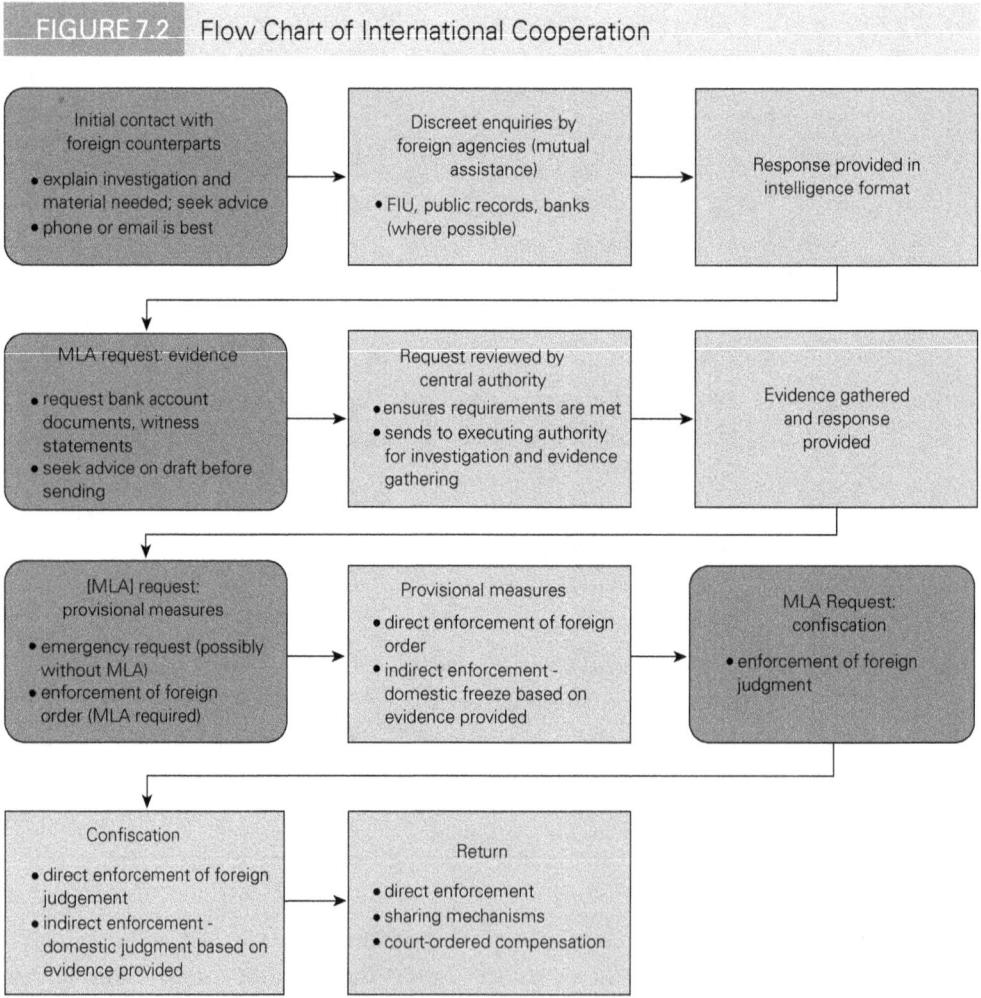

FIGURE 7.2 Flow Chart of International Cooperation

Source: Authors' illustration.
Note: FIU = financial intelligence unit. In some jurisdictions, evidence and provisional measures can be requested at the same time.

FIGURE 7.3

FIGURE 7.3 Informal Assistance and Formal MLA Requests—What Can Be Requested?

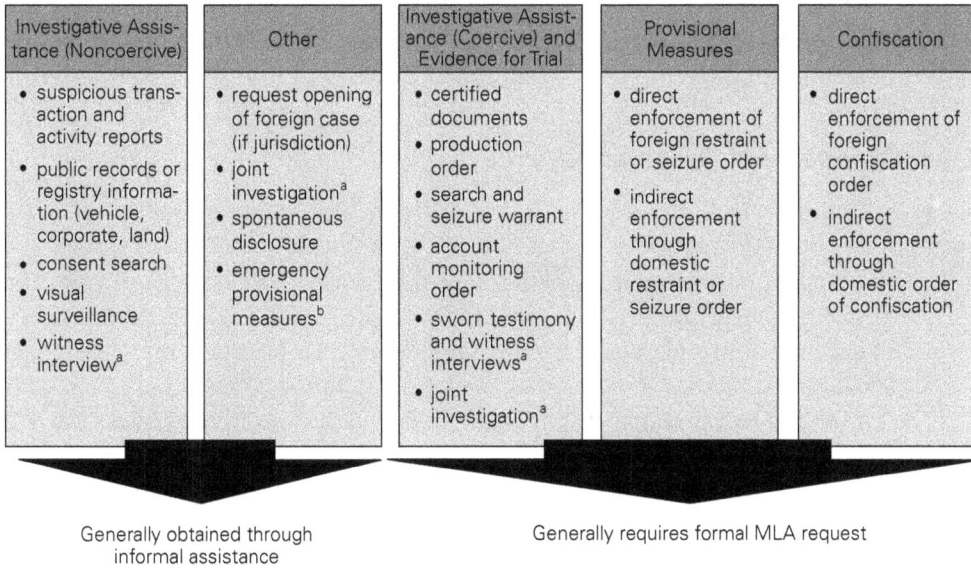

Investigative Assistance (Noncoercive)	Other	Investigative Assistance (Coercive) and Evidence for Trial	Provisional Measures	Confiscation
• suspicious transaction and activity reports • public records or registry information (vehicle, corporate, land) • consent search • visual surveillance • witness interview[a]	• request opening of foreign case (if jurisdiction) • joint investigation[a] • spontaneous disclosure • emergency provisional measures[b]	• certified documents • production order • search and seizure warrant • account monitoring order • sworn testimony and witness interviews[a] • joint investigation[a]	• direct enforcement of foreign restraint or seizure order • indirect enforcement through domestic restraint or seizure order	• direct enforcement of foreign confiscation order • indirect enforcement through domestic order of confiscation

Generally obtained through informal assistance

Generally requires formal MLA request

Source: Authors' illustration.
a. Either informal assistance or formal MLA request (or both), depending on the jurisdiction.
b. May not require formal MLA request for the initial order, but will require one to retain the order.

7.2.2 What Can Be Requested?

The information, evidence, or judicial measures that can be requested vary from jurisdiction to jurisdiction and ultimately depend on treaty agreements and domestic laws. In addition, jurisdictions differ on whether requests may be addressed through informal assistance or whether an MLA request is required. For example, some jurisdictions permit the possibility of emergency provisional measures using informal assistance channels—through a financial intelligence unit (FIU), ministry of justice, prosecutor, or an investigating magistrate. For additional information, see section 7.3.4.

At the same time, there are general areas of agreement on what can be requested and the process through which it is achieved (see figure 7.3). Noncoercive investigative techniques, for example, can usually be obtained through informal assistance; coercive investigative techniques and judicial measures typically require an MLA request. These measures are set out in greater detail in the following sections on informal assistance and MLA requests.

7.3 Informal Assistance

Below is a more detailed review of the channels for this cooperation and some of the specific forms of informal assistance that may be helpful in asset recovery cases—specifically, asset tracing, emergency provisional measures, spontaneous disclosures, and asking another jurisdiction to open a case. A joint investigation, one form of cooperation that may be initiated through informal assistance or an MLA request, is discussed in section 2.2.3 of chapter 2. A checklist in appendix H lists some of the talking points and issues that practitioners can use to begin discussions with their counterparts.

7.3.1 Channels for Cooperation

The most common channels for informal assistance include the following:

- **Counterpart practitioners,** whether law enforcement officials, prosecutors, or investigating magistrates. Also helpful in this regard are law enforcement attachés and liaison magistrates. Based in embassies or consulates abroad, these individuals facilitate contact with counterparts to provide informal assistance, help with MLA request preparations, and assist in following up MLA requests (see box 7.2 for some of the jurisdictions that have these resource persons).
- **FIUs.** The amount and type of assistance they provide will vary, depending on the style of the FIU (administrative or law enforcement); but generally they will be able to share financial intelligence with other FIUs. Some FIUs have authority to restrain funds or operate in a consent regime (see section 7.3.4).
- **Regulatory authorities,** such as bank, securities, and company regulators. This cooperation is more limited because it usually requires a memorandum of understanding and may have restrictions in sharing for law enforcement purposes.

How does one initiate cooperation with foreign agencies? This is often accomplished through personal contacts from previous cases, either directly or through networks to which the agencies are members (for example, Interpol and the World Customs Organization for law enforcement, the Egmont Group for FIUs, and the Camden Assets Recovery Inter-Agency Network or the Organization of American States' network for prosecutors and investigating magistrates (see box 7.2 for a wider list of networks). One problem for practitioners seeking to contact their counterparts is that many jurisdictions have multiple law enforcement agencies, and it may be difficult to determine which one(s) to contact (see box 7.4 for examples from four countries). These agencies could include federal, state or provincial, and municipal police; anticorruption offices; customs agencies; drug control offices; or tax agencies. This means that practitioners may need to contact multiple agencies, and should seek guidance from their counterparts whether other agencies might be relevant.

7.3.2 General Considerations

Although there are fewer restrictions to informal assistance than to MLA requests, there are some restrictions that practitioners will need to consider. Information requested or shared must be gathered lawfully in both the requested and requesting jurisdictions, and communications among counterparts must be authorized. And because cooperation is

BOX 7.4 **Investigative Jurisdiction in France, Switzerland, the United Kingdom, and the United States**

Many jurisdictions have multiple law enforcement agencies with authority to investigate and prosecute corruption and money laundering. Some examples are below.

France
- Customs
- Gendarmerie Nationale
- Interregional specialized courts for organized and financial crime
- Investigating judges
- Judicial police, specifically l'Office Central de Repression de la Grand Delinquance Financiere
- Prosecution offices

Switzerland
- Federal Police Office
- Federal investigating magistrates (*juges d'instruction*)[a]
- Ministère public de la Confédération (federal prosecution)

Each of the cantons (states) has its own prosecutors, law enforcement agencies, and investigating magistrates authorities.

United Kingdom (England and Wales)
- Crown Prosecution Service and the Revenue and Customs Prosecution Office
- Her Majesty's Revenue and Customs for England and Wales
- Serious Fraud Office
- Serious Organised Crime Agency

In addition, there are 43 regional police forces in England and Wales—some of which have dedicated units to fighting corruption and money laundering. They include the Metropolitan Police and the City of London Police.

United States
- Customs and Border Protection
- Department of Homeland Security
- Department of Justice (the central authority)
- Department of the Treasury
- Drug Enforcement Agency
- Federal Bureau of Investigation
- Immigration and Customs Enforcement

(continued next page)

- Internal Revenue Service Criminal Investigation
- U.S. Postal Service

In addition, there are state and local police forces.

Note: a. In 2011, the system of investigating magistrates (federal and cantonal) will be removed. Prosecutors will remain.

BOX 7.5   Facilitating Informal Assistance

Informal assistance is generally conducted on a counterpart-to-counterpart basis, a process that introduces a middleman in some exchanges because law enforcement must go through its domestic financial intelligence unit (FIU) to obtain information from an FIU in a foreign jurisdiction. Some jurisdictions have moved to facilitate informal exchanges by permitting direct cooperation, regardless of whether the foreign agency is a counterpart. For example, the U.S. Financial Crimes Enforcement Network cooperates directly with foreign law enforcement agencies from the European Union in certain circumstances, and similar cooperation is reciprocated.

usually counterpart-to-counterpart, the appropriate practitioners will need to go through the relevant domestic agency for their foreign counterparts (see box 7.5 for an example of how some jurisdictions are moving to eliminate this requirement). For example, instead of a law enforcement agency contacting a foreign FIU, the domestic FIU may use the Egmont Group channels to obtain information from the foreign FIU and then give that information to law enforcement officials. In some cases, in addition to Egmont membership, counterpart agencies must sign a memorandum of understanding or confidentiality undertakings.

Practitioners must always weigh the risks and benefits of proceeding with informal assistance. For example, interviewing voluntary witnesses or even breaches of confidentiality by the foreign counterparts may alert targets to the investigation and give them a chance to destroy evidence, move assets, or flee the jurisdiction.

7.3.3 Asset Tracing and Other Investigations

Because the tracing of assets is so time-sensitive and crucial to asset recovery, some jurisdictions have developed tools to allow rapid access to limited information before an MLA request is submitted. This may include suspicious transaction report (STR) information, data from public records (for example, land, vehicle, and legal person registries), and limited information on bank accounts. Practitioners will need to consult with their counterparts to determine what may be available without an MLA request and what information will need to be followed up with such a request.

Asset tracing is often stymied because there is insufficient information to narrow the search to a particular bank, branch, or location. Such information is generally required in jurisdictions with large numbers of financial institutions and branches (none of which share information); otherwise, the request is too onerous in its breadth. A tool that has helped overcome this barrier is a central registry of bank accounts.[182] Operated in Brazil, Chile, France, Italy, and Germany,[183] these registries hold limited information (for example, account number, name, and branch location); and they have safeguards to ensure that privacy is protected and that access is limited to specific agencies and circumstances. In France, for example, the FIU may conduct searches on the databases only when there is a reasonable suspicion of money laundering or terrorist financing. Foreign practitioners would have to provide sufficient information to meet requirements, and an MLA request may be necessary.

7.3.4 Emergency Provisional Measures

Although there are situations where funds may be preserved through a domestic restraint order submitted for enforcement through an MLA request, there are also circumstances that require greater urgency. The target may be tipped off to the investigation through an arrest or leak. Because of the speed with which targets and their associates can move proceeds from one jurisdiction to another, practitioners must be prepared to act quickly. Fortunately, a number of jurisdictions have measures that enable a swift seizure or restraint of funds in emergency situations. This rapid action often takes the form of a temporary measure executed on the expectation that an MLA request will follow within a specified period of time.[184] If the request is not provided in time, the money may be released. Some examples of emergency provisional measures are

- **Administrative orders.** An administrative official (typically associated with the FIU) may issue a preservation order instructing a financial institution to restrain funds for a brief period of time. These administrative orders are sometimes limited to cases involving specified underlying offenses.[185] Some jurisdictions operate under a "consent regime" that requires the financial institution, on the filing of an STR, to hold the funds until the FIU provides consent to release them or

---

182. The FATF recently recognized establishment of central registries as a best practice in "Best Practices: Confiscation (Recommendations 3 and 38)," adopted by the plenary in February 2010. The document is available at http://www.fatf-gafi.org/dataoecd/39/57/44655136.pdf.

183. Legislation permitting central registries is currently before the Spanish parliament.

184. A time extension may be granted on application in some jurisdictions.

185. The Anti-Money Laundering Act, 1999 (Thailand), sec. 48, empowers the Transaction Committee to restrain or seize for a period not exceeding 90 days "if there is a probable cause to believe that there may be a transfer, distribution, placement, layering or concealment of any asset related to predicate offense." In case of emergency, the secretary-general may issue the order. Relevant regulations relating to the procedure for taking into custody, preservation, maintenance, auction, and so forth may apply.

hold them for a specified period of time (thereby allowing the FIU or law enforcement to implement provisional measures).

- **Provisional orders of investigating magistrates.** In civil law jurisdictions that have investigating magistrates, the magistrate may be able to issue orders authorizing provisional measures if there is reason to believe that a confiscation order may ultimately be issued, that assets are likely to be dissipated, or both.[186]
- **Provisional measures on instigation of charges or arrest.** Some jurisdictions permit a temporary restraint or seizure of assets subject to confiscation following an arrest in another jurisdiction.[187] The requesting jurisdiction must provide evidence of the arrest and a summary of the facts of the case. The funds will be restrained to await further evidence, and this period of restraint can be extended on application. Generally, assets need not be traced to a crime and no treaty arrangement is necessary, and the proceeding is conducted without notice to the asset holder (*ex parte*).
- **Direct referral to prosecutors.** In some jurisdictions, incoming requests for restraint and confiscation are referred to prosecutors to provide the same level of international cooperation in obtaining provisional measures and confiscating proceeds and instrumentalities of crime as is available in domestic cases.[188] Evidence of crime and benefit or evidence that assets are proceeds or an instrumentality of crime may be required.

Some jurisdictions will require an MLA request to obtain any provisional measure, but a hearing can be obtained on short notice and *ex parte*.[189] Other jurisdictions may have stricter conditions, such as the requirement of an arrest or charges. If that is the case, the practitioner may have to consider other options—perhaps initiating a joint investigation or supplying the foreign jurisdiction with sufficient information through informal assistance channels to enable provisional measures under domestic law. These options are possible only if the foreign authority has jurisdiction over some element of the underlying crime, such as money laundering.

7.3.5 Spontaneous Disclosures

Another form of informal assistance that has aided in recovering proceeds of corruption is spontaneous disclosures.[190] A proactive form of assistance used by competent authorities and FIUs, a spontaneous disclosure alerts a foreign jurisdiction to an ongoing investigation of money laundering in the disclosing jurisdiction; and indicates that existing evidence could be of interest, such as the bank account of a corrupt politically exposed

---

186. This applies in Switzerland, and can be achieved by sending a fax to the Federal Office of Justice.
187. The United States has a temporary restraint order (30 days) that can be issued upon notice of charges being filed or arrest: Title 18, United States Code, sec. 984(b)(4).
188. Proceeds of Crime Act, 2002 (External Requests and Orders), order 2005, sec. 6.
189. Hong Kong SAR, China, will provide for a hearing on short notice.
190. UNCAC art. 46(4) and 56 require that states parties try to provide such disclosures of information.

Spontaneous Disclosures from Switzerland

A spontaneous disclosure from Switzerland could include

- information on the investigation, including the name of the accused and a summary of the facts and the offense(s);
- a description of evidence that might be of interest, including the name of the bank and account holder, account number, amount of funds frozen, and relevant transactions;
- reasons for transmission (for example, pending or possible investigation in the receiving jurisdiction);
- an invitation to present an MLA request; and
- a request that the information not be used for any other purpose.

person. Box 7.6 describes the information that may be transmitted by Switzerland.[191] The receiving jurisdiction then may use the information to further its own investigation and eventually submit an MLA request. Such disclosures are particularly helpful in corruption cases because the international media coverage that such cases attract may prompt a foreign bank to file an STR (subsequently leading to a foreign investigation) or a foreign practitioner to initiate an investigation independently.[192]

Recipients of spontaneous disclosures should contact the author to clarify the disclosure, find out about the foreign case, ensure that the assets will remain frozen, and discuss the next steps to be taken.

7.3.6 Requesting the Opening of a Foreign Case

In some circumstances, the authorities may not have the ability to pursue a domestic case of criminal or non-conviction based (NCB) confiscation or civil proceedings. Perhaps this is because of a lack of capacity, political will, or an effective legislative framework. In these circumstances, the authorities may provide the case materials to their foreign counterparts and request that those authorities initiate domestic proceedings. Ultimately, the foreign authorities will determine whether to proceed and how the proceedings will be conducted (see chapter 9 for details on this option).

---

191. The enabling legislation for spontaneous disclosures in Switzerland is art. 67a of the Federal Act on International Mutual Assistance in Criminal Matters. It grants the authority to spontaneously transmit to a foreign authority any prosecuting offenses information or evidence that is gathered in the course of its own investigation, when it determines that the transmission will (1) permit the opening of a criminal proceeding or (2) facilitate a pending criminal investigation. The transmission will not affect the domestic criminal proceedings in Switzerland.

192. A spontaneous disclosure was the catalyst for international cooperation between Peru and Switzerland in the Montesinos case.

7.4 MLA Requests

As previously discussed, practitioners should generally *not* begin their international cooperation efforts with the submission of an MLA request. If available, informal assistance channels should be explored first so that practitioners connect with their counterparts to discuss what will be needed to execute the request and to address potential barriers. Once a practitioner determines that an MLA is required for certain needed action—such as the production of financial records, obtaining compulsory testimony or a search and seizure warrant, or enforcing a provisional restraint order—numerous requirements and procedures must be fulfilled. Some of those are described below.

Requirements will vary from jurisdiction to jurisdiction, so practitioners should confirm their applicability beforehand with the foreign central authority. Consulting with foreign counterparts or other contacts can be helpful in this regard, although many jurisdictions will require the practitioner to proceed on a formal basis through their own central authority when a formal request is being prepared or has been sent. In addition, many jurisdictions publish information on their central authority's Web site that may state the requirements, and some even provide sample forms for preparing an MLA request that is acceptable (see appendix J for a list of helpful Web sites in a selection of jurisdictions, and appendix I for a sample MLA request).[193] The United Nations Office on Drugs and Crime operates a directory of central authorities and has developed an MLA request writer tool[194] to assist practitioners.[195] Finally, publications by nongovernmental or multilateral organizations may also provide assistance.[196]

7.4.1 Legal Basis for International Cooperation

To proceed with an MLA request, there must be a legal basis for cooperation; and this must be specified in the request. This legal basis may come through (1) multilateral conventions, treaties, or agreements containing provisions on MLA in criminal matters;

---

193. For example, Hong Kong SAR, China, and the United Kingdom have booklets that are available to assist practitioners.

194. The United Nations Office on Drugs and Crime's Mutual Legal Assistance Request Writer Tool (which can be downloaded through http://www.unodc.org/mla/en/index.html) is a software program that generates an MLA request after prompting the user for information. The request must be tailored for each jurisdiction, but the tool will assist with the organization of the request. This tool is currently being expanded to include asset recovery features.

195. Other multilateral organizations provide lists of central authorities, including the Organisation for Economic Co-operation and Development (OECD), the Organization of American States, and the Asociación Iberoamericana de Ministerios Públicos.

196. The StAR Initiative's forthcoming publication of its study of the barriers to asset recovery will include MLA information on 15 financial center jurisdictions. See footnote 28 for publication details. Other pertinent publications include the Asian Development Bank (ADB)/OECD Anti-Corruption Initiative for Asia and the Pacific, "Mutual Legal Assistance, Extradition and Recovery of Proceeds of Corruption in Asia and the Pacific: Frameworks and Practices in 27 Asian and Pacific Jurisdictions" (Manila, 2007); and the ADB/OECD Anti-Corruption Initiative for Asia and the Pacific, "Asset Recovery and Mutual Legal Assistance in Asia and the Pacific" (Manila, 2008).

(2) bilateral MLA treaties and agreements; (3) domestic legislation allowing for international cooperation in criminal cases; or (4) a promise of reciprocity through diplomatic channels (referred to as "letters rogatory" or "comity" in some jurisdictions). It should be noted that the above-mentioned legal avenues are not mutually exclusive; and an MLA request may use one or more of these avenues, depending on the subject matter of the case and the expected outcomes (see box 7.7). Each avenue is discussed below.

Multilateral Conventions, Treaties, or Agreements

Multilateral conventions, treaties, or agreements contain binding provisions that oblige signatories to provide MLA under international law. The provisions define areas of cooperation and contain governing procedures, thereby bringing clarity and predictability to the process. These agreements often permit more extensive forms of cooperation than the traditional promise of reciprocity or letters rogatory, such as communication between central authorities (rather than through formal diplomatic channels).

UNCAC is the most applicable multilateral treaty for recovery of the proceeds of corruption and the MLA required for success. It has been ratified by more than 140 jurisdictions and obliges states parties to afford one another the widest measure of assistance in investigations, prosecutions, and judicial proceedings concerning corruption matters. In addition to UNCAC and other United Nations treaties, a legal basis can be provided through some regional MLA treaties or agreements—such as the Southeast Asian Mutual Legal Assistance in Criminal Matters Treaty and the Inter-American Convention against Corruption.

One issue that practitioners must consider with international conventions, treaties, and agreements is how, if at all, their relevant obligations have been incorporated into domestic legislation in the other jurisdiction—a process referred to as "domestication."

In theory, MLA requests submitted under a multilateral treaty (such as UNCAC, UNTOC, or the United Nations Convention against Narcotic Drugs and Psychotropic Substances) can be applied directly, as a long as both jurisdictions have ratified the treaty.[197] However, the mandatory provisions of these treaties are typically formulated in a general manner, leaving room for interpretation and uncertainty. For example, the treaty may not specify the channels for communication, the procedures and documents for enforcement, or the particular types of evidence or procedures requiring judicial authorization. Some jurisdictions enact detailed domestic legislation to provide the specifics; others have limited or no legislation domesticating the treaty and rely on direct application through existing criminal laws and procedures, with modifications based on the treaty. Because some authorities will prefer that the requested jurisdiction have domesticated the treaty, it will be important for practitioners to consider this issue and to look to domestic laws for details on the implementation of multilateral treaties.

In addition, there may be voluntary arrangements with other jurisdictions or regional groups (such as the Commonwealth Secretariat's Scheme on Mutual Assistance in Criminal Matters [Harare Scheme], which is a commitment of the Commonwealth Law Ministers). Although not a binding legal instrument or treaty, parties are expected to implement the provisions in domestic legislation; and assistance is rendered through these provisions.

Bilateral Mutual Legal Assistance Treaties and Agreements
Similar to the multilateral treaties, bilateral MLA treaties contain binding provisions that oblige the signatories to provide assistance and that define the procedures for practitioners to follow. In addition, they may provide forms of cooperation that are not available under other arrangements, such as direct contact between the practitioners, competent authorities, and members of the judiciary (with limited central authority involvement).

Domestic Legislation
A number of jurisdictions have passed legislation that provides an MLA process for jurisdictions without a bilateral treaty, often on the condition of reciprocity (that is, the requesting jurisdiction will provide MLA in similar situations). Unlike a treaty arrangement, there is no international obligation to provide requested assistance; such flexibility makes it uncertain that the request will be acceptable.[198]

Promise of Reciprocity through Diplomatic Channels (Letters Rogatory)
This traditional form of assistance may be useful if there is neither an existing treaty between the jurisdictions nor domestic legislation in the requested jurisdiction (although some jurisdictions require the reciprocity undertaking even when using a

---

197. UNCAC, art. 46 and 55; UNTOC, art. 18; and United Nations Convention against Narcotic Drugs and Psychotropic Substances, art. 7.

198. Some examples include the Mutual Assistance in Criminal Matters Act (Singapore); Law on International Mutual Legal Assistance in Criminal Matters (Liechtenstein); Mutual Legal Assistance in Criminal Matters Ordinance, cap. 525 (Hong Kong SAR, China); and the Federal Act on International Mutual Assistance in Criminal Matters (Switzerland).

multilateral or bilateral treaty as a basis for the request). It permits formal communication among the judiciary, a prosecutor or law enforcement official of one jurisdiction, and his or her counterpart in another jurisdiction. It is a longer process because it requires the inclusion of an additional party, the ministry of foreign affairs, and diplomatic formalities.

7.4.2 General Requirements

Each jurisdiction will have a number of legal requirements that requesting jurisdictions must meet in submitting an MLA request. Below are some of those requirements and the considerations practitioners can make in meeting them.

Nature of the Matter

Generally, the request must be related to a criminal matter, although some jurisdictions will provide assistance on NCB confiscation requests (because they usually arise in connection with a criminal investigation) and in civil and administrative cases.[199] Jurisdictions differ as to the point in criminal investigations or proceedings when assistance can be provided. Although most jurisdictions will permit requests during the investigation stages, others will have more onerous requirements for the provisional seizure or restraint of assets (such as requiring that charges have been filed or final confiscation has been ordered). Many jurisdictions will not provide assistance if the criminal proceedings have been concluded. For the more onerous requirements, practitioners should consider timing and coordinating the request for provisional measures and arrest to avoid the dissipation of funds.

Dual Criminality

Many jurisdictions require some showing of dual criminality (or dual confiscation if confiscation assistance is sought), meaning that the conduct underlying the request for assistance is criminalized in both jurisdictions. Some jurisdictions will waive the requirement in certain circumstances.[200] Some jurisdictions may apply this in a more restrictive matter (that is, requiring a match in the names or essential elements of the offense). However, jurisdictions more frequently apply a conduct-based approach (that is, they look behind the terminology to the conduct and require that the conduct is a criminal offense under the laws of both jurisdictions).[201] In any event, the use of informal assistance is paramount to discuss, identify, and overcome (if possible) any potential barriers that the dual criminality requirement may pose.

The conduct-based approach may help in corruption cases because some of the more specific offenses involved are not criminalized in all jurisdictions (for example, illicit enrichment, bribery of foreign public officials, tax avoidance, or extended confiscation).

---

199. See sections 7.5 and 7.6 for a discussion of international cooperation in NCB confiscation and civil cases. In addition, UNCAC art. 43(1) and 54(1)(c) require states parties to consider assisting each other in civil and administrative matters and to permit NCB confiscation.

200. Jersey is a jurisdiction that does not require dual criminality.

201. International conventions and agreements require that states parties apply this conduct-based approach. UNCAC, art. 43(2); recommendation 37 of FATF 40+9 Recommendations.

BOX 7.8 **Overcoming Dual Criminality—Illicit Enrichment and Corruption of Foreign Public Officials**

The offenses of illicit enrichment (a significant increase in the assets of a public official that the official cannot reasonably explain as being derived from lawful earnings) and bribery of foreign public officials have not been criminalized in a number of jurisdictions. If strictly interpreted on the basis of terms, there would be no dual criminality—and thus no assistance available—from those jurisdictions.

This barrier may be overcome when dual criminality is assessed on the basis of conduct because the facts under investigation in the requesting jurisdiction may constitute another offense in the requested jurisdiction. For illicit enrichment, the conduct that results in the illicit enrichment may constitute another offense under domestic law (for example, accepting a bribe). With bribery of foreign public officials, the requested jurisdiction may consider the offense to be bribery of a *national* official, not a foreign official.[a] Once the parallel offenses—based on the same *conduct*—are determined, the dual criminality requirement is met.

Practitioners using this approach must take care in stating the facts and offenses in their MLA requests. For example, it may not be sufficient to submit a request that states

> Mr. X is a public official who earns $3,000 per month at the Ministry of Transportation. When he began his position five years ago, he had no savings; now he has $5 million. He was unable to explain and is guilty.

Instead, it will be important to include additional facts that may support an offense in the foreign jurisdiction:

> Mr. X is responsible for procurement of construction contracts. In the past three years, he has awarded three major contracts to new companies. His bank account statement shows he received two deposits of $400,000 just prior to the awards. Recently, $1 million was wired to a bank account in jurisdiction Y.

Asking counterparts in the requested jurisdiction to review a draft of the MLA request prior to submission may facilitate this procedure. The counterpart may be able to offer drafting suggestions that make the request more easily enforceable.

a. This approach was confirmed in a 2003 ruling of the Swiss Federal Supreme Court (ATF 129 II 462). The Court held that dual criminality was met on corruption charges, despite not having an offense for corruption of foreign public officials in Swiss law. In reaching this verdict, the Court looked at the facts and conduct, and held that the requesting jurisdiction was able to fulfill the requirement on the basis of another offense: *passive corruption of national public officials was an offense under the Swiss system.*

It will be important to describe rather than merely list the offenses because the requested jurisdiction may not have the relevant expertise of the legal system of the requesting country and may have to assess whether the conduct is punishable under a different name under its domestic laws (see box 7.8). It will also be important to put the offense into context, demonstrating its connection to the criminal conduct in explaining the request's subject matter. In addition, practitioners should avoid the use of certain words and phrases that may prompt confusion in terminology. For example, "illicit flows" can be problematic in some jurisdictions because the term often refers to tax evasion and capital flight. It would be better to use "criminal flows."

International conventions and standards also require that assistance for noncoercive measures be provided in the absence of dual criminality.[202]

Assurances and Undertakings (Reciprocity, Confidentiality, Limits on Use [Specialty], and Commitment to Pay Costs or Damages)

Many jurisdictions require a reciprocity assurance, a written statement that the requesting jurisdiction will provide the requested jurisdiction with the same type of cooperation in a similar case in the future. And many jurisdictions require the requesting jurisdiction to specify if it wishes the request to be treated as confidential. In addition, jurisdictions may require an assurance that the requesting jurisdiction will use the information supplied only for the case described in the request for assistance—not as evidence in another case and not disclosed to a third party. Finally, some jurisdictions may require a commitment to pay any costs and damages incurred by the requested party during the course of executing the request.[203]

These assurances may be waived on a case-by-case basis, but waivers must be discussed with the other jurisdiction. Some practitioners hesitate or refuse to provide these assurances because they are not used in their own jurisdiction (many civil law jurisdictions do not use them), and the practitioner is unsure whether he or she has the authority to provide them. However, these assurances are often not optional, and assistance may be refused if they are not provided or addressed prior to the submission of the request.

7.4.3 Evidentiary Requirements

Practitioners usually have to provide sufficient admissible evidence to officials in the requested jurisdiction to enable them to meet the evidentiary threshold mandated by their courts in executing a request. This can be challenging because admissibility requirements vary among jurisdictions. Requested jurisdictions may require standards for some measures that are more demanding than those in the requesting jurisdiction. What may be an appropriate request in one jurisdiction is considered overly broad—a fishing expedition—in another.

This difficulty is augmented when the exchange is between civil and common law jurisdictions or between different confiscation systems (value-based versus property-based system, or criminal confiscation versus NCB confiscation) because standards of proof, evidentiary tests, and requirements for admissibility may differ widely. For example, if

---

202. UNCAC, art. 46(9); recommendation 37 of FATF 40+9 Recommendations. UNCAC art. 46(9)(a) also requires states parties to take into account the purposes of the Convention when applying dual criminality.
203. One of the rationales is that the requested jurisdiction may take action and expose itself to liability, and the requesting state could fail to follow through in providing promised proof. Through no fault of its own, the requested state would then face an award of costs against it.

facts about the case are to be admissible as evidence, common law jurisdictions generally require statements in affidavit or certificate format; civil law jurisdictions, however, generally will not impose that requirement (for information on drafting affidavits, see box 4.1 in chapter 4).

Failure to include sufficient admissible evidence to meet the applicable threshold or to use the least intrusive means as a first step in gathering evidence may result in the request being returned or refused. Thus, practitioners should discuss evidentiary requirements, standards, and examples of admissible evidence with their foreign counterparts prior to sending an MLA request. Once it is determined that an MLA request is required, the following three-step process should be considered prior to submission of the request:

- **Step 1.** Determine what is needed (for example, production or seizure of financial or business records, search of a location, seizure or restraint of assets, or confiscation). It is often best to use a step-by-step approach to requesting MLA, rather than to request everything at once.
- **Step 2.** Determine the least intrusive means for obtaining the needed information, as well as the standard of proof and evidence required by the requested jurisdiction (for example, specific facts, location of the assets, link between asset and offense, and final court order).
- **Step 3.** Determine the format for admissible evidence in the requested jurisdiction and any other documents required (see section 7.4.4 below for additional details on form and content).

Generally speaking, the more intrusive the measure, the higher the evidentiary standard of proof required to demonstrate, among other things, (1) that an offense has been committed; (2) that the assets sought are linked to the offense or offender, or are otherwise subject to confiscation in the practitioner's jurisdiction; and (3) specifically where the assets sought to be restrained or recovered are located. Common law jurisdictions typically permit investigative and provisional measures on a "reasonable grounds to believe" or "probable cause" standard; a higher standard is required for confiscation, namely the "balance of probabilities" or "preponderance of the evidence" standard. With some exceptions, most civil law jurisdictions provide investigative and provisional measures on the reasonable grounds to believe standard; but they require a higher level of proof ("intimate conviction") for confiscation. Figure 2.1 in chapter 2 illustrates the different standards of proof that may be required. Section 7.4.6 below describes more specifically the evidentiary requirements for asset tracing, provisional measures, and confiscation; the standards of proof that must be reached; and other relevant information.

7.4.4 Form and Content Requirements

MLA requests must be in writing and must meet the language, content, and format requirements of the requested jurisdiction, applicable treaty, or practitioner's domestic central authority. As noted previously, practitioners should determine these requirements and obtain sample requests before writing and sending the request. Where permitted and available, practitioners should maximize opportunities to send drafts of the MLA request to the requested jurisdiction's central authority or the authority that will be implementing the request. This drafting process and resulting assistance helps to ensure that requirements are met, the facts of the case are clear, and the terminology is correct. It also helps the requesting practitioner avoid unnecessary delays or refusals of assistance, and gives the requested jurisdiction the opportunity to prepare its responsive actions.

With regard to language, requests should be provided in a language that is acceptable to the requested jurisdiction. Responsibility for arranging translation lies with the requesting jurisdiction, although some jurisdictions provide translation services if the requesting jurisdiction agrees to pay the fees. In some past cases, developed jurisdictions have agreed to cover these costs for developing jurisdictions. If conducting the translation services, it is important to use professional services that are familiar with the legal terminology because mistakes in translation may result in ambiguities that need clarification by the requesting jurisdiction and will delay the process. Also, the authority responsible for drafting the request in the original language should bear in mind that translation will be necessary; and should write concisely, objectively, and with simple language to facilitate the work of the translators and avoid problems of misinterpretation. Short, declarative sentences set out in chronological order translate well.

Contact information for the lead investigator or prosecutor should also be included in the request.

Practitioners should also determine any preferences for the format of the request and any additional documentation that is required. Some jurisdictions provide template headings to assist in this process (see appendix J for a sample MLA request). It may be necessary to include additional documents such as affidavits and certified copies or originals of court orders for production or seizure of documents, breach of bank secrecy, provisional measures, or confiscation. These documents may need to be certified by a court or signed by the author, witness, and taker of oaths.[204]

Finally, if there are any legal requirements from the requesting jurisdiction to the requested jurisdiction in carrying out the request (for example, a specific warning to an interviewee), these must be specified in the request. Practitioners should also specify if the circumstances require greater urgency, and they should provide details on when and why the information is needed (for example, upcoming trial dates).

7.4.5 Reasons for Refusal

In addition to the general and evidentiary requirements, most MLA arrangements will allow the requested jurisdiction the discretion to refuse assistance in certain circumstances,

---

204. An affidavit requires a sworn statement of the author, witnessed by a taker of oaths (such as a notary public or a commissioner of oaths). Certification can be provided by a judge, magistrate, or officer of the court.

Bank secrecy and fiscal offenses are generally prohibited by United Nations conventions as reasons for refusing to provide MLA. Where applicable, practitioners should refer to treaty provisions:

- **Fiscal offenses.** UNCAC article 46(22), UNTOC article 18(22), and United Nations Convention against Narcotic Drugs and Psychotropic Substances article 3(10) prohibit MLA refusals on the sole ground that the offense involves fiscal matters.
- **Bank secrecy.**
  - OECD Bribery Convention article 9(3), UNCAC article 46(8), and UNTOC Article 18(8) expressly prohibit MLA refusals on the ground of bank secrecy.
  - UNCAC article 31(7) and UNTOC article 12(6) require states parties to empower courts or other competent authorities to order seizure of bank, financial, or commercial records in domestic cases and in international cooperation.
  - UNCAC article 40 requires states parties to ensure there are appropriate mechanisms to overcome obstacles that arise from bank secrecy in domestic criminal investigations. Although this provision applies to domestic investigations, it demonstrates efforts toward reducing bank secrecy, and would help in cases where the requested jurisdiction is asked or opts to pursue a domestic case for money laundering on the basis of the foreign predicate.

on a case-by-case basis.[205] Some treaties (including United Nations conventions) elaborate prohibited grounds for refusal, such as the involvement of fiscal offenses or bank secrecy (see examples in box 7.9). Practitioners should address these potential obstacles proactively and before the request is sent (if possible) because it becomes much more difficult to overcome a refusal when it has been issued. Consulting with foreign counterparts will be important in this regard. Elaborated below are some reasons for refusals that jurisdictions may use, and some suggestions for addressing them.

Essential Interests. Assistance may be denied if execution of the request would prejudice the "essential interests" of the requested jurisdiction. Essential interests are not specifically defined in any convention, but may include sovereignty, public order, security, and excessive burden on resources. Unfortunately, a broad interpretation of essential interests can impair international cooperation. For example, a requested jurisdiction

---

205. For example, UNCAC permits refusals if the request involves matters of a de minimis nature or there are other ways to obtain the assistance; the request does not conform to the procedural or substantive requirements (for example, dual criminality); the execution of the request would prejudice the sovereignty, security, public order, or other essential interests of the requested state; or the action requested is prohibited under domestic law. UNCAC, art. 46(9)(b) and (21); see also UNCAC, art. 46(23), which requires states parties to provide reasons for any refusal to provide MLA.

could refuse to cooperate in a bribery case that would result in disclosure of information on natural resources.

Assets of De Minimis Value. As indicated earlier, the process for gaining international cooperation is lengthy and resource intensive for both the requested and requesting jurisdictions; and a requested jurisdiction may have monetary thresholds or other criteria that must be met (such as the seriousness of the offense).[206] Practitioners should prioritize and filter MLA requests where the assets are of de minimis value or where there is no reasonable prospect of conviction. The value considered to be de minimis will vary among jurisdictions, and most jurisdictions will consider requests that are below this threshold if there is a strong public interest in responding, such as a request involving the corruption of a senior political figure.

Double Jeopardy and Ongoing Proceedings or Investigations in Requested Jurisdiction. When the target has already been convicted or acquitted of the same crime or there are ongoing proceedings or investigations of the same conduct in the requested jurisdiction, that jurisdiction may refuse to provide assistance. This is particularly problematic in MLA requests because the request itself may give the requested jurisdiction sufficient information to open a domestic case and issue the following response: "Thank you for your request. We cannot provide assistance because we have started an investigation based on the information you provided." It will be important to assess this issue prior to sending the request (through use of either personal contacts or networks), and to determine how this will affect case strategy.

Nature and Severity of the Penalty. Some jurisdictions will refuse to cooperate if the offense carries a punishment that is deemed too severe, such as the death penalty. More specifically on asset confiscation, the nature of the penalty may impair cooperation when the same penalty does not exist in the requested jurisdiction (for example, extended confiscation). This issue may be resolved with an assurance or undertaking that a specific penalty will not be imposed or carried out.

Immunities. Jurisdictions generally refuse to provide assistance if the target has immunity from prosecution. This may be resolved through a waiver of immunity by the requesting jurisdiction. For example, in the Ferdinand Marcos case, the subsequent government of the Philippines provided a waiver of immunity to enable action by one of the foreign jurisdictions involved. For more information, see the discussion of immunities in section 2.6.2 of chapter 2.

Lack of Due Process. Practitioners often have to make a showing to the requested jurisdiction that due process will be or has been given to the offender. In requests for provisional measures and confiscation, due process must also be afforded any third

---

206. Refusals on such a basis are permitted under UNCAC art. 46(9)(b) and 55(7). In addition to reasons for refusal outlined in UNCAC art. 46, art. 55(7) and 55(8) provide that cooperation may be refused or provisional measures may be lifted if sufficient and timely evidence is not received or if the property is of a de minimis value.

parties with an interest in the assets. Due process generally includes a fair hearing; sufficient time to prepare a case; third-party protections; protection of the right against self-incrimination; and nondiscrimination on the bases of race, nationality, sex, or religion.[207] It is important for practitioners to note that the due process issue, like other reasons for refusal, must be looked at on a case-by-case basis—not as an analysis of an entire legal system. As a result, it is important that the request clearly elaborates the domestic proceedings, the rights afforded the parties (for example, notice and the opportunity to be heard), and any procedural decisions made.

Additional reasons for refusal will apply in cases of extradition.[208]

7.4.6 Specific Considerations: Tracing, Provisional Measures, and Confiscation

Investigations and Asset Tracing

As outlined in chapter 3, there are numerous investigative tools for tracing assets and obtaining information and evidence relevant to the investigation. Many of these tools will require an MLA request, including (1) production or seizure orders to compel financial institutions to produce or surrender relevant documents, (2) account monitoring orders to compel a financial institution to provide account activity and transactions data over a period of time, (3) search and seizure warrants for physical evidence and documents held by private parties or businesses, and (4) interviews with witnesses. Examples of conditions commonly necessary to give effect to such requests are:

- General requirements for MLA requests are met and there are no grounds for refusal.
- There are reasonable grounds to suspect (or believe) that the requested information is relevant to the investigation and that it can be found in the bank account or place to be searched.
- There is as much information as possible on the location of the assets to be monitored, the bank account records to be produced, and the time periods to be examined to avoid being accused of making an overly broad request (see box 7.10 for tips on avoiding such refusals).

In some civil law jurisdictions, certain orders can be effected by a prosecutor or investigating magistrate; in common law jurisdictions, these orders are usually issued by a court. Who issues the orders may affect the request form and requirements, as well as the length of time it takes to process the request (that is, greater formality and time will be needed in requests that require court authorization).

---

207. See, for example, the United Nations International Covenant on Civil and Political Rights and the Universal Declaration of Human Rights.

208. Extradition may be refused if the offense was committed (even partly) in the requested jurisdiction or if the offense is of a political nature. In this regard, it is important to note that UNCAC art. 44(4) states that offenses under the convention are not considered political offenses.

BOX 7.10 Avoiding Rejections of MLA Requests That Are Overly Broad

One of the common reasons cited for the refusal of an MLA request or a request for additional information is that the request is a "fishing expedition"—a request that is overly broad and goes beyond the scope of the offense being investigated. For example, the following request could uncover accounts that are outside the investigation and therefore is overly broad: "Mr. X is suspected of corruption. Please provide a list of all accounts he has in your jurisdiction and restrain them immediately." More important, in jurisdictions with thousands of financial institutions and tens of thousands of intermediaries, gathering this information would be too onerous a task. Even if there are only a few large financial institutions, each with hundreds of branches, the request would be too burdensome because banks generally do not hold information in a central database.

To avoid a refusal or delay on grounds of a fishing expedition, the request must be as precise as possible in its description of the assets and their location(s), and often will require an established link between those assets and the offense being investigated. The request should include the bank or financial intermediary where assets may be located and the names of possible proxies (spouses, children, shell companies, trusts, close associates, lawyers, and so forth). It may be difficult to assemble this information, but it is essential to the request. Below are a few suggestions to assist in gathering this information:

- Use the domestic investigation and informal assistance channels, including an Egmont Group request through your domestic FIU, to gather as much information as possible.
- When the bank account number or branch location cannot be obtained, look to other information that could assist the requested jurisdiction in identifying the location of the accounts—for example, a phone or fax number of the bank, an account manager's name or business card, travel destinations, hotel bills, credit card records, copies of checks or bank transfer information, and the like.

A few jurisdictions may be able to help when only a minimum amount of evidence is provided—namely, the smaller jurisdictions or those with national registries of bank accounts (Brazil, Chile, France, Italy, Germany, and Spain). However, certain conditions, such as a link between the assets and the offense, will have to be established in these jurisdictions as they are in others.

In larger or particularly complicated cases with a vast amount of financial and bank documentation, practitioners should consider participating in the execution of the request.

Where permitted, participation by the investigating practitioners in executing search and seizure orders, seizing and sorting documents, and questioning witnesses and experts may greatly facilitate the execution of a request.[209] The requesting jurisdiction is more familiar with the case and requirements regarding admissibility of evidence, so it is in a better position to identify relevant documents and ensure that procedural safeguards are followed (for example, reading a warning to a witness). Direct participation also avoids the need for follow-up requests because relevant leads can be followed. Participants can include the judge in charge of the investigation, representatives of the authority conducting the proceedings (public ministry, state prosecutor), law enforcement officers (including analysts and technicians), the accused person and his or her lawyer(s), and civil parties and their lawyers. Certain safeguards are in place to ensure the MLA process is respected: although foreign practitioners may be able to view the documents, copies of the documents will not be sent until the MLA request is received and approved. An undertaking is often required to ensure that information will not be used before the official response is received.

Also in large cases, practitioners should consider narrowing the scope of their request. Many corruption investigations will span a number of years—possibly decades—and involve multiple accounts, account holders, products, companies, and corporate vehicles. If a requesting jurisdiction were to request bank and other documents for the duration of this period, it could take months or years to assemble all the information. And when the information is received, practitioners will have to sift through boxes and boxes of documents, many of which will be irrelevant. It is important to prioritize requests and avoid framing requests that are so broad that vast amounts of documentation will be required (for example, 10 years of account materials on a number of individuals and companies). It would be more appropriate first to request only bank statements and significant transactions, and then request additional documents based on a review of the first batch of materials. Not only does this narrowing of scope make it possible to process the request more quickly, but it also avoids unnecessary requests for and effort expended on irrelevant documents. In jurisdictions that require disclosure to the asset holder, a focused request makes it more difficult for the asset holder to contest on the grounds that the request is overly broad.

For guidance in seeking relevant documents that may be requested to assist with asset tracing, see section 3.4 in chapter 3.

Provisional Measures
Once the assets are identified, authorities must take steps to seize or restrain the assets to prevent dissipation before the eventual confiscation. Practitioners should consider

---

209. This is permitted in Switzerland, the United Kingdom, and other jurisdictions. In Switzerland, foreign investigators are forbidden access to "information within the scope of secrecy" (Federal Act on International Mutual Assistance in Criminal Matters [Switzerland], sec. 65[3]). "Secrecy" is information protected by law, notably bank information and commercial secrets; "access" is handing out copies of documents, taking written notes, taping audiences, or gathering any similar material element of proof to be used in court. Therefore, to safeguard these limits, the foreign authority may participate on condition that it will not use information before closure of the regular MLA procedure.

options for administrative or emergency provisional measures by the foreign authorities (through either the FIU, law enforcement officials, or other authority under that jurisdiction's domestic law), if available, prior to making an MLA request.[210] Ultimately, an MLA request for the provisional measures (seizure or restraint) must be submitted to retain the measures.

Depending on the jurisdiction, fulfilling an MLA request for provisional measures typically involves either the requested jurisdiction's "direct" enforcement of the requesting jurisdiction's order, or "indirect" enforcement whereby the evidence submitted by the requesting jurisdiction is used to support an application for a domestic order to restrain or seize assets.[211]

If the requested jurisdiction is enforcing the order indirectly (that is, domesticating the confiscation by filing its own case in domestic courts), the requesting jurisdiction will have to provide the evidence necessary for practitioners in the requested jurisdiction to prove their case. The burden of proof and type of evidence will be what is required under the requested jurisdiction's laws, even if a confiscation order was obtained separately in the requesting jurisdiction. If the requested jurisdiction has a lower burden of proof on NCB confiscation, this process may be useful.

Direct enforcement of foreign seizure or restraint orders allows the requested jurisdiction to register the foreign order in its courts and subsequently enforce the order in the same way as a domestic court order. The requesting jurisdiction will need to provide the restraint or seizure order, as well as information on the proceedings and grounds to believe that a confiscation order may be made (in affidavit or certificate format in common law jurisdictions). Some jurisdictions will permit the registration of a faxed copy of the order; however, an official copy of the order must be filed to retain the restraint or seizure. The requesting jurisdiction can then register the foreign order in its courts.[212] The process is simpler and quicker than indirect enforcement because it avoids duplicating efforts and relitigating the order; however, it will not be possible in every case. There may not be a legal basis for direct enforcement in a treaty or legislation, or the requesting jurisdiction may have concerns about the process through which the orders were obtained.

---

210. UNCAC art. 54(2) outlines provisional measures for freezing or seizure on the basis of a foreign order or request or where necessary to preserve property on the basis of a foreign arrest or criminal charge related to the assets.

211. UNCAC art. 54(1)(a) and (b) and 55(1)(a) and (b) outline these general obligations of requested jurisdictions. See also United Nations Convention against Narcotic Drugs and Psychotropic Substances, art. 5; UNTOC, art. 13; and art. 8 of the Terrorist Financing Convention.

212. Laws that permit a registration and enforcement of the foreign confiscation judgment usually provide that the courts in the requested jurisdiction not be permitted to entertain challenges to the confiscation that may be raised in the requested jurisdiction's courts. Even if not explicitly provided for in the law, practitioners should argue that courts in the requested jurisdiction not hear the same type of challenge that has been raised or could be raised in the requesting jurisdiction's courts, as long as all potential claimants have been sufficiently notified of the proceeding and have been given the opportunity to raise a challenge.

Examples of conditions commonly necessary to give effect to such requests are:

- General requirements for MLA requests are met and there are no grounds for refusal.
- There are reasonable grounds to believe that the assets being sought are linked to the criminal activities, or that the target has committed an offense from which a benefit has been derived.
- There are reasonable grounds to believe the assets will be confiscated.
- The location of the assets to be restrained is provided.
- The relief sought could also be obtained if proceedings had been brought in the requested jurisdiction (or the assets subject to confiscation are also subject to confiscation in the requested jurisdiction).[213]
- Copies (certified, if necessary) of relevant court orders are included, and are enforceable in the requested jurisdiction.

Similar to investigative orders, provisional measures can be taken by a prosecutor or investigating magistrate in civil law jurisdictions; common law jurisdictions generally require authorization by a court. As stated above, this may affect the form and requirements for the request, as well as the time it takes to process the request.

Additional points for practitioners to consider include these:

- **Notice to the asset holder.** Most jurisdictions will issue provisional orders *ex parte,* but laws typically require that notice be given within a certain period of time to the asset holder and others with a legal interest in the asset. Notices in foreign jurisdictions must be translated (if necessary) and published—another cost consideration for practitioners. Some jurisdictions permit use of the Internet to publish notice, a process that is more cost effective. Some jurisdictions do not permit foreign authorities to publish or serve legal notices (even by mail or shipper) within their borders, and an MLA request to serve notice must be made through the central authority. Some jurisdictions require that the MLA request, application, and order be disclosed to the asset holder (see box 7.3).
- **Additional dissipation risks.** Some jurisdictions allow for legal fees and living expenses (schooling, leases, mortgage) to be paid out of seized or restrained assets; and, over time, that can significantly reduce the assets available for confiscation. Courts in the requested jurisdiction may order these fees to be paid, even if not permitted under the law of the requesting jurisdiction.[214]
- **Different features of confiscation models.** Where the cooperating jurisdictions have different models for asset confiscation, practitioners must be aware of the

---

213. This condition can be difficult to fulfill, especially because jurisdictions differ in the types of relief that are permitted. This generally includes anything of value obtained directly or indirectly from an offense and instrumentalities used in connection with an offense. However, relief may extend to incorporate fines, substitute assets, extended confiscation, and assets intended for use in an offense.

214. In some jurisdictions, an argument can be made that if the requesting jurisdiction is "enforcing" the requested state's order, it should follow the procedural and substantive law provisions of the requesting state.

BOX 7.11   Worldwide Orders in the United Kingdom

In cases involving assets in the United Kingdom, consider requesting a worldwide freezing or disclosure order (see section 8.2.2 of chapter 8). The order requires that the target repatriate funds or disclose documents (such as bank statements) held in foreign jurisdictions so that they form a single group of assets in the one jurisdiction.

Sometimes a receiver is appointed to pursue the repatriation of assets during the provisional restraint or seizure phase through the use of a power of attorney.

The effect of these orders may be limited because they rely on the compliance of the target and others who are named in the order. At the same time, the prospect of additional charges for contempt or failure to comply has proved sufficient to gain compliance in some cases.

differences in evidential requirements and standards of proof. For example, one jurisdiction may apply value-based confiscation, which requires evidence that the defendant financially benefited from his or her crime and that he or she owns the assets; another jurisdiction may use property-based confiscation, which requires evidence of a link between the asset and the offense. In addition, some jurisdictions permit provisional measures that apply more broadly (see box 7.11 for worldwide orders available in the United Kingdom).

Confiscation

Ultimately, practitioners must submit an MLA request for confiscation of the assets. Similar to orders for provisional measures, a confiscation order may be enforced directly through registration and enforcement of the order in the requested jurisdiction, or indirectly through an application for a domestic order in the requested jurisdiction whereby the evidence submitted by the requesting jurisdiction is used to support an application for a domestic confiscation order (see the section on "Provisional Measures" above for descriptions of direct and indirect enforcement). For information on what is required to obtain confiscation in the United Kingdom and the United States, see box 7.12.

Examples of conditions typically necessary to obtain a confiscation judgment include:

- the conditions as outlined above for provisional measures applications,
- a provisional restraint during the course of the litigation to ensure assets are not moved or dissipated,
- a final order of judgment of confiscation that is not subject to any possible appeal, and
- proof that notice was provided to all potential claimants and that they were given an opportunity to present any challenges recognized by law.

Requirements for Direct Enforcement of MLA Requests for Confiscation in the United Kingdom and the United States

In the United States, an MLA request to register and enforce a foreign court confiscation judgment must meet certain statutory requirements[a] and be certified by the U.S. attorney general. U.S. authorities will file an application to enforce the order as if it had been rendered by a court in the United States. The district court will order that the judgment be enforced on behalf of the foreign jurisdiction, unless it finds that the judgment was rendered under a system incompatible with the requirements of the due process of law, that it was obtained by fraud, or that the foreign court lacked subject-matter jurisdiction or personal jurisdiction.

In the United Kingdom, the Secretary of State refers the processing of confiscation orders arising from a criminal conviction in a foreign jurisdiction to the Director of the Agency, the Director of Public Prosecution, or the Director of Revenue and Customs Prosecutions. The Crown Court decides whether to seek registration of an external order, thus giving it effect. It will register only an order made consequent to the final conviction of the person named in it, not subject to appeal, and compatible with the Human Rights Act of 1998. Appeals to the Court of Appeal and the House of Lords are possible.

a. MLA requests for enforcement of a foreign order in the United States require a treaty agreement and must include a case summary, a description of the legal proceedings that resulted in the confiscation order, a certified copy of the confiscation order, and an affidavit that notice was provided and that the decision rendered is in force and not subject to appeal.

Some jurisdictions will require additional information, such as the amount that remains unpaid from the requesting jurisdiction's confiscation order or confirmation that the person has been convicted of an offense. This latter requirement can be a barrier if a conviction is not possible because the accused has died, fled the jurisdiction, or is immune from prosecution. Many jurisdictions cannot convict in absentia or through absconding provisions, but are able to issue a final order of confiscation using criminal law provisions or NCB confiscation.

7.4.7 Submission of an MLA Request, Follow-Up, and Addressing of Refusals

When finalized, an MLA request must be signed by appropriate authorities in the requesting jurisdiction and then transmitted through the authorities listed in the applicable treaty, legislation, or agreement—often the central authorities, although some bilateral and multilateral treaties (such as the Council of Europe conventions) allow the request to go directly to law enforcement practitioners, with a copy sent to the central authority. Other jurisdictions may require the more traditional processing through diplomatic channels (that is, through the ministry of foreign affairs). Figure 7.4 demonstrates the flow of a request.

Following submission, the practitioner will have to follow up on its progress. If possible, practitioners should speak directly with the person assigned to execute the request because this opens the opportunity to clarify any terminology or translation issues,

FIGURE 7.4 **Flow of an MLA Request in the Presence of a Treaty or Domestic Legislation**

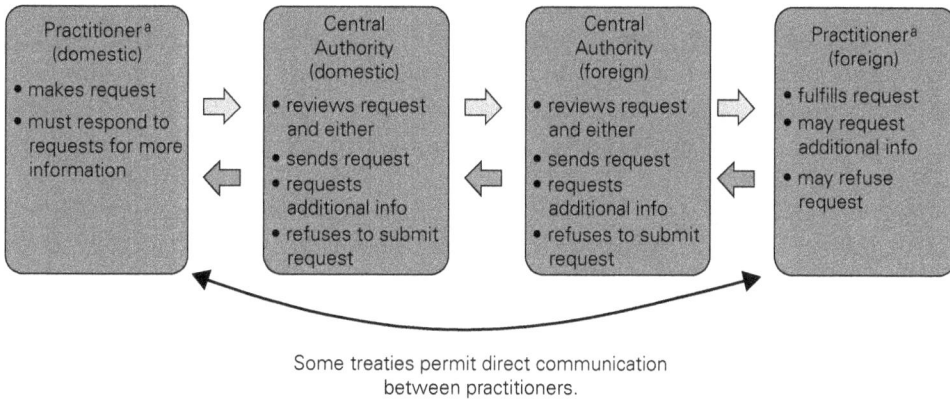

Practitioner[a] (domestic)	Central Authority (domestic)	Central Authority (foreign)	Practitioner[a] (foreign)
• makes request • must respond to requests for more information	• reviews request and either • sends request • requests additional info • refuses to submit request	• reviews request and either • sends request • requests additional info • refuses to submit request	• fulfills request • may request additional info • may refuse request

Some treaties permit direct communication between practitioners.

Source: Authors' illustration.
Note: If letters rogatory are required, the domestic and foreign ministries of foreign affairs must be added to the process.
a. Practitioners could include prosecutors, investigating magistrates, or law enforcement officials.

check if requirements are met, and offer additional information. The requesting jurisdiction may be asked for more information to support the request. Such a request is *not* a refusal and should not be perceived as one: the number of requirements and opportunities for misunderstanding mean that requests often need more information, even among jurisdictions with a lot of experience in transmitting requests. Clarify the information needed with personal contacts and provide the information as soon as possible to avoid further delay.

If no response is received or an MLA request is refused, practitioners should contact counterparts in the requested jurisdiction to determine the reasons for the lack of a response or for a refusal. United Nations conventions require states parties to provide the reason(s) for any refusal.[215] It is possible that the refusal is not warranted. Perhaps it is based on a prohibited ground (for example, fiscal offenses or bank secrecy), a misinterpretation or misapplication of the facts, or on a general opinion of the legal system and due process rather than the facts of the case. If there is an error, requesting practitioners should respectfully bring this to the attention of the requested jurisdiction and seek guidance on how best to proceed. The request may be resurrected and repaired, administratively appealed, or replaced by a new request.

If there is still no response or a refusal to address possible errors in the reasons for refusal, look for other avenues. Applying third-party pressure through other jurisdictions or international organizations has been helpful in some cases, particularly in multijurisdictional

---

215. UNCAC, art. 46(23); UNTOC, art. 18(23); United Nations Convention against Narcotic Drugs and Psychotropic Substances, art. 7(16). Note that it is most helpful if requesting jurisdictions receive the reasons for refusal prior to the official response so that they have the opportunity to make necessary revisions.

cases. One requested jurisdiction may have greater success than the requesting jurisdiction in reaching out to another requested jurisdiction that is refusing to help, especially if there is an existing relationship between the two requested jurisdictions. In one example, Jurisdiction x applied to two major financial centers for assistance, jurisdiction y and jurisdiction z (all UNCAC signatories). Jurisdiction y responded with an offer to help and jurisdiction z refused. Jurisdiction y, which had worked with jurisdiction z on other cases, wrote to jurisdiction z to indicate that it was assisting jurisdiction x and urged officials there to reconsider assistance because the reasons for their refusal were against UNCAC.

Another option for assistance with request drafting, submission, and follow-up is to hire an attorney from the requested jurisdiction. The benefit of such an arrangement is that this person is on the ground, has contacts, and knows the language. The disadvantage is the cost.

7.5 Cooperation in Cases of Confiscation without a Conviction

Although an increasing number of jurisdictions are adopting legislation that permits confiscation without a conviction and it is encouraged in multilateral treaties and by international standard setters,[216] international cooperation in NCB confiscation cases remains quite challenging for a number of reasons. First, although it is a growing area of law, it is not yet universal; therefore, not all jurisdictions have adopted legislation permitting NCB confiscation, enforcement of foreign NCB orders, or both. Second, even where NCB confiscation exists, the systems vary significantly. Some jurisdictions conduct NCB confiscation as a separate proceeding in civil courts (confiscation known as "civil confiscation"), with a lower standard of proof than in criminal cases (specifically, a "balance of probabilities" or "preponderance of the evidence"); others use NCB confiscation in criminal courts and require the higher criminal standard of proof. Some jurisdictions will pursue NCB confiscation only after criminal proceedings have been abandoned or unsuccessful, whereas others pursue NCB confiscation in a proceeding parallel to the related criminal proceeding.[217]

There have been some successes in overcoming these barriers. Some jurisdictions have been able to incorporate cooperation on NCB confiscation into bilateral treaties or agreements. Other jurisdictions have provided the case information to the foreign jurisdiction, and the foreign jurisdiction has been able to pursue the case under domestic legislation. Finally, some jurisdictions have been able to enforce foreign NCB confiscation orders in

---

216. UNCAC art. 54(1)(c) requires that states parties consider such cooperation in cases of death, flight, or absence, or in other appropriate cases. Recommendation 3 of the FATF 40+9 Recommendations requires that countries consider allowing confiscation without a conviction. The FATF has also introduced best practices on NCB confiscation, including recognition of foreign NCB confiscation orders. See "Best Practices: Confiscation (Recommendations 3 and 38)," adopted by the plenary in February 2010.

217. The United Kingdom generally pursues NCB confiscation only after criminal proceedings are abandoned or unsuccessful. The United States often pursues NCB confiscation parallel to the related criminal proceeding.

spite of differences in pertinent systems[218] or even in the absence of a domestic NCB confiscation system.[219]

Even if the requesting jurisdiction does not have NCB confiscation, it may be possible to use NCB confiscation in a requested jurisdiction that does have it. Doing so will require a request to the other jurisdiction to open a foreign case in the requested jurisdiction. This may be the only way to recover assets in some cases, particularly if the offender has died, fled the jurisdiction, or is immune from prosecution (see chapter 9 for information on this option).[220]

7.6 Cooperation in Civil Recovery (Private Law) Cases

International cooperation in civil recovery (private law) cases may be difficult, even when the jurisdiction is a litigant in a private case. Although information gathered through informal assistance channels could help in developing the investigation, many MLA agreements have limits on the use of information and do not permit its use in actions by private litigators to obtain civil judgments. Civil judgments can be enforced between jurisdictions through processes such as reciprocal enforcement of judgments and related laws.

At the same time, the international community has recognized that civil recovery is often the only recourse in cases of corruption and has recommended cooperation in civil and administrative matters.[221] As a result, it has become increasingly common for jurisdictions to consent to such use either generally in a treaty or on a case-by-case basis.

---

218. In a case involving a request by the United States (in an NCB confiscation case) to Switzerland (in which criminal proceeds were restrained in a criminal court), the Supreme Court of Switzerland held that there can be circumstances in which confiscation may be likened to a case of "criminal character"—even in the absence of a criminal proceeding in the foreign state (*A____ Company v. Federal Office of Justice* [U.S.A.] [1A.326 12005, ATF 132 II 178]). The jurisdiction must have the right to punish, even if the authorities do not intend to exercise it. Although this requirement can be met in the United States (a jurisdiction which usually conducts NCB confiscation parallel with or prior to the conclusion of criminal proceedings), it would not be met in jurisdictions that pursue NCB confiscation only after a criminal case has been dropped or unsuccessful.

219. Hong Kong SAR, China, and Jersey have legislation permitting enforcement of foreign NCB confiscation orders, but do not permit NCB confiscation domestically: Civil Asset Recovery (International Cooperation) Law 2007 (Jersey). Some Latin American countries will accept an NCB confiscation order and file it in a civil court for enforcement. In France, courts recognized and executed a foreign NCB confiscation order from Italy, pursuant to the 1990 Council of Europe Convention on Laundering, Search, Seizure and Confiscation of the Proceeds of Crime, despite the fact that France did not have a system for NCB confiscation: Cour de cassation, November 13, 2003, No. 3 03-80371, case Crisafulli. The court recognized the decision because of two factors: First, the evidence establishing that the property was the product of a criminal offense was sufficiently similar to that required for a criminal decision, thus likened to a criminal case. Second, the consequences on the property of the person were similar to a criminal penalty.

220. This method has been used in a number of cases: $20 million was returned to Peru from the United States in the case of Victor Venero Garrido, an associate of Montesinos; $2.7 million was returned to Nicaragua from the United States in the case of Bryon Jerez, former Nicaraguan director of taxation; and funds were returned to Ukraine from Antigua and Barbuda and the United States in the case against Pavlo Lazarenko, former prime minister of Ukraine.

221. See UNCAC, art. 43(1); also see recommendation 37 of the Commonwealth Secretariat's August 2005 "Report of the Commonwealth Working Group on Asset Repatriation," which states, "The mutual legal

Asset Recovery Pursuant to an MLA Request in France

In France, an MLA request based on a foreign court decision is sent by the Ministry of Justice to the competent prosecutor's office, which will ask the court to confiscate the assets. If the court decides to do so, the confiscated assets become the property of the French government. The competent officials (in particular, those within the Treasury Department) will determine whether France is obliged to return the assets under an international agreement. Even if there is no such obligation, the assets may be returned at the discretion of the government or under an ad hoc agreement with the requesting jurisdiction.

7.7 Asset Return

In general, there are two methods for asset return if an MLA request is used for confiscation or compensation. The first method is direct recovery through the judicial process. Such recovery can occur if the requested jurisdiction permits the court to order compensation or damages directly to the foreign jurisdiction, or permits the court or competent authority to recognize the foreign jurisdiction as a legitimate owner in a confiscation action. Direct recovery may also occur "voluntarily" through plea agreements by which a defendant agrees to voluntarily repatriate assets located in a foreign jurisdiction to the court in which he or she is convicted.[222] In such a case, a practitioner must request that the foreign jurisdiction lift any provisional restraint order that it had previously requested be imposed on the assets. Also, worldwide confiscation orders may be enforced directly by a court without the need for a treaty (see box 7.13 for an example).

The second, more common, method of asset return is pursuant to treaties, agreements, or statutory authority to distribute assets after a final order of confiscation. If an MLA request has been submitted pursuant to UNCAC, states parties have an obligation to return confiscated assets in cases of public corruption or when the requesting party reasonably establishes prior ownership or damages to the state.[223] In other cases, multilateral and bilateral treaties, asset sharing agreements (either on a case-by-case basis or by permanent agreement), and statutory authorities may be used to share or return the recovered funds (see chapter 9 for additional information on these avenues).

---

assistance regimes in Commonwealth countries should permit evidence gathered for a criminal proceeding to be subsequently used in civil proceedings and requests for such use should be granted in corruption cases."

222. In the Montesinos case in Peru, money was recovered from Switzerland through a system of waivers (that is, those who pleaded guilty provided information and signed waivers giving Peru the rights to the funds).

223. UNCAC, art. 57(3)(a) and 57(3)(b). In both cases, the obligation applies only to the convention's offenses and requires compliance with UNCAC's provisions on international cooperation and a final judgment in the requesting jurisdiction (requirement for judgment can be waived).

8. Civil Proceedings

In most jurisdictions, authorities seeking to recover the proceeds of corruption have the option to initiate civil proceedings[224] in domestic or foreign civil courts in the same way as a private citizen.[225] In some cases, the authorities may decide to pursue a criminal conviction and use civil proceedings to recover the proceeds of corruption.[226]

Civil proceedings may be considered for a number of reasons, including the inability to obtain criminal confiscation, non-conviction based (NCB) confiscation, or the successfully obtaining of mutual legal assistance (MLA) for the enforcement of confiscation orders (see chapter 1 for these and other obstacles that may lead to the selection of one confiscation approach over another). In addition, there are procedural advantages. Civil proceedings may take place in the absence of defendants who have been properly notified; and, at least in common law jurisdictions, the case will be adjudicated on a lower standard of proof (usually the balance of probabilities). With respect to third parties, intermediaries, and professionals who facilitated, participated in, or assisted in the reception, transfer, or management of suspicious assets, civil actions can be launched more easily than criminal proceedings in some jurisdictions.[227] In cases that cross borders, a civil action affords a jurisdiction seeking to recover assets greater control of the process, compared with criminal proceedings in foreign jurisdictions; and may offer a more expedient route than waiting for enforcement action by the foreign jurisdiction.

The drawbacks to civil proceedings are the cost of tracing assets and the legal fees entailed in obtaining relevant court orders. In addition, civil cases may extend over many years, and private investigators do not typically have the range of investigative tools or access to intelligence that is available to law enforcement.

When the decision is made to bring a civil lawsuit in a domestic or foreign court, practitioners must explore the potential claims and remedies (including ownership of misappropriated assets, disgorgement of illicit profits, compensation for damages, and invalidity of contracts) or other options (such as insolvency proceedings). Practitioners

---

224. "Civil proceedings" are separate and distinct from "civil confiscation," "civil forfeiture," or other forms of non-conviction based (NCB) confiscation.

225. United Nations Convention against Corruption (UNCAC), art. 53 requires that states parties take measures to permit another state party to initiate civil actions in domestic courts and to recover compensation or damages.

226. In some jurisdictions, the proceedings will go forward in parallel. In others, the civil proceeding will be stayed until the conclusion of the criminal matter. In addition, the award of civil damages may affect a confiscation order. In some jurisdictions, confiscation is discretionary rather than mandatory when civil damages are ordered.

227. In this situation, it may be difficult to prove criminal intent to participate in a conspiracy, and easier to establish civil liability.

then have to determine how they will initiate the lawsuit, collect evidence, secure assets, and enforce foreign judgments. These various options and techniques are discussed in this chapter.

8.1 Potential Claims and Remedies

A number of claims and remedies exist in the civil proceedings context, including proprietary claims for assets and actions in tort, actions based on invalidity or breach of contract, and illicit or unjust enrichment.

8.1.1 Proprietary (Ownership) Claims

Cause of Action

In most jurisdictions, misappropriated assets and bribes paid to government officials may be claimed by the jurisdiction seeking redress as the legitimate and true owner. Three examples of civil actions to claim ownership of assets in corruption cases are presented in box 8.1.

BOX 8.1 **Case Examples of Proprietary (Ownership) Claims**

Case 1: *Federal Republic of Nigeria v. Santolina Investment Corp., Solomon & Peters, and Diepreye Alamieyeseigha* (2007)[a]

In December 2007, the London High Court of Justice held that Nigeria was the true owner of three residential properties in London and of the credit balances of certain bank accounts. The properties and funds were officially held by two companies incorporated in the Seychelles and the Virgin Islands. These companies were controlled by Diepreye Alamieyeseigha, the governor of Nigeria's Bayelsa State from May 1999 until his impeachment and dismissal in September 2005.

In separate proceedings in Nigeria, the two companies, represented by Alamieyeseigha, pleaded guilty to money laundering charges related to bribes obtained for the awarding of government contracts.

Based on this Nigerian proceeding and other circumstantial evidence, the London High Court inferred that the bank balances and real estate investments held by the two companies controlled by Alamieyeseigha were bribes and secret profits to be returned to the government of Nigeria as the legitimate owner of those assets.

Case 2: *Kartika Ratna Thahir v. Pertamina* (1992–94)[b]

Pertamina—an Indonesian state-owned enterprise whose principal business was the exploration, processing, and marketing of oil and natural gas—sought to recover bribes paid to Pertamina executive Haji Achmad Thahir by contractors

(continued next page)

BOX 8.1   *(continued)*

hoping for better contractual terms and preferential treatment. The bribes were deposited by the executive into a bank in Singapore. Pertamina learned about the bank accounts (owned jointly by Thahir and his wife Kartika Ratna Thahir) in Singapore after the death of the executive and brought an action in Singapore claiming to be entitled to the funds.

The court of first instance ruled that the bribes and all earned interest were held by the executive as a constructive trustee. The court of appeal upheld the ruling and confirmed that a fiduciary who accepted a bribe in breach of his or her duty held that bribe "in trust for the person to whom the duty was owed." As a result, Pertamina was entitled to a proprietary claim to the money in Singapore.

Case 3: *Attorney General of Hong Kong, SAR, China v. Reid* (1994)[c]

In this case, the Independent Commission against Corruption of Hong Kong SAR, China, sought to recover properties purchased in New Zealand by a former prosecutor, Warwick Reid. The purchases were made with bribes received in exchange for not prosecuting certain offenders. Two properties had been assigned to Reid and his wife, and one had been assigned to his solicitor. The judge ruled that these properties, as far as they represented bribes accepted by Reid, were held in trust for the Crown. As the Court explained it,

> When a bribe is accepted by a fiduciary in breach of his duty, he holds that bribe in trust for the person to whom the duty was owed. If the property representing the bribe decreases in value, the fiduciary must pay the difference between that value and the initial amount of the bribe because he should not have accepted the bribe or incurred the risk of loss. If the property increases in value, the fiduciary is not entitled to any surplus in excess of the initial value of the bribe because he is not allowed by any means to make a profit out of a breach of duty.

This case is still considered one of the leading common law authorities on the use of constructive trusts to recover bribery proceeds from an unfaithful fiduciary.

a. *Federal Republic of Nigeria v. Santolina Investment Corp., Solomon & Peters and Diepreye Alamieyeseigha* [2007] EWHC 437 (Ch.) (U.K.). b. *Kartika Ratna Thahir v. PT Pertambangan Minyak dan Gas Bumi Negara (Pertamina)* [1994] 3 SLR 257; [1994] SGCA 105 (Singapore). c. *Attorney General of Hong Kong v. Reid* [1994] 1 AC 324 PC (U.K.).

Remedies

A court will consider the return or restitution of assets to their legitimate owner through a variety of available proprietary remedies. These remedies have significant advantages over compensation or contractual remedies in that the claimant's rights are not in competition with those of other creditors, and civil procedures frequently allow courts to issue seizure and restraint orders even if the claimant does not demonstrate a risk of dissipation. If the proceeds of corruption were invested, the claimant may also be entitled to recover interest or profits earned by the defendant, as demonstrated by the *Pertamina* and *Attorney General of Hong Kong SAR, China,* cases discussed in box 8.1.

It should be noted, however, that these proprietary claims and remedies may not be available if the proceeds cannot be traced to the corruption offense because they have been laundered around the world. In addition, some jurisdictions will not recognize bribes received by government officials or profits derived from fraudulent contracts as property of the state or government.

8.1.2 Actions in Tort

Cause of Action

According to the United Nations Convention against Corruption, states parties should allow requesting jurisdictions to claim compensation for damages caused by a corrupt act.[228] Tort damages are paid to compensate a plaintiff for loss, injury, or harm directly caused by a breach of duty, including criminal wrongdoing, immoral conduct, and pre-contractual fault. Where a corrupt act has occurred, a plaintiff generally has to prove that it suffered compensable damage, that the defendant breached a duty, and that there is a causal link between corruption and the damage.

Legal persons and individuals who directly and knowingly participate in the corrupt act are primarily liable for the damage. In addition, courts may hold liable those who facilitated the corrupt act or failed to take appropriate steps to prevent corruption. This may be the case for lawyers or intermediaries who assisted in corrupt acts or for parent companies and employers who failed to exert appropriate control over their subsidiaries or employees.

In some civil law jurisdictions, any person who suffers direct harm caused by an offense can claim damages for tort in civil or criminal court after a defendant has been convicted.[229] To recover from the defendant in other jurisdictions, general liability statutes simply require the plaintiff to show that an act or omission by the defendant caused the plaintiff's damages.

In bribery cases, courts in some jurisdictions may consider that a briber and the person receiving the bribe have committed a joint tort for which the victim is entitled to recover the entire loss from either party.[230] Once the bribe is established, there is an irrefutable presumption that it was given with an intention to induce the agent to act favorably to the payer and, thereafter, unfavorably to the principal. This presumption will be sufficient to prove that the act was affected and influenced by the payment.[231] In other jurisdictions, a principal or employer also has a claim against an employee who takes a bribe

---

228. See UNCAC, art. 53; and the Council of Europe Civil Law Convention on Corruption, art. 5 (Strasbourg, 4.XI.1999).

229. In Panama, for example, the commission of a crime or any unlawful act gives rise to a claim for damages that can be sought through proceedings in criminal courts or by filing a civil claim for damages in a civil court. France permits plaintiffs to claim for damage in criminal courts (see art. 2, Criminal Code of Procedure [France]).

230. In the United Kingdom, the defendant may then seek contribution from the joint tort under the Civil Liability (Contributions) Act of 1978.

231. *Industries & General Mortgage Co. Ltd. v. Lewis* [1949] 2 All ER 573 (U.K.).

In the United States, foreign governments or foreign nationals acting as civil plaintiffs may seek compensation for harm resulting from tortuous corrupt practices. They may also use the Alien Tort Claims Act (enacted in 1789) to bring a tort claim based on violations of international conventions, including corrupt or fraudulent activity. Courts have held that there is no private right of action under the Foreign Corrupt Practices Act (FCPA), which is essentially enforced by criminal or civil actions from government agencies. However, plaintiffs could receive civil compensation under the RICO statute for damages caused by corruption.

The RICO statute makes it unlawful to participate, directly or indirectly, in an enterprise through a pattern of racketeering activity or collection of unlawful debt. Racketeering activities that could be considered "predicate acts" of RICO violations include bribery, theft, embezzlement, extortion under the color of official rights, fraud, obstruction of justice, and money laundering. Predicate acts form a pattern if they "have the same or similar purposes, results, participants, victims, or methods of commission." The statute is applicable to defendants who committed two predicate acts within a 10-year period of time. In practice, courts have ruled that violations of the FCPA may serve as predicate acts for civil liability in RICO actions. Treble damages are available, although some foreign jurisdictions view these as punitive and will not enforce them.

on the basis of loyalty owed in application of an employment contract. In practice, however, it may be difficult to prove that an act of bribery is the direct cause of a material loss.[232] Box 8.2 describes examples of tort actions in the United States.

Remedies

In most jurisdictions, the basic rule for determining damages is that the victim must be placed as closely as possible in the circumstances in which he or she would have been if the corrupt act that caused the damage had not taken place. Courts may be authorized to compensate loss of profits reasonably expected but not gained as a result of corruption and nonpecuniary damages that cannot be immediately calculated. The plaintiff's right to compensation may be reduced or even disallowed in cases of negligence. With respect to corruption cases (as the example in box 8.3 demonstrates), some common law jurisdictions have ordered compensation by an equivalent sum of monetary damages.

Specific difficulties in calculating damages may arise in bribery cases. In some jurisdictions, the loss sustained is equivalent to the value of the bribes. However, that amount may not be sufficient if undue advantages were included in a government decision or

---

232. For example, in a case where the city of Cannes, France, sued the mayor after he had been convicted for corruption, courts held that damages were the result of a ministerial decision to revoke and refuse a license (not an act of bribery). Damages awarded for the town's loss of reputation were quantified at €100,000 (approximately $128,300).

contract. The bribe may have resulted in a price for goods and services that is above market value or may have permitted the use or the sale of government resources at less than market value. In addition, there may be social or environmental damage that has been incurred as a result of the contract award.

To be fully compensated in these situations, government authorities or entities may have to establish the difference between the benefits that would have been received if bribery had not taken place and those received after entering into the fraudulent contract.[233] It may not be sufficient to show that prices for goods and services were set above market rates. Courts may require a more precise measure of rates that a hypothetical prudent negotiator would have accepted, given the market for goods and services of the same quality. Determining this measure will be particularly challenging in specific circumstances and in the absence of clear market references.[234] In these situations, establishing the financial damage will frequently require evidence of a secret agreement between the briber and the corrupt agent and/or of technical or accounting assistance.[235]

In some jurisdictions, when the corrupt act is uncovered years after it has taken place, courts may presume that the bribe was incorporated into the contractual prices. Other losses must be proved and quantified by the plaintiff.[236]

---

233. Kevin E. Davis, "Civil Remedies for Corruption in Government Contracting: Zero Tolerance Versus Proportional Liability," International Law and Justice Working Paper 2009/4 (New York: New York University School of Law, 2009).

234. In particular, for specific constructions or equipment and for "intellectual" services, including consulting studies.

235. For example, such evidence could be documents showing that the briber and the corrupt agent secretly agreed to increase usual rates by a specific amount or percentage, comparisons with bids from competitors in the same bidding process, or transcripts of conversations or reports on meetings where the corrupt agreement was discussed.

236. O. Meyer, ed., *Civil Law Consequences of Corruption* (Baden Baden: Nomos Verlag, 2009).

In other jurisdictions, the briber may be held liable for the loss sustained by the victim in entering a contract with unfavorable terms.[237] Some courts have assumed that the true price of any goods bought by the principal in application of a fraudulent contract was increased by at least the amount of the bribe,[238] and any loss beyond this amount must be proved.[239]

In the context of employee/employer relations, other jurisdictions have found that both the employee who was bribed and the briber are liable to the employer at least in the amount of the bribe,[240] and companies are liable for any tortuous act committed by their employees.[241] In the absence of a more precise yardstick, a reasonable measure of damages may be the bribe itself,[242] an accounting of profits,[243] or the harm caused by predicate acts constituting an illegal pattern.[244] The case *Fyffes v. Templeman and Others* (box 8.4) highlights how courts may identify and quantify such damages.

8.1.3 Actions Based on Invalidity or Breach of Contract

Cause of Action

Courts or arbitration tribunals may hold that contracts awarded after corruption of a government official are illegal, thus invalid or unenforceable.[245] Invalidity may be based on the facts that the contract was extorted by fraud and that consent was vitiated by corruption.

Breach of contract is another possible action in some jurisdictions, particularly if a contract included clauses wherein the contractor promised not to provide any inducements to public officials in connection with the award or performance of the contract. Violation of this particular prohibition gives the government an entitlement to terminate the contract, avoid its own obligations, and claim damages.[246]

Remedies

Remedies for invalidity or breach of contract will include monetary damages, such as compensatory, incidental, and other (for example, liquidated or punitive) damages. In

---

237. *Salford Corporation v. Lever* (No. 2) (1891) 1 QB 168 (U.K.).

238. Ibid.

239. *Solland International Ltd. v. Daraydan Holdings Ltd.* [2002] EWHC 220 (TCC) (U.K.).

240. *Williams Electronic Games, Inc. v. Garrity,* 479 F.3d 904 (7th Cir., 2007) (U.S. Court of Appeals).

241. For example, Germany applies these principles.

242. *Continental Management, Inc. v. United States,* 527 F.2d 613, 620, 208 (Ct. Cl. 501 1975) (U.S. Court of Claims).

243. U.S. courts have concluded that an accounting of profits may be a reasonable measure of damages because it ensures compensation to the plaintiff, prevents unjust enrichment by a defendant, and deters willful violations of law.

244. In *County of Oakland, et al. v. Vista Disposal, Inc., et al.,* 900 F. Supp. 879 (E.D. Mich. 1995) (U.S. District Court), a district court held that the measure of civil damage in Racketeer Influenced and Corrupt Organizations Act cases is the harm caused by predicate acts constituting an illegal pattern. In the case of a contract to treat a county's waste, the damage was the difference between the price charged and the price that would have been charged in the absence of corruption.

245. UNCAC art. 34 permits such actions by states parties.

246. Reference is made to the United Kingdom.

Fyffes v. Templeman and Others (2000)[a]

Fyffes, a company involved in the banana trade, claimed that an employee who negotiated a service agreement with a shipping contractor took bribes amounting to more than $1.4 million between 1992 and 1996. The bribes were revealed when the U.S. Internal Revenue Service was tipped about undeclared payments that the employee received in the United States from a company incorporated in Cyprus.

Fyffes sought to recover damages from the employee, the shipping company, and its agents. All defendants were found jointly liable for the value of the bribes. The court ruled that "there can be no dispute that they were taken into account by *the contractor* in agreeing the amount of the freight for each year, which would have been correspondingly less for Fyffes if they had only had to pay the net sum which *the contractor* were prepared to accept."

The shipping company and its agents were liable to pay additional compensation for the loss that Fyffes suffered from entering into the contract under unfavorable terms. For each year, the court determined what Fyffes would have normally agreed to pay if it had been represented by a prudent and honest negotiator. There was no evidence that actual payments would have been different in 1992, 1994, and 1995. But the court ruled that payments were inflated by $830,022 in 1993 and by $1.1 million in 1996.

An account of all profits made by the contractor was rejected because it was "highly probable that Fyffes would have entered into a service agreement with the contractor if the employee had not been dishonest." As a result, "ordinary" profit from the contract was not caused by bribery, but by "the provision of services for which there would have been a contract in any event."

a. *Fyffes Group Ltd. v. Templeman* [2000] 2 Lloyd's Rep 643 (U.K.).

some cases, courts have limited damages to contractual fees already paid, and they have excluded unpaid fees.[247] Rescission of contract is also possible in some jurisdictions, particularly in cases of bribery and collusion in bidding.[248] A claim for rescission requires proof that the government entity would have refused the contract in the absence of any fraudulent acts. If this is not the case, the government entity would only be entitled to damages for entering the contract under less favorable terms than what would have been agreed to in the absence of the act causing the breach.

---

247. In *S.T. Grand, Inc. v. City of New York*, 32 NY2d 300, 344 NYS2d 938 (1973) (U.S.), the court ruled that a contractor who paid a bribe to obtain a contract to clean the New York City reservoir could not recover unpaid fees; but the city could recover all of the fees it had already paid to the vendor. Other courts have ruled that a municipality was only entitled to compensation for the harm caused by an illegally awarded contract.

248. *Ross River Ltd. v. Cambridge City Football Club Ltd.* [2007] EWHC 2115 (Ch) (U.K.). In addition, French courts have ruled that government entities that entered a contract after bidders colluded to suppress competition in the bidding process are entitled to rescission of contracts or damages.

World Duty Free Company Limited v. The Republic of Kenya (2006)[a]

In 1989, Kenya initially entered into an agreement with World Duty Free Company (WDF) for construction, maintenance, and operation of duty-free complexes at Nairobi and Mombasa international airports. In obtaining the contract, WDF paid bribes to the former Kenyan president, Daniel arap Moi. Subsequently, in 1998, WDF was placed under receivership by the High Court in Kenya; and a formal judgment and decree was made in 2001, transferring beneficial ownership to the receiver.

In disputing the order before the ICSID, WDF claimed that Kenya had unlawfully destroyed its contractual rights through the receivership order. The government of Kenya argued that WDF's procurement of the agreement through bribes was a breach of the English and Kenyan laws applicable to the contract, as well as a breach of international public policy; and that the government was lawfully entitled to avoid contract obligations.

The tribunal ruled that Kenya was legally entitled to avoid, and it did legally avoid its obligations.

a. *World Duty Free Company Limited v. The Republic of Kenya,* ICSID Case No. ARB/00/7, Award of September 25, 2006, http://ita.law.uvic.ca/documents/WDFv.KenyaAward.pdf.

In disputes arising from international investment contracts, the principle of "state responsibility" obliging governments to assume full responsibility for the actions of their agents may be taken into account.[249] The results are that contracts could remain valid in spite of illegality or defect of consent caused by corruption and that remedies should be limited to damages, adaptation of the contract, and reduction in prices.[250] On the other hand, "international public policy" (also referred to as "ordre public international") has been used to support the avoidance of contracts in a case before the International Centre for Settlement of Investment Disputes (ICSID) arbitration panel (see box 8.5).[251]

Nongovernmental organizations, including Transparency International, have encouraged the use of so-called integrity pacts by which government entities and bidders to public tenders agree on pre-announced sanctions for violations of commitments not to bribe public officials. Depending on the agreement, sanctions applied by courts or arbitration tribunals may include denial or loss of the contract, liability for damages to the principal and the competing bidders, and debarment of the violator for an appropriate

---

249. Hilmar Raeschke-Kessler and Dorothee Gottwald, "Corruption," in *The Oxford Handbook of International Investment Law,* ed. Peter Muchlinski, Federico Ortino, and Christoph Schreuer (Oxford, U.K.: Oxford University Press, 2008), 584–616.
250. Davis, "Civil Remedies for Corruption in Government Contracting."
251. It is not clear whether international commercial arbitration would uphold this result in the absence of an applicable national law containing the voidability rule.

period of time. To avoid overly complicated arguments about the level of damages, clauses may predetermine the value of "liquidated damages" that could be based on a percentage of the contract revenues or profits (or a multiplication of the bribe, such as 200 percent or 300 percent of the bribe). Integrity pacts have been used in Argentina, China, Colombia, Ecuador, Germany, India, Mexico, Pakistan, and other jurisdictions. When applicable, they may help governments recover undue payments or advantages awarded in application of corrupt payments to public officials.[252]

8.1.4 Actions Based on Illicit or Unjust Enrichment

Claims for disgorgement or restitution of profits obtained by illegal or unethical acts are based on the legal and moral principle that no one should benefit from his or her wrongdoing or from illicit or unjust enrichment (see the example in box 8.6). Courts may order defendants to pay back illegal profits, even if the victim did not suffer loss or any other disadvantage.[253]

In certain jurisdictions, courts have ruled that the receipt of bribes gives rise to liability based on dishonesty or claims for restitution of profits, independent of any harm.[254] As a result, a briber is liable to account for the amount of the bribe. Any loss in excess of the bribe must be recovered as damages.

---

252. Transparency International, "The Integrity Pact, a Powerful Tool for Clean Bidding," http://www.transparency.org.
253. In principle, German civil law upholds the view that an agent or wrongdoer must not be allowed to retain the proceeds from a bribe.
254. *Dubai Aluminum Company Ltd. v. Salaam and Others* [2002] All ER (D) 60 (Dec) (U.K.).

8.2 Bringing a Civil Action to Recover Assets

8.2.1 Initiating a Civil Action

A civil action to recover assets may be brought to courts or to arbitration. Courts of a foreign jurisdiction may be competent if a defendant is living (an individual), was incorporated or does business (an entity) in the jurisdiction; if the assets are within or have transited the jurisdiction; or if an act of corruption or money laundering was committed within the jurisdiction. It is generally possible to use evidence gathered in the course of a criminal proceeding in a civil litigation.

Arbitration may be used when an international contract provides for an arbitration clause; alternatively, a bilateral investment treaty may be the basis for investment arbitration. Most bilateral investment treaties provide for mandatory dispute resolution mechanisms or permit recourse to international arbitration under the auspices of the ICSID. The center's jurisdiction extends to any legal dispute arising directly out of an investment between a contracting state (or any constituent subdivision or agency of a contracting state designated to the center by that state) and a national of another contracting state, which the parties to the dispute consent in writing to submit to the center.

8.2.2 Collecting Evidence and Securing Assets

As with criminal proceedings, the plaintiff in a civil court will have to provide direct or circumstantial evidence to establish the cause of action. Box 8.7 describes the use of circumstantial evidence in private civil proceedings.

Using Evidence Gathered in Criminal Proceedings
Although it generally is possible to use evidence gathered in the course of a criminal proceeding in a civil action, it may not be permitted in some jurisdictions because of the secrecy and confidentiality of investigation laws.[255] Similarly, evidence initially gathered to support foreign criminal investigations and prosecutions may be used in civil proceedings initiated in some common law jurisdictions.[256]

---

255. In France, for example, it is a crime to disclose elements of ongoing criminal proceedings to third parties. However, when criminal proceedings are completed, civil parties to the criminal procedure are allowed to use and disclose related documents in a civil proceeding.

256. In *Federal Republic of Nigeria v. Santolina, Solomon & Peters and Diepreye Alamieyeseigha,* the Proceeds of Corruption Unit of the Metropolitan Police gathered information about the corrupt assets and activities of Alamieyeseigha in support of its own criminal investigations and pursuant to requests for MLA from the federal government of Nigeria. Alamieyeseigha fled the United Kingdom before prosecution could be brought, and he enjoyed immunity from prosecution in Nigeria while in office. Nigeria brought civil proceedings in England to recover its assets. The High Court of England ordered the Metropolitan Police to disclose to Nigeria the information gathered during the criminal investigations on confirmation by the police agency that such disclosure would not prejudice its investigations.

Circumstantial Evidence Considered in *Federal Republic of Nigeria v. Santolina Investment Corp., Solomon & Peters, and Diepreye Alamieyeseigha* (2007)[a]

The case was adjudicated in the absence of defendants who were notified of the proceedings. The court relied on inferences to find that funds deposited in London bank accounts and properties held by the two companies controlled by Diepreye Alamieyeseigha were bribes and secret profits to be returned to the government of Nigeria. To explain this conclusion, the court mentioned several elements that served as circumstantial evidence:

- There was a huge discrepancy between assets and income officially declared by Alamieyeseigha and the funds deposited in foreign bank accounts.
- The defendant held these foreign bank accounts in breach of a constitutional prohibition.
- The defendant could not give any plausible and legitimate explanation of his ability to acquire such amount of assets outside Nigeria.
- Funds were transferred by government contractors in separate transactions and held by offshore corporate vehicles.
- Residential properties were purchased with transfers or loans from those corporate vehicles.

a. *Federal Republic of Nigeria v. Santolina Investment Corp., Solomon & Peters and Diepreye Alamieyeseigha* [2007] EWHC 437 (Ch.) (U.K.).

Disclosure and No-Say (or "Gag") Orders

Depending on the applicable civil procedure, documents held by the parties and third parties are subject to disclosure. In asset recovery cases, it is particularly useful to request disclosure of documents held by third parties—banking and financial documents, including account-opening forms, the identity of beneficial owners of accounts or of companies and trusts, bank statements, and know-your-customer information. A third party could also be ordered to disclose the identity of a wrongdoer.[257]

In some civil law jurisdictions, disclosure is ordered by a judge, and the application can be made without any formality.[258] In other civil law jurisdictions, any interested party may make an *ex parte* request in a civil court to issue orders for the taking of evidence prior to filing a civil action. In common law jurisdictions, the parties must usually provide their opponents with all relevant documents under their control, and applications can be made to the court for disclosure of third-party documents.

In some jurisdictions, courts are permitted to order worldwide disclosure of assets (see box 7.11 of chapter 7). To be truly effective in the foreign jurisdiction, such worldwide orders must also be enforced by foreign courts. Such orders are typically made *ex parte*.

---

257. *Norwich Pharmacal Co. v. Customs and Excise Commissioners* [1974] AC 133 (U.K.).
258. Code of Civil Procedure (France), art. 139.

Requirements for Restraint Orders in France, Panama, and the United Kingdom

In France, courts[a] may order the restraint or seizure of assets (movable or immovable, tangible or intangible) pending the outcome of a trial when the applicant shows that there is a risk of dissipation. For funds in bank accounts, the applicant must demonstrate that the order would be "justified in principle" and that there is "peril with respect to the recovery of the obligation."

In Panama, the plaintiff must meet the basic pleading requirements and post an adequate bond, set by the court. Furthermore, the plaintiff must follow the restraint order with an action at law against the defendant. The restraint order remains in place unless these requirements are not met. When a favorable judgment is obtained, the prevailing plaintiff is entitled to recover from the frozen assets if the defendant does not pay the judgment. If, however, the ruling favors the defendant, on a showing of bad faith, the party whose assets were frozen may recover from the bond posted by the plaintiff.

In the United Kingdom, the applicant must show a good, arguable case, sufficient evidence identifying and locating the assets, and the existence of a real risk of asset dissipation. The applicant must give an undertaking that he or she will compensate the defendant for losses suffered if the court finds that it should not have granted the restraint order.

a. In France, the court is referred to as *le juge de l'exécution*.

To prevent third parties, including banks, from informing a defendant that a disclosure order exists, the court may impose a "gag" or "no-say" order. Any breach of confidentiality may be considered contempt of court. Courts may also order disclosure and restraint of bank accounts prior to service of the proceedings on the defendants.[259]

Restraint Orders

Interim injunctions or restraint orders are frequently used to restrain assets suspected of being the proceeds of crime.[260] A restraint order may also be obtained during the proceedings (to ensure that a defendant has sufficient assets to satisfy a judgment against him or her) or after judgment (to enforce the court's decision).

The applicant must meet certain requirements to obtain the order, and these requirements will vary among jurisdictions. Generally, the applicant must establish that there is justification for the order (an arguable case) and a risk of dissipation of the assets. The applicant may also be required to give an undertaking or post a bond that he or she will compensate the defendant for losses suffered in the event the court finds that it should not have granted the order (see box 8.8 for examples of some requirements).

259. These orders are referred to as "bankers trust" orders in some jurisdictions.
260. These are often referred to as "Mareva injunctions," after *Mareva Compania Naviera S.A. v. International Bulk Carriers S.A.* [1980] 1 All ER 213; [1975] 2 Lloyd's Rep. 509 (CA) (U.K.).

Ex parte applications may be permitted in both civil and common law jurisdictions to avoid tipping off the asset holder and risking the dissipation of assets. In some jurisdictions, that requires the applicant to give full and frank disclosure of all factual elements and evidence in his or her possession.[261] Others require evidence of the risk of dissipation in the event of notice.

Some jurisdictions permit courts to order worldwide restraint to cover assets in both the jurisdiction in question and foreign jurisdictions, and may reach defendants who are not resident within the jurisdiction (see box 7.11 in chapter 7).[262] Similar to the worldwide disclosure orders outlined above, worldwide restraint orders must be enforced by foreign courts to be truly effective in the foreign jurisdiction. Defendants or third parties (including banks or lawyers) who are notified may be held in contempt of court for failing to comply with such orders; possible sanctions include imprisonment, fines, or seizure of assets.

A victim of corruption may also employ a "Mareva by Letter," a technique that puts a third-party guardian or holder of assets on notice that he or she holds potentially corrupt proceeds.[263] Such notice effectively constitutes an immediate and de facto restraint of assets and avoids the costly and lengthy process of making an application with a court to restrain assets. It operates by triggering the due diligence and reporting requirements that financial institutions and some non-financial businesses have in place for detecting and preventing the laundering of crime proceeds. Receipt of notice that an account holder or beneficial owner (who is neither the current guardian nor the holder of the assets) holds the proceeds of crime is typically sufficient for the financial institution or business to report the suspicious activity and hold the funds; otherwise, it is opening itself to potential liability as an accessory to the crime. A Mareva by Letter can be effected by sending a letter to the current guardian or asset holder, notifying him or her that the true or beneficial owner holds the proceeds of crime and providing an advisory warning that he or she may be an accessory to civil or criminal liability (or both) if the funds are disposed of or transferred. The letter should be accompanied by adequate proof of the true or beneficial owner's link to criminal activity to give the third-party holder sufficient justification for the restraint.

In some cases, the plaintiff may benefit from the restraint of assets that has occurred on the basis of criminal law provisions (see box 8.9).

Search and Seizure Orders
Civil proceedings may permit a plaintiff's lawyer to enter premises to preserve evidence that might be destroyed (also referred to as an "Anton Piller order"). In some jurisdictions,

---

261. These are the requirements in the United Kingdom. See U.K. Ministry of Justice, Rules of Civil Procedure, Practice Direction, Freezing Injunctions.

262. In *International Bulk Carriers S.A.*, 1 All ER at 213 and 2 Lloyd's Rep. at 509, the court covered assets in both England and foreign jurisdictions.

263. See also Martin S. Kenney, "'Mareva by Letter'—Preserving Assets Extra-Judicially—Destroying a Bank's Defence of Good Faith by Exposing It to Actual Knowledge of Fraud" (November 27, 2006), http://www.martindale.com/international-law/article_Martin-Kenney-Co._258798.htm (2010).

BOX 8.9   **The Ao Man Long Case**

In 2008, Ao Man Long, former minister of transport and public works in Macao SAR, China, was convicted of corruption offenses involving about HK$800 million (approximately $103 million). He was sentenced in Macao SAR, China, to 27 years' imprisonment; and a confiscation order of approximately HK$250 million (roughly $32 million) was entered.

A significant amount of his bribery proceeds had been deposited into accounts in Hong Kong SAR, China. There was no MLA agreement between the jurisdictions, but authorities in Macao SAR, China, used informal channels (the Hong Kong Independent Commission against Corruption) to restrain the proceeds and obtain search warrants. Because MLA channels were unavailable to recover the proceeds, Macao SAR, China, subsequently launched a civil suit in Hong Kong SAR, China, for more than HK$230 million (approximately $30 million). The original restraint order, obtained pursuant to antibribery legislation in Hong Kong SAR, China, remained in place even though a criminal prosecution was not launched in that jurisdiction.[a]

a. Simon N. M. Young, "Why Civil Actions against Corruption?" *Journal of Financial Crime* 16, no. 2 (2009): 144–59.

courts may grant such orders if there is strong prima facie evidence that incriminating documents are in the defendant's possession and there is a real possibility that such material will be destroyed. In addition, the defendant's activities must cause very serious potential or actual harm to the plaintiff's interest.[264]

8.3 Final Dispositions

In many cases, the disputing parties will choose to settle the matter before or after the court proceedings have begun. Both sides typically have a strong incentive to settle to avoid the costs (such as fees for lawyers and expert witnesses), time, and stress associated with a trial; and to maintain some control over the amount of the final order. Authorities should verify that settlements do not include a waiver of future claims related to assets that were not fully disclosed at the time of the agreement.

Alternatively, the parties will have to await the judgment of the court. This may occur at the end of trial proceedings. Summary judgments may be sought when the jurisdiction seeking redress shows strong evidence, and where the defendants do not present a reasonable

---

264. Applications for search orders (as well as freezing injunctions) submitted to competent judges must be supported by affidavit evidence. Urgent applications can be made without notice and even before a claim form has been issued. Where it is not possible to arrange a hearing, applications may also be made by telephone or by fax sent to a duty judge. See U.K. Ministry of Justice, Rules of Civil Procedure, Freezing and Search Orders and Practice Direction 25A (Supplements), para. 4.5. For additional details, see http://www.justice.gov.uk/civil/procrules_fin/contents/practice_directions/pd_part25a.htm.

Enforcement of Judgments When the Defendant Is Absent from the Proceeding

In *Attorney General of Zambia v. Meer Care & Desai & Others* (2007),[a] a civil action was brought in the United Kingdom against the former president of Zambia, Frederick Chiluba, and his associates (see section 1.3.2 of chapter 1 for additional details on this case). Because the terms of bail required the defendants to remain in Zambia, the court made special arrangements to address the situation. These arrangements included sitting in Zambia as a special examiner to hear evidence and, for proceedings in London, setting up a live video link between London and Zambia and recording daily transcripts.

The London court held in favor of the attorney general of Zambia, who then registered the judgment in the Lusaka High Court in Zambia. The former president applied to set aside the judgment on the basis that he was not able to participate in the hearings in London and was not afforded the opportunity to be heard by the National Assembly (which had stripped him of his immunity against criminal prosecution in Zambia). In 2010, Zambia's Supreme Court rejected Chiluba's appeal on the basis that sufficient actions had been taken.

a. *Attorney General of Zambia v. Meer Care & Desai & Others* [2007] EWHC 952 (Ch.) (U.K.).

defense. Similarly, judgments by default may be obtained when defendants do not comply with court orders asking for detailed explanations on facts and documents. Both summary and default judgments allow courts to shorten the process and grant decisions without a full trial.

In civil actions, the absence of the defendant is much less likely to be a barrier to adjudicating a case than it would be in a criminal action. However, it may complicate enforcement in foreign jurisdictions (see box 8.10).

8.4 Formal Insolvency Processes

Insolvency processes are class remedies. Therefore, they will not provide recovery for one creditor (or victim) alone. However, the fact that those formal insolvency regimes provide powerful tools for investigation, preservation, and recovery of assets often outweighs the class nature of these processes.

Under many formal insolvency processes, there is an automatic moratorium on dissipation of assets when an officeholder has been appointed. As a result, if a perpetrator has assets within the jurisdiction in which he or she has been made bankrupt, insolvency regimes will prevent any further dissipation. The effect of such a moratorium internationally is often complex, but the existence of international regimes such as the Council of the European Union's regulation on insolvency proceedings[265] and the Model Law on Cross-Border Insolvency of the United Nations Commission on International Trade Law often gives this stay on proceedings extraterritorial effect.

Investigatory powers frequently include the ability to cross-examine the bankrupt party and directors of the insolvent entity, as well as any person with information related to the person or entity (including accountants and lawyers). Such powers are wide-ranging and may be enforced by court order. Many of them are also backed by the ability to arrest and imprison a recalcitrant debtor.[266] Investigatory powers also usually involve the ability to compel production of books and records, including those from lawyers and banks. Any legal privilege of the bankrupt person or insolvent entity is typically overridden, denying a perpetrator of crime the ability to hide behind his or her legal advisers.

Generally, the definition of property owned by a bankrupt person or insolvent entity is interpreted broadly to include not only tangible property, but also intangible property and any assets that are the traceable products of such property. Insolvency officeholders (the trustees, administrators, liquidators, insolvency representatives, or similar functionaries who make many insolvency systems work in insolvency cases), too, may have specific claims to recover assets—some of which are unavailable to any other party. Examples of such claims include claims for misfeasance, preferences, transactions that were undervalued, and wrongful and fraudulent trading. Remedies for such claims often include the ability to undo transactions, reverse transfers of property to third parties, and void security rights.

---

265. Council Regulation (EC) No. 1346/2000 of May 29, 2000, on insolvency proceedings.
266. In the United Kingdom, for example, there is no privilege against self-incrimination; and failure to answer questions may lead to imprisonment for contempt of court.

9. Domestic Confiscation Proceedings Undertaken in Foreign Jurisdictions

Practitioners may find themselves in circumstances where obtaining a domestic criminal or non-conviction based (NCB) confiscation order and foreign enforcement pursuant to a mutual legal assistance (MLA) request and civil proceedings is not possible. There may be an insufficient legal framework, legal obstacles (for example, immunities, statute of limitations, or refusal to extradite), and a lack of resources and political will (see chapter 2 for a description of these obstacles). In those circumstances and where offenses have crossed into other jurisdictions (such as with bribery or the laundering of proceeds of corruption), practitioners may decide to support the efforts of a foreign authority to bring confiscation or civil proceedings against those individuals and assets over which they have jurisdiction. Alternatively, a foreign authority may decide independently to initiate criminal or NCB confiscation or civil proceedings.

When a foreign jurisdiction brings confiscation or civil proceedings against a target, the authority in the jurisdiction harmed by corruption offenses effectively loses control over the case. Because the case is a domestic proceeding of the foreign jurisdiction, the jurisdiction harmed by corruption offenses has no authority to choose the direction of the proceedings or to decide how the case is conducted. It has limited standing (if any) and may have fewer options for the recovery of assets. As a result, practitioners often choose this method only after they have considered or attempted all other mechanisms, including domestic criminal or NCB confiscation (and enforcement pursuant to an MLA request) or civil proceedings. Proactively selecting this approach will depend on a number of factors that should be verified at the outset, including the foreign jurisdiction's capacity and willingness to undertake investigation and confiscation proceedings, the commitment by the jurisdiction harmed by corruption offenses to provide requested MLA in the foreign proceedings, and an agreement on the return of assets.

9.1 Jurisdiction

The foreign authority must have jurisdiction to investigate and prosecute the offense. International treaties require or encourage states parties to adopt measures that establish broad jurisdiction over corruption offenses.[267] States parties to the United Nations

---

267. United Nations Convention against Corruption (UNCAC), art. 42; United Nations Convention against Transnational Organized Crime (UNTOC), art. 15; United Nations Convention against Narcotic Drugs and Psychotropic Substances, art. 4. See also the Organisation for Economic Co-operation and Development (OECD) Bribery Convention, art. 4. Recommendation 1 of the Financial Action Task Force 40+9 Recommendations states that "predicate offences for money laundering should extend to conduct that

Convention against Corruption (UNCAC), for example, must have jurisdiction over corruption offenses committed within their territory, by or against one of their nationals, or by or against a stateless person who has his or her habitual residence in their territory.[268] In cases of "extradite or prosecute" (described below), jurisdiction is established by virtue of the delegation of legal proceedings.

In cases that do not involve nationals and where only some of the elements of a criminal offense are committed in or to the detriment of a foreign jurisdiction, establishing jurisdiction may still be possible. Some authorities will claim jurisdiction even if only peripheral acts related to the offense have "touched" their territory (see box 9.1).

Most laws extend jurisdiction beyond nationals to include companies incorporated (or simply active) in the jurisdiction for acts of bribery committed in another jurisdiction (see box 9.2).[269]

Legislation may also use broadly defined money laundering offenses to establish jurisdiction—such as legislation that permits money laundering predicates to have been committed in another jurisdiction (see box 9.3). In some jurisdictions, authorities will prosecute ancillary offenses committed domestically that are intended to prepare or promote acts of corruption committed in another jurisdiction—for example, conspiracy, receipt of criminally derived assets, and complicity.[270] Finally, some jurisdictions permit NCB confiscation proceedings against correspondent accounts of foreign banks holding illicit proceeds in a customer account abroad.[271]

9.2 Procedure for Beginning an Action

It is important for practitioners to recognize that domestic confiscation proceedings in foreign jurisdictions are not solely dependent on a request from the jurisdiction that has been harmed by corruption offenses. The foreign authorities may initiate a case

---

occurred in another country, which constitute an offence in that country, and which would have constituted a predicate offence had it occurred domestically."

268. UNCAC, art. 42. Offenses under UNCAC include bribery of national and foreign public officials (art. 15–16); the embezzlement, misappropriation, or other diversion of property by a public official (art. 17); and the knowing acquisition, possession, or use of the proceeds of crime and money laundering (art. 23). Possible offenses that UNCAC encourages states parties to legislate include influence peddling, abuse of functions, illicit enrichment, and private sector bribery or embezzlement.

269. Thirty-seven of the 38 OECD parties have jurisdiction over nationals and companies.

270. For example, French authorities may bring charges against a foreigner for participating in a conspiracy intended to prepare a money laundering operation in France, even if he or she did not commit the actual criminal act in France. Cassation Court, February 20, 1990.

271. Under Title 18, United States Code, sec. 981(k), courts in the United States have jurisdiction to order the confiscation of an amount of funds located in a foreign bank's U.S. correspondent account that is equivalent to the amount of illicit proceeds deposited by a customer in the foreign bank. The provision is generally used only if the foreign jurisdiction is unable or unwilling to provide MLA to restrain and confiscate those assets.

Establishing Jurisdiction Where Limited Acts Have Occurred in the Territory

It may appear to be difficult to establish jurisdiction in cases that do not involve nationals and where only some of the elements of the offense are committed in or against a particular jurisdiction. However, many jurisdictions have found innovative ways to accomplish this. Here are some factors on which they have focused:

- **Financial transactions in the territory.** The U.S. Supreme Court has upheld convictions of defendants who used interstate wires to execute a scheme to defraud a foreign government of tax revenue.[a]
- **Origin of activities.** In Brazil, a telephone call, fax, or e-mail emanating from Brazil would be sufficient to establish jurisdiction over an act of foreign bribery.
- **Links to other crimes committed in the territory.** In France, jurisdiction can be established over crimes committed in a foreign jurisdiction if those crimes can be linked to crimes committed in France.[b]
- **Transfers of national currency (even if outside the territory).** In 2009, the U.S. Department of Justice filed a confiscation action against bribery proceeds paid (in Singapore, with U.S. currency) by a foreign company to the son of the former prime minister of Bangladesh.[c] The Department of Justice successfully argued that the transfer of U.S. currency between financial institutions outside the United States necessarily transited through U.S. correspondent banks. Also supporting the establishment of jurisdiction was the fact that the foreign company making the bribe was registered on the New York Stock Exchange and subject to U.S. laws and regulations.
- **Offenses against national interests.** Foreign nationals are criminally liable for offenses committed outside Ukraine if they commit grave offenses against rights and freedoms of Ukrainian nationals or against the interests of Ukraine.

a. *Pasquantino v. United States*, 544 U.S. 349 (2005) (U.S.). b. Cour de cassation, April 23, 1981, January 15, 1990 (France). c. Title 18, United States Code, sec. 981(a)(1)(C): any property.

independently based on information obtained through various avenues (see box 9.4). As indicated above, the foreign authorities ultimately decide whether to pursue the case and how it is conducted.

9.3 Role of the Jurisdiction Harmed by Corruption Offenses in Foreign Investigation and Prosecution

Once a foreign investigation is initiated, practitioners in the foreign jurisdiction will need to gather evidence in the jurisdiction harmed by corruption to prove corruption or the predicate crimes of money laundering offenses. Even if the jurisdiction harmed

In the United Kingdom, the Bribery Act, 2010,[a] imposes criminal penalties on organizations or companies whose employees, subsidiaries, agents, or consultants pay bribes in the context of the organization's business activities anywhere in the world. A foreign bank operating a small branch in London will be criminally liable if an employee, agent, or subsidiary pays a bribe in any country, even if the bribe is not approved by or paid through the branch in the United Kingdom. The mere existence of the branch office will give jurisdiction to U.K. prosecutors and courts.

In the United States, the Foreign Corrupt Practices Act (FCPA) establishes jurisdiction over any individual, firm, officer, director, employee, or agent of a corporation that issues securities registered in the United States; any legal person established under U.S. law or headquartered in the United States; and any U.S. citizen for acts related to a corrupt payment, even where those acts took place outside the United States. The FCPA also holds liable foreign nationals or companies who take an action in furtherance of a corrupt payment while in the United States or who cause an international or interstate wire communication into or through the United States. Foreign officials who receive the corrupt payments are exempt from prosecution under the FCPA, but can be prosecuted for money laundering in relation to the payment if the United States otherwise has jurisdiction over the money laundering. In addition, a foreign official receiving a corrupt payment may be prosecuted under the Travel Act (Title 18, United States Code, sec. 1952) or for wire or mail fraud (Title 18, United States Code, sec. 1341 and 1343) and related statutes, even where they cannot be prosecuted under the FCPA.

a. The Bribery Act, 2010 (United Kingdom), is expected to enter into force in April 2011.

by corruption offenses has provided the case file at the outset, the foreign jurisdiction likely needs additional information and legal assistance (including witness statements, financial records, and banking or corporate documents). This information may be sought through informal assistance or an MLA request. However the information is requested, it is imperative that a response be transmitted. Without continued attention to the case and responses to foreign requests, success in the foreign case will be limited or impossible (see box 9.5).

In most countries, a foreign jurisdiction that has been harmed by corruption offenses can participate as a complainant or victim (referred to in some jurisdictions as "the plaintiff") to some extent in the investigation, trial, and sentencing or confiscation proceedings. Complainants and victims may attend trial proceedings and consult with practitioners on the progress of the investigation and prosecution. Many jurisdictions encourage practitioners to involve victims in all phases—particularly in the sentencing or confiscation proceedings to facilitate direct recovery from the court. Victims may be consulted on orders to be requested of the court or may be given the opportunity to

Jurisdiction to Prosecute Money Laundering Offenses in France, the United Kingdom, and the United States

In France, courts have convicted defendants accused of receiving the proceeds of crimes committed overseas[a] when circumstantial evidence proved that they knew or should have known that the asset was of illegal origin.[b] Similarly, France criminalizes the laundering of proceeds of predicate offenses committed abroad. For example, French courts convicted a former Nigerian minister who used bribes collected in Nigeria to purchase residences in France. All elements of the bribery offense were committed in Nigeria, but French courts took jurisdiction on the money laundering activities.[c]

In the United Kingdom, authorities may prosecute the concealing, disguising, converting, or transferring of criminal assets derived from crimes committed abroad if the predicate offense also constitutes an offense under U.K. law.[d] Prosecutors can rely on circumstantial evidence to prove that the asset is generally derived from "criminal conduct"; they are not required to show that the asset was acquired by means of a specific criminal act.[e]

In the United States, money laundering predicates include bribery of foreign officials, embezzlement of public funds, fraud by or against a foreign bank, and any crime for which the United States will be obliged to extradite under an international treaty.[f] In the prosecution of the former Ukraine prime minister, Pavlo Lazarenko, for money laundering, prosecutors established jurisdiction by demonstrating that funds received through banks in San Francisco, California, were the proceeds of acts of extortion and bribery committed in Ukraine.[g]

a. Article 321–1 of France's Criminal Code criminalizes *recel*—the receiving, retaining, concealing, or transferring of ill-gotten items or acting as an intermediary therein, knowing that the items were obtained by a felony or misdemeanor.
b. Tribunal of Paris, 11th chamber, 3d section, October 29, 2009, "Angolagate." c. Court of Appeals of Paris, criminal chamber, section A, March 8, 2009 (France). d. Title 18, United States Code, sec. 1956(c)(7)(B) and sec. 981. NCB confiscation actions may be used to confiscate the proceeds of those same foreign criminal offenses, as well as assets involved in money laundering transactions (sec. 981[a][1][C]). In such cases, the United States can seek confiscation of corruption proceeds held inside and outside of the United States if the underlying crime occurred in the United States (sec. 1355[b][2]). e. *United States of America v. Lazarenko,* 564 F.3d 1026 (9th Cir., 2009) (U.S.). f. Proceeds of Crime Act, 2002 (United Kingdom), sec. 327 and 340(2). g. Crown Prosecution Service, Proceeds of Crime Act, 2002, Money Laundering Offenses (United Kingdom).

testify. However, decisions on how to proceed, the people to interview, the records to obtain, and the compensation or damages to be requested of the court ultimately lie with practitioners.

In civil law jurisdictions or mixed systems, victims (including a state or government) may initiate criminal investigations or proceedings in the foreign jurisdiction as a civil party. Civil parties may be permitted to submit evidence or claims to the prosecutor or investigative magistrate, participate in interviews of witnesses and targets, and have access to the case file. The prosecutor or investigating magistrate ultimately determines if the case has sufficient evidence to proceed to trial. If a trial proceeds, civil parties may apply to the court for a judgment awarding damages in the same manner that they would before a civil court (see chapter 8 for more information on this topic). The action for damages proceeds with the criminal case, on the same basis and evidence.

BOX 9.4 | Confiscation Proceedings Initiated by Foreign Authorities

- **A jurisdiction harmed by corruption offenses files a complaint or shares evidence and case file with authorities in a foreign jurisdiction.** This source is most often used when the jurisdiction harmed by corruption offenses is seeking to have the case proceed in a foreign jurisdiction. In civil law jurisdictions, those jurisdictions seeking the return of corruptly acquired assets may also be permitted to initiate (as a civil party) criminal investigations or proceedings concerning those assets. For example, investigations into or proceeding against the laundering of those assets.

- **An MLA request is submitted by a jurisdiction harmed by corruption offenses.** An MLA request typically contains detailed information on targets, alleged offenses, and money flows; and this information may lead a requested jurisdiction to initiate its own investigation into money laundering, foreign bribery, or other offenses that may have been undertaken within its territory or involving its nationals. This is done almost systematically in Switzerland, and relatively frequently in other jurisdictions. In most cases, two different proceedings will be conducted in the requested jurisdiction: the first will respond to the request for MLA and the second will pursue the domestic charges of money laundering.

- **Media report on corruption or money laundering.** Corruption cases—particularly those involving politically exposed persons—typically attract substantial media coverage. That coverage may reveal links to foreign jurisdictions, and those links may be picked up by foreign practitioners who decide to initiate a case or by bank compliance officers who file a suspicious transaction report (STR) that ultimately leads to an investigation.

- **STRs are filed.** Financial institutions that suspect activity or transactions are involved in money laundering or terrorist financing must report their suspicions to financial intelligence units (FIUs) by filing STRs. The FIUs are required to analyze the STRs and disseminate reports to law enforcement or through the Egmont Group to other FIUs. Law enforcement agencies may subsequently decide to open an investigation based on information provided by the FIU.

- **The "extradite or prosecute" principle is applied.** Jurisdictions that refuse to grant extradition of nationals under the United Nations Convention against Corruption (UNCAC) have an obligation to submit the case to their domestic authorities for prosecution, if asked by the requesting jurisdiction.[a] In France, offenses carrying a penalty of at least five years in prison will be prosecuted whenever an extradition requested by a foreign jurisdiction is refused on the grounds of due process or if the penalty in the requesting country is not compatible with French public order.[b]

- **Transfer of proceedings.** Pursuant to article 47 of UNCAC, states parties shall consider transferring cases established in accordance with the convention where such a transfer is in the interests of the proper administration of justice. When several jurisdictions are involved, this serves to concentrate the prosecution of such cases.

a. UNCAC, art. 44(11); United Nations Convention against Transnational Organized Crime, art. 16(12); United Nations Convention against Narcotic Drugs and Psychotropic Substances, art. 6(9)2. b. Criminal Code (France), art. 113–8–1.

Important Role of the Jurisdiction Harmed by Corruption—A Case Example from Haiti

From May 2001 to April 2003, Robert Antoine, the former director of international affairs for Haiti's state-owned national telecommunications company, accepted bribes from three U.S. telecommunications companies and laundered the bribes through intermediaries.

Haiti was unable to proceed against Antoine or any of the intermediaries involved because it did not have sufficient legal provisions in place, including the necessary anti-corruption offense legislation and investigative tools required to establish an offense. Haitian authorities reviewed the case with U.S. personnel and ultimately decided that the best course of action would be to support a case initiated by the United States.

The United States initiated a case against Antoine for money laundering conspiracy in connection with the foreign bribery scheme and cases against the briber and the intermediaries for conspiracy to commit violations of the FCPA and money laundering. Haitian authorities collaborated by actively seeking and providing all evidence and expertise required by the U.S. prosecutors. Assistance was required from and provided by a range of authorities, including the financial intelligence unit, national police, and the Ministry of Justice and Public Security. Without that specific collaboration, it would have been impossible to proceed in the United States.

Antoine pleaded guilty to the offenses and was sentenced in June 2010 to 48 months in prison. He was ordered to pay $1,852,209 in restitution and more than $1,500,000 was confiscated.[a] A discussion of the sharing of the proceeds is ongoing.

a. Department of Justice, Office of Public Affairs, "Former Haitian Government Official Sentenced for His Role in Money Laundering Conspiracy Related to Foreign Bribery Scheme," news release, June 2, 2010, http://www.justice.gov/opa/pr/2010/June/10-crm-639.html.

Some jurisdictions will allow complainants and civil parties access to case information, including a copy of the case file. For example, if a prosecutor or investigating magistrate is appointed, a copy of the case file will be provided, on request, to attorneys representing victims who have joined the action as civil parties.[272]

9.4 Ensuring Recovery of Assets from the Foreign Jurisdiction

In some jurisdictions, the courts or other competent authorities will order victim restitution from any seized or restrained assets as part of the criminal proceeding. Such an order may take the form of an order for compensation, damages, or claims of legitimate ownership; and it can be awarded to a jurisdiction harmed by corruption

---

272. Code of Criminal Procedure (France), art. 114, R.155, R.165.

offenses.[273] Any assets not ordered returned through such an order is likely to become the property of the foreign jurisdiction. As a result, the jurisdiction seeking to recover assets should consider, at the outset, whether recovery or sharing of these confiscated proceeds will be possible. Depending on the jurisdiction and the procedures followed, recovery may be available through international conventions, MLA treaties, asset sharing agreements, or legislation. Even if a foreign jurisdiction independently initiates a case, the jurisdiction harmed by corruption offenses may be able to avail itself of procedures to obtain restitution of the assets.

9.4.1 Claiming Ownership of Stolen Assets during Criminal Investigations

In some jurisdictions, claiming ownership of stolen assets is possible at an early stage of an investigation.[274] When assets are found and the offender remains unknown, the prosecutor or investigating magistrate will attempt to establish or determine whether the assets are the proceeds or an instrumentality of the alleged offense. If a connection is established, restitution of the restrained assets may be ordered. These orders can be appealed.

9.4.2 Direct Recovery of Assets through Foreign Courts

Many courts will order direct recovery to a foreign jurisdiction that can demonstrate its status as a victim or a legitimate owner of the asset. This practice is included in international agreements and will permit courts to order compensation or damages to the jurisdiction harmed by corruption offenses and allow courts or competent authorities to recognize the jurisdiction's claim as a legitimate owner of an asset in confiscation proceedings.[275]

Direct recovery is often facilitated through the participation of the jurisdiction harmed by corruption offenses, whether as a plaintiff in a civil action, a complainant or victim (plaintiff) in a domestic proceeding, or a civil party to a criminal action. In jurisdictions that allow the injured party to join as a civil party, the jurisdiction harmed by corruption offenses has the opportunity to apply to the court for damages or compensation. Otherwise, the jurisdiction will need to discuss potential compensation or damages with the prosecutor, who can then apply to the court for the order. Box 9.6 offers examples of direct recovery in practice.

The treatment of a claim for damages in the event of acquittal varies among jurisdictions. In some places, the claim cannot be considered and the injured party must file a civil action for damages. In others, the court may reach a decision on damages despite the acquittal if the facts are sufficiently established.

---

273. UNCAC, art. 53.
274. France and Switzerland permit this procedure.
275. UNCAC, art. 53.

- **Civil party to criminal proceedings.** In France, article 2 of the Code of Criminal Procedure provides that a victim may obtain civil compensation from a criminal law court offense if the plaintiff is able to prove personal and direct damage resulting from the corrupt act. In a corruption case involving the former mayor of Cannes, the city of Cannes—which joined as a civil party to the criminal action—was able to obtain from the court an order for damages, but was not granted material compensation. The damages were awarded on the basis of the loss of reputation; the compensation order was refused on the basis that the damage suffered was the consequence of a ministerial decision to revoke and refuse a license rather than a consequence of corruption.
- **Compensation pursuant to a criminal plea agreement.** In the United Kingdom, a bridge-building company, Mabey & Johnson Ltd., pled guilty to conspiracy relating to the payment of bribes to public officials in Ghana and Jamaica and to "making funds available" in connection with illegal kickbacks to the Saddam Hussein regime in Iraq through contracts awarded under the United Nations Oil-for-Food Program. The company admitted that, but for the bribe, the contract would have been for less money and that the Iraqi people lost out on funds diverted to pay the kickback.[a]

  The settlement included £4.6 million (approximately $7.2 million) in criminal penalties and an additional £2 million (approximately $3.1 million) in reparations and costs to be paid to the governments of Ghana, Iraq, and Jamaica. With regard to the Iraq case, confiscation was awarded for the value of the contract, €4.22 million plus interest (approximately $5.41 million), and compensation of £618,484 (approximately $969,100) was awarded to the Iraqi people (Development Fund for Iraq).
- **Compensation through a civil action.** In a case involving funds and real estate in London held in the name of a corrupt Nigerian official, investigations conducted by the Metropolitan London Police resulted in a property manager being criminally convicted of money laundering. Following this conviction, a civil action brought in the London High Court by a U.K. law firm resulted in the recovery of stolen assets to the benefit of Nigeria.

a. A news release and the prosecution's opening statements are available at http://www.sfo.gov.uk/press-room/latest-press-releases/press-releases-2009/mabey—johnson-ltd-sentencing-.aspx.

9.4.3 Recovering Assets Pursuant to Treaties, Agreements, or Statutory Authorities

Several international conventions introduce obligations on the return of assets.[276] To enforce these international conventions—or when international conventions do not

276. UNCAC, art. 57; UNTOC, art. 14; United Nations Convention against Narcotic Drugs and Psychotropic Substances, art. 5. Note that the UNCAC provisions set forth mandatory requirements on the return of

apply—multilateral and bilateral treaties (such as MLA treaties), agreements, and statutory authorities are often used to allow for the return of assets.

If no obligation to return confiscated assets is in place, multilateral and bilateral asset sharing agreements between jurisdictions may set out specific procedures for these sharing mechanisms.[277] Such agreements may be negotiated on a case-by-case basis or, more expediently, through an ongoing sharing agreement designed to cover all sharing cases that arise.[278] Some jurisdictions prefer to negotiate a sharing arrangement either before providing the requested restraint or following the restraint but before the entry of a final order of confiscation.

Confiscated assets may also be returned under an ad hoc agreement with the requesting jurisdiction. In the absence of a treaty or agreement, some jurisdictions will have statutory provisions that give the state, the government, or a competent authority the discretion to return assets. Box 9.7 describes some of the asset return options that are available in Switzerland.

---

assets, as opposed to the discretionary requirements outlined in UNTOC and the United Nations Convention against Narcotic Drugs and Psychotropic Substances.

277. Sharing agreements are also included in the following international agreements: UNCAC, art. 57; UNTOC, art. 14; United Nations Convention against Narcotic Drugs and Psychotropic Substances, art. 5.

278. In the United States, the formal sharing agreement is not confirmed until the conclusion of the case, and it is based on the amount of cooperation provided by each jurisdiction: 50–80 percent of confiscated assets if the foreign jurisdiction provided essential assistance, 40–50 percent in the case of "major assistance," and up to 40 percent if the foreign jurisdiction provided "facilitating" assistance.

Appendix A. Offenses to Consider in Criminal Prosecution

Misappropriation or Diversion of Funds and Property
- theft or larceny
- embezzlement
- fraud, false pretenses, misrepresentation

Bribery and Related Offenses
- bribery (national and foreign public officials)
- trading in influence
- abuse of functions
- illicit enrichment
- conflict of interest
- illegal financing of political parties or campaigns
- extorting

Possible Corruption Case Charges

Laundering, Concealment, Acquisition, Possession, or Use of Proceeds of Crime
- conversion or transfer of property
- concealment and disguise
- acquisition, possession, or use of proceeds of crime

Facilitating Crimes
- breach of public procurement regulations
- collusion
- forgery / falsification of documents
- accounting crimes
- tax violations
- customs fraud / smuggling
- mail and wire fraud
- conspiracy
- assistance by aiding or abetting
- obstruction of justice

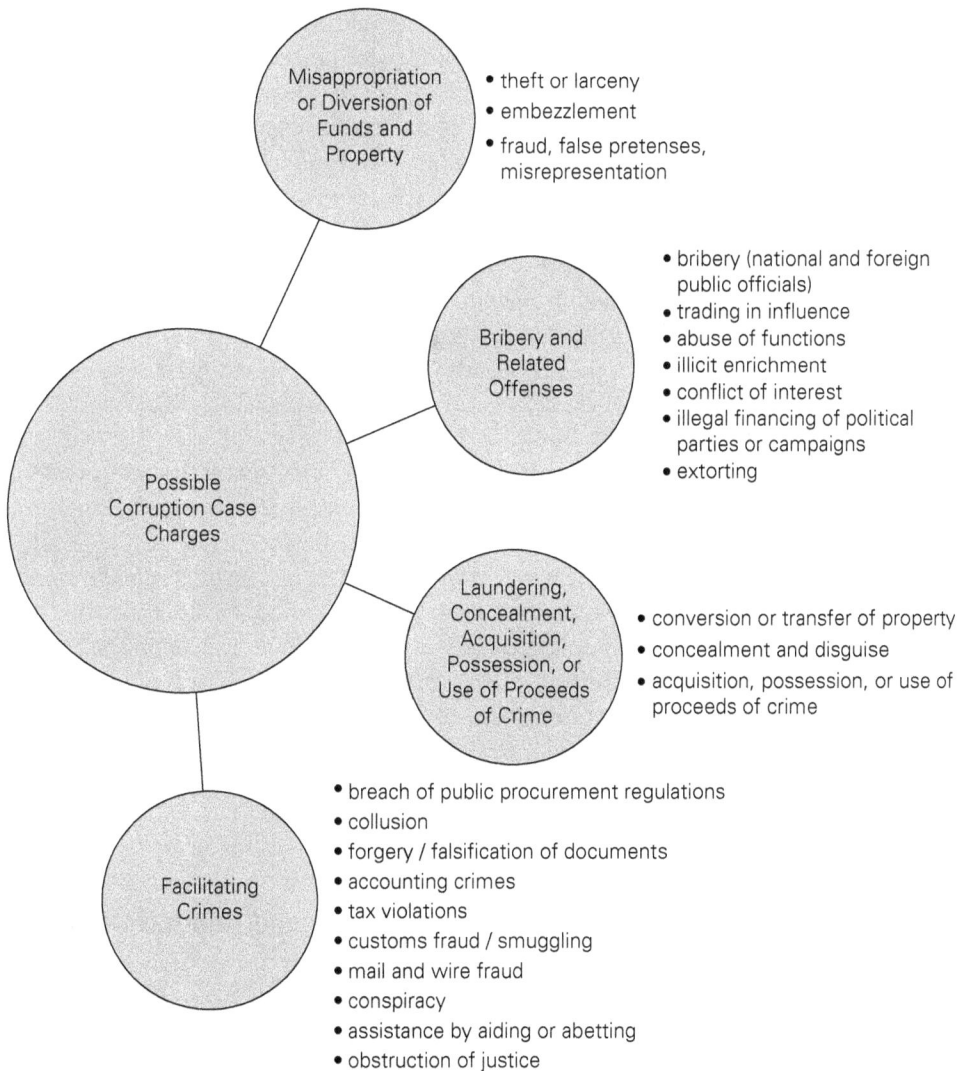

Source: Authors' illustration.

Misappropriation or Diversion of Funds and Property (United Nations Convention against Corruption [UNCAC], article 17)

- **Theft or larceny.** These crimes are generally defined as the unlawful appropriation of personal and tangible assets with the intention of depriving the legitimate owner of this property. In this case, assets are simply taken without the consent of the legitimate owner (or, in some jurisdictions, with consent obtained by fraud). Unauthorized harvesting in protected areas or public forests, or looting cash, checks, and other financial instruments from a central bank are well-known examples of theft committed by public officials. In many jurisdictions, real property, services or intangible assets are not included in the definition of larceny.
- **Embezzlement.** This offense is generally defined as the fraudulent transfer of property by an individual or legal entity in lawful possession of assets belonging to another individual or legal entity. This criminal offense applies to public officials or executives who misappropriate or misuse funds or property that they are supposed to manage for a government entity (central, local, or city government; government agency; or state-owned company). It involves violation of the terms of a trust agreement authorizing the offender to hold the assets and manage them in the interest of the legitimate owner. In several jurisdictions, embezzlement does not apply to the misappropriation of real estate or services. Examples of embezzlement include hiring and paying employees who do not perform their duties (no-show jobs), purchasing goods or services at above-market rates (over-billing), paying fees for nonexistent goods or services that do not correspond to a real counterpart (fictitious billing).
- **Fraud, false pretenses, and misrepresentation.** These offenses are generally defined as the acquisition of a title or the possession of property belonging to another person by intentional deception, or false statements of past or existing fact. In some jurisdictions, the applicable offense may be considered to be larceny or theft by trick if only possession of property is obtained. In other jurisdictions, the crime will extend to obtaining possession of the property even in the absence of title. Although the definition of this offense is always based on intentional deception, the specific legal definition of deceptive actions may vary. Here is a typical example: a public official instructs his subordinates to pay money or grant loans to fictitious companies that have no real business activity and are managed by straw men or the official's relatives.

Bribery, Trading in Influence, Abuse of Functions, and Related Offenses

- **Bribery of national public officials (UNCAC, article 15).** Consists of intentionally,
  - (a) directly or indirectly promising, offering, or giving to a public official an undue advantage for the official himself or herself or for another person or entity in return for the official acting or refraining from acting in the exercise of his or her official duties;

(b) directly or indirectly soliciting or accepting as a public official an undue advantage for oneself or for another person or entity in return for acting or refraining from acting in the exercise of one's official duties.

- **Bribery of foreign public officials and officials of public international organizations (UNCAC, article 16).** Consists of intentionally,
  (a) either directly or indirectly promising, offering, or giving a foreign public official or an official of a public international organization an undue advantage for the official himself or herself or for another person or entity in return for the official acting or refraining from acting in the exercise of his or her official duties in a way that enables the offender to obtain or retain business or other undue advantage in relation to the conduct of international business;
  (b) either directly or indirectly soliciting or accepting as a foreign public official or an official of a public international organization an undue advantage for oneself or for another person or entity in return for acting or refraining from acting in the exercise of one's official duties.

- **Trading in influence (UNCAC, article 18).** Consists of intentionally,
  (a) directly or indirectly promising, offering, or giving a public official or any other person an undue advantage in return for the public official or other person abusing his or her real or supposed influence with a view to obtaining from an administration or public authority of the state party an undue advantage for the original instigator of the act or for any other person;
  (b) directly or indirectly soliciting or accepting as a public official or any other person an undue advantage for oneself or for another person in return for abusing one's real or supposed influence with a view to obtaining an undue advantage from an administration or public authority of the state party.

- **Abuse of functions (UNCAC, article 19).** Consists of a public official performing or failing to perform an act, in violation of laws, in the discharge of his or her functions, for the purpose of obtaining an undue advantage for himself or herself or for another person or entity.

- **Illicit enrichment (UNCAC, article 20).** Generally defined as "a significant increase in the assets of a public official that he or she cannot reasonably explain in relation to his or her lawful income." Authorities prosecuting illicit enrichment are not required to demonstrate the illegal origin of property to obtain convictions or confiscation orders. It will be sufficient to show that the legitimate income of a public official cannot explain an increase in assets or expenditures. The public official must then explain how the property in question accrued from legal sources (see box A.1 for an example from France).

- **Conflict of interest.** In some jurisdictions, it is a crime for public officials to take or accept any direct or indirect interest in any grant, contract, or decision subject to his or her opinion, supervision, control, or administration. In many jurisdictions, it is a crime for public servants whose duties include supervising private activities or companies to take a financial interest in those activities or companies. The typical example of conflict of interest is a public official's awarding of a government contract to a company for which the official has direct or indirect ownership or control.

In France, the following two provisions of the Criminal Code are relevant in the context of illicit enrichment:

- **Conviction proceedings.** Article 321-6 provides that a person can be convicted because of his or her "inability to justify an income corresponding to his lifestyle or the origin of a property, while maintaining regular relationships with one or more persons involved in felonies or misdemeanors punishable by at least five years imprisonment and from which they drew a direct or indirect benefit, or who are the victims of these offences." This offense is punishable by three to seven years' imprisonment and allows the confiscation of the convicted person's entire assets.
- **Confiscation proceedings.** Article 131-21 provides that confiscation may be carried out on all properties of the defendant, unless he or she can justify those properties are of legitimate origin. The offense must be punishable by at least five years' imprisonment and must have procured a direct or indirect profit.

- **Illegal financing of political parties or campaigns.** Covered by statutes proscribing the illicit financing of political activities and those relating to corruption, these schemes typically involve contractors who inflate the price of government contracts. From the proceeds of overbilling, these contractors relay funds to "taxi" firms (so called because they receive the equivalent of illicit taxes) that submit forged invoices. In return, these taxi firms finance political activities. These schemes also fall under racketeering or extortion statutes when it is clear that reluctant contractors will lose government business if they refuse to participate in these schemes.
- **Extortion.** In some jurisdictions, this crime is defined as the collection of unlawful fees by a public official in his or her official capacity by means of oral or written threats, fear, coercion, and intimidation.

Laundering, Concealment, Acquisition, Possession, or Use of the Proceeds of Crime

- These offenses are defined in UNCAC, articles 23 and 24 as the
  - (a) conversion or transfer of property, knowing that such property is the proceeds of crime, for the purpose of concealing or disguising the illicit origin of the property or of helping any person who is involved in the commission of the predicate offense to evade the legal consequences of his or her action;
  - (b) concealment or disguise of the true nature, source, location, disposition, movement, or ownership of or rights with respect to property, knowing that such property is the proceeds of crime;

(c)   acquisition, possession, or use of property, knowing at the time of receipt that such property is the proceeds of crime;

(d)   participation in; association with; conspiracy to commit; attempts to commit; and aiding, abetting, facilitating, and counseling the commission of any of the offenses established in accordance with this article; and

(e)   concealment or continued retention of property when the person involved knows that such property is the result of corruption offenses.

- Money laundering offenses will usually be applicable to all financial or nonfinancial institutions, businesses, individuals, and intermediaries who knowingly engage in transactions intended to disguise the illicit source of the property. Money laundering charges should be considered in plotting asset recovery strategy because corrupt officials need to invest or to spend illegally derived property in financial centers. In many corruption cases, money laundering schemes facilitate the commission of the corruption offense. In particular, a company may pay fictitious invoices, with the funds going to offshore accounts held by contractors or consultants. Those intermediaries then use the funds to bribe corrupt public officials on behalf of the company. In most legal jurisdictions, the organization of such slush funds falls under money laundering statutes.

Facilitating Crimes

- **Breach of public procurement regulations.** When public officials fail to comply with procurement regulations, they frequently intend to grant an undue advantage to certain government contractors. As an example, a public official in charge of procurement operations may provide a bidder with sensitive information, including government cost estimates, to ensure that this potential contractor will enjoy a significant advantage. Similarly, large procurement contracts may be artificially divided into smaller "slices" to avoid a competitive bidding process that would be mandatory, given the total cost of the project. Or, during the execution of a contract, administrative officers may agree to pay for goods that are not delivered, for services that are not rendered, or for a quantity or quality of goods that does not correspond to the provisions of the contract. Government contracts awarded or executed at significantly inflated costs illicitly benefit the contractor. In return, kickbacks or other advantages received from this contractor may reward the public official.
- **Collusion.** This offense criminalizes (usually secretive) agreements that occur between two or more persons to deceive, mislead, or defraud others of their legal rights; to obtain an objective forbidden by law; or to gain an unfair advantage. In particular, secret agreements among firms or between a firm and a public official to limit or organize competition or set prices in public procurement will be frequently encountered in corruption cases. A public official who drafts work statements or terms of reference for a competitive bidding process based on information provided by a potential bidder commits collusion.
- **Forgery/falsification of documents.** This offense involves forging or altering the substance, the date, or the signatures of parties or witnesses in any private or public documents having the effect of an obligation, discharge, or disposition.

- **Accounting crimes.** A very common tool to organize or facilitate corruption or misappropriation of funds, accounting crimes include falsifying accounts, books, records, or financial statements. In particular, companies will issue or record fictitious or false invoices to justify and conceal improper payments to intermediaries, to manage slush funds, and to pay bribes. A very common scheme consists of private firms paying false invoices submitted by intermediaries posing as consultants who use the funds to bribe officials. In this case, the accounts of both the company and the "consultant" will record fictitious transactions.
- **Tax violations.** Schemes involving the misrepresentation of transactions in the accounts or the financial records of a company will result in the over- or underestimation of assets, revenues, or expenses; and illegally will modify taxable revenues or deductible expenses. This is typically the case for fictitious or falsified invoices that increase purchase accounts, reducing the taxable profit of an entity.
- **Customs fraud/smuggling.** Corruption, misappropriation of assets, and money laundering frequently involve illegal transportation of money or the transfer of goods out of or into the victim country. Customs fraud may also involve the duty-free import of goods that will supposedly transit the country, but are actually illegally sold within the country.
- **Mail and wire fraud.** Some jurisdictions criminalize mail and wire fraud. For example, in the United States it is a crime to devise a scheme to defraud or to obtain money or property by means of false or fraudulent pretenses, and to use the mail or telecommunications infrastructure (telephone, facsimile transmissions, and e-mail) to execute the plan. This criminal offense is also applicable to public officials who obtain money in ways that may not be commonly defined as illicit.
- **Conspiracy.** This offense involves agreements between two or more persons to break the law at some time in the future. Actions agreed to in conspiracy often include fraud, corruption, and misappropriation of property. In some jurisdictions, conspiracy charges can be lodged only if malefactors commit at least one overt act in furtherance of the conspiracy agreement.
- **Assistance by aiding or abetting.** An accomplice takes no part in a criminal offense, but participates by assisting the principal offender. Subject to prosecution for the same crime, the accomplice faces the same criminal penalties.
- **Obstruction of justice (UNCAC, article 25).** Consists of
  (a) the use of physical force, threats, or intimidation; or the promise, offering, or giving of an undue advantage to induce false testimony or to interfere in the giving of testimony or the production of evidence in a proceeding in relation to the commission of offenses established in accordance with this convention; and
  (b) the use of physical force, threats, or intimidation to interfere with the exercise of official duties by a justice or law enforcement official in relation to the commission of offenses established in accordance with this convention.

Appendix B. Explanation of Selected Corporate Vehicles and Business Terms

"Corporate vehicle" is a broad concept that refers to all forms of legal entities and legal arrangements through which a wide variety of commercial activities are conducted and assets are held. Below are definitions, descriptions, and examples of a range of such vehicles and related business terms.

Agency: Under an agency relationship, the principal (normally, the client) engages an agent to perform duties by agreement. Examples of a principal agent relationship are client and attorney/accountant or employer and employee. An agent may create a corporate vehicle or open a bank account or perform management services on behalf of the principal, but may not do so in his or her own name. Unlike a trust, there is no conveyance of title to the account assets when the agency relationship is established; legal title to the property remains with the principal.

Association: This is a membership-based organization whose members (legal or natural persons) or their elected representatives constitute the highest governing body of the organization. An association may be formed to serve the public benefit or the mutual interest of members. Whether an association is a legal entity often depends on registration. Registered associations may enjoy the same benefits as other legal entities.

Bearer share: This negotiable instrument accords ownership of a corporation to the person who possesses the bearer share certificate. The person who has physical possession of the bearer share certificate is deemed to be the lawful shareholder of the corporation that issues such bearer share, and he or she is entitled to all of the rights of a shareholder. Many jurisdictions have introduced safeguards to ensure that these instruments are not abused—for example, immobilization or dematerialism. Immobilization requires that bearer shares be deposited with the authorities or a licensed corporate service provider. Bearer shares are dematerialized when the bearer shareholder must report his or her identity to vote the shares, collect their dividends, or hold a certain level of control.

Beneficial owner: A beneficial owner is the natural person who ultimately owns or controls the corporate vehicle or benefits from its assets, the person on whose behalf a transaction is being conducted, or both. The term also encompasses those persons who exercise ultimate effective control over a legal person or arrangement.

Chain of corporate vehicles: This term generally refers to groups of two or more corporate vehicles connected through legal ownership.

Control: The term means the direct or indirect possession of the power to direct or cause the direction of the management and policies of a corporate vehicle.

Corporate director: These are corporate entities, not natural persons, that serve as and perform the duties of a director for another corporate entity.

Corporation: Corporations maintain a legal personality separate from their shareholders, the owners. Control of a corporation is ordinarily vested in the board of directors, and shareholders have limited power to manage the corporation directly. Powers granted to shareholders usually include the right to elect directors, to participate and vote in general shareholders' meetings, and to approve extraordinary transactions that effectively result in the sale of the company. A corporation typically enjoys unlimited duration. In most cases, the shareholders of a corporation are granted limited liability protection, which means that their liability to the company and the company's creditors is limited to their investment. Many offshore jurisdictions offer registration for foreign/offshore companies and international business corporations/exempt companies. Foreign/offshore companies are companies incorporated in a different jurisdiction, but registered to do business in the host jurisdiction. International business corporations/exempt companies are companies incorporated in the host jurisdiction, but not permitted to do local business. These latter firms generally receive an exemption from local taxes.

Designated nonfinancial businesses and professions: This term encompasses casinos (including Internet-based casinos), real estate agents, dealers in precious metals, dealers in precious stones, lawyers, notaries, other independent legal professionals and accountants, and trust and company service providers.

Enforcer: For a purpose trust or a foundation, an enforcer is the person who holds the rights to enforce the trust and to apply to the courts, if necessary. For charitable trusts, the enforcer is usually the senior law officer of the jurisdiction—the attorney general or some equivalent authority. But for non-charitable purpose trusts, a separate person, accountable to the court, is appointed.

Foreign/offshore company: These companies are incorporated in a different jurisdiction, but registered to do business in the host jurisdiction.

Foundation: A foundation is a legal entity that consists of a property that has been transferred into it to serve a particular purpose and has no owners or shareholders. Foundations are ordinarily managed by a board of directors, according to the terms of a foundation document or constitution. Some jurisdictions restrict foundations to public purposes (public foundations); other jurisdictions allow foundations to be established to fulfill private purposes (private foundations). Common law jurisdictions generally permit the formation of companies limited by guarantee (essentially equivalent to a civil law foundation), but regulated by company law. Some of these jurisdictions also permit companies to be limited by guarantee and have shares (hybrid companies). A hybrid functions as a foundation, but issues shares like a company.

International business corporation (IBC): This vehicle, sometimes called an exempt company, is the primary corporate form employed by nonresidents in offshore financial centers. An IBC has the features of a corporation, but is not permitted to conduct business within the incorporating jurisdiction and is generally exempt from local income taxes. In most jurisdictions, an IBC is not permitted to engage in banking, insurance, and other financial services.

Legal owner: The legal owner of a corporate vehicle is defined as the natural person, legal entity, or combination of both recognized by law as the owner of the corporate vehicle.

Legal person: The term refers to bodies corporate, foundations, anstalts, partnerships, associations, or any similar bodies that may establish a permanent customer relationship with a financial institution or otherwise own property.

Letter of wishes: This letter, which often accompanies discretionary trusts, sets out the settlor's wishes regarding how he or she desires the trustee to carry out trustee duties, from whom the trustee should accept instructions, and who the beneficiaries should be (may include the settlor himself or herself). Although a letter of wishes is not legally binding on trustees, the trustee usually follows the wishes expressed there.

Limited liability company (LLC): This is a business entity that provides limited liability to its owners (known as members). Unlike a corporation that has a legal personality separate from its owners, an LLC is deemed to be a flow-through vehicle for tax purposes. Therefore, it permits profits and losses to be allocated to, and taxed at, the member level. An LLC may be managed either by members themselves or by one or more separate managers engaged by the LLC under the terms contained within its articles of organization.

Nominee director: This person appears as the registered director in a company on behalf of another person (normally undisclosed) who is called the beneficial owner. In some nominee director arrangements, a confidential legal document (such as a mandate agreement, a nominee services agreement, or something similar) is issued by the nominee and held by the beneficial owner. When the nominee director is a corporate entity, the nominee is referred to as a corporate director. Certain jurisdictions do not recognize nominee directors. Consequently, a person who accepts a directorship is subject to all of the requirements and obligations of a director (including fiduciary obligations), notwithstanding the fact that he or she is acting as a nominee. In certain jurisdictions, nominee directors cannot be indemnified by the beneficial owner.

Nominee shareholder: This is a company or person who appears as the registered shareholder in a company, but who holds the shares on behalf of another person (normally undisclosed) who is called the beneficial owner. Sometimes, in a nominee shareholder arrangement, a confidential legal document (such as a declaration of trust, a deed of transfer, a nominee services agreement, or something similar) is issued by the nominee and held by the beneficial owner. With respect to publicly traded shares, nominees who, for example, are registering shares in the names of stockbrokers are commonly and legitimately used to facilitate the clearance and settlement of trades.

Partnership: A partnership is an association of two or more individuals or entities formed for the purpose of carrying out business activity. In contrast to corporations, traditional partnerships are entities in which at least one (in the case of limited partnerships) or all (in the case of general partnerships) partners have unlimited liability for the obligations of the partnership. In a limited partnership, the limited partners enjoy limited liability, provided that they do not participate actively in management decisions or bind the partnership. In recent years, certain jurisdictions have introduced limited liability partnerships whereby all partners, regardless of the extent of their involvement in the management of the partnership, have limited liability. For tax purposes, partnerships are deemed to be flow-through vehicles that permit profits and losses to be allocated to and taxed at the partner level.

Power of attorney: A power of attorney or letter of attorney in common law systems, or a mandate in civil law systems, is an authorization to act on someone else's behalf in a legal or business matter. The person authorizing the other to act is the principal, grantor, or donor of the power; and the one authorized to act is the agent, the attorney-in-fact, or (in many common law jurisdictions) simply the attorney.

Private trust company (PTC): This vehicle is a corporation formed for the express and sole purpose of acting as the trustee of a specific trust or a group of trusts, where each trust beneficiary is a connected person in relation to the settlor of the trust, and each settlor of such a trust is a connected person in relation to any other settlor of any other trust to which that corporation provides trust business services. "Connected person" includes all relationships established by blood, marriage, and adoption. PTCs must not solicit trust business from nor provide trust business services to the public. Normally, a PTC will be managed by its board of directors, comprising a combination of family members or representatives and professionals who are experienced in trust law and administration.

Protector: The protector to a company, trust, or foundation is the person who is given supervisory power over the company, trust, or foundation. The supervisory power granted to the protector is determined by the incorporator, settlor, or founder. Although the protector is not a trustee, director, or foundation council, he or she does have the right to full information—including the right to attend organizational meetings. The protector may also have veto powers in certain key areas, such as fees, the timing and recipients of distributions, and the appointment of beneficiaries; and may have the power to hire and fire trustees and directors.

Purpose trust: In this trust, the trust fund is held by the trustees to meet prescribed purposes rather than for the benefit of the beneficiaries. Purpose trusts may be charitable or non-charitable, depending on the jurisdiction. Asset protection trusts are a type of purpose trust.

Shelf company: This term is generally used to describe an arrangement where a company is incorporated (with a standard memorandum or articles of association and with inactive shareholders, directors, and secretary) and left dormant for the purpose of later being sold. When the shelf company is sold, the inactive shareholders transfer their shares to the purchaser, and the directors and secretary submit their resignations. On transfer, the purchaser also receives the companies' credit and tax history.

Shell company: This company has no independent operations, significant assets, ongoing business activities, or employees. Shell companies are not illegal and may have legitimate business purposes.

Trust: This vehicle provides for the separation of legal ownership from beneficial ownership. It is an arrangement whereby property (including real, tangible, and intangible) is managed by one person for the benefit of others. A trust is created by one or more settlors who entrust property to the trustee or trustees. The trustees hold legal title to the trust property, but are obliged to hold the property for the benefit of the beneficiaries (usually specified by the settlors who hold what is termed equitable title). The trustees owe a fiduciary duty to the beneficiaries, who are the beneficial owners of the trust property. The trust is not, of itself, an entity having legal personality. Any transactions undertaken by the trust are undertaken in the names of the trustees. Although the trustees are the legal owners, the trust property constitutes a separate fund that does not form part of the trustees' personal estates. Thus, neither the personal assets nor the personal liabilities of the trustees attach to the trust, and the trust assets are accordingly insulated from any personal creditors of the trustees.

Trust and company service provider: The term refers to any person or business providing any of the following services to third parties: acting as a formation agent of legal persons; acting as (or arranging for another person to act as) a director or secretary of a company, a partner of a partnership, or a similar position in relation to other legal persons; providing a registered office, business address or accommodation, a correspondence address, or an administrative address for a company, partnership, or any other legal person or arrangement; acting as (or arranging for another person to act as) a trustee of an express trust; acting as (or arranging for another person to act as) a nominee shareholder for another person.

Appendix C. Sample Financial Intelligence Unit Report

Financial Intelligence Unit

To   :   Chief of Police, Prosecutor's Office, or Other Competent Authority
From   :   Director, Financial Intelligence Unit
Date   :   March 1, 2010
Subject :   **John Smith Charity Fund**

STRICTLY CONFIDENTIAL

This document is confidential and is to be considered as law enforcement–sensitive financial information. The data contained in this document are to be used only for intelligence purposes; are not to be disseminated or disclosed, in whole or in part, to any person, agency, or organization; and may not be used in any judicial or administrative proceeding, without the prior written consent of the financial intelligence unit.

This case was initiated by the financial intelligence unit (FIU) after the FIU received a suspicious transaction report (STR) indicating there are irregularities in an account related to the **John Smith Charity Fund**. The irregularities indicate that the **John Smith Charity Fund** could be involved in possible money laundering violations or in violation of other provisions of the Money Laundering Act.

On January 25, 2010, the FIU received an STR concerning suspicious transactions of the **John Smith Charity Fund**. The FIU discovered that account number **17026557** was involved in roughly **48** suspicious transactions of **$9,000.00** each. This account number belongs to a nongovernmental organization (NGO) named the **John Smith Charity Fund**. This NGO was registered with number **5110282** as the **John Smith Charity Fund** on March 23, 2007, under Regulation 1985, section 18 on the Registration and Operation of NGOs. Registration certificate carries serial number **99951**. Contact address of this NGO is **100 Palm Street, Smithville, Smith Islands,** mobile number **255-401-050**, fax number **251-401-202**. General activity of this NGO as stipulated within the registration documents is "Developing of donations from Smith Island citizens, and from institutions and nongovernment organizations and charity organizations, organizing of concerts, theatre plays, and sports matches." There are three founders of this NGO:

1. **Robert FRANK,** D.O.B. May 1, 1970, in Jonesville, Smith Islands; **ID 1000718145;** address 195 Palm Street, Smithville; mobile 255-505-233; current minister of

sports and gaming; member of Alliance for the Smith Islands (ASI) political party; first cousin of the current prime minister, Thomas MARK.

2. **Betty FRANK**, D.O.B. May 17, 1975, in Jonesville, Smith Islands; **ID 1009875847**; address 195 Palm Street, Smithville; mobile 255-211-440; email betty.frank@ gmail.com; spouse of Robert FRANK.

3. **Anthony SMITH**, D.O.B. June 14, 1965, in Marksville, Smith Islands; **ID 1000719109;** address 8097 Yankee Way, Marksville; mobile 255-540-050; email tony.smith@gmail.com; person authorized to open and operate the **John Smith Charity Fund** bank accounts in Peoples Bank, Mountain Bank, and River Bank; businessman, co-owner of Smithville Brewery; second cousin of Robert FRANK; current adviser to Prime Minister MARK, and treasurer of ASI political party.

Account 17026557 opened in Peoples Bank. Peoples Bank holds the above-mentioned account, no. **17026557**. Between March 31, 2008, and January 3, 2009, it recorded a total cash flow of $733,987.52. **Anthony SMITH** signed the deposit orders for the suspicious deposits described above. On at least three occasions, **SMITH** went to Peoples Bank with several hundred thousand dollars in new $100 notes in stacks of 100 notes each. He told bank officials that the money represented donations to the **John Smith Charity Fund** from several people, and that he was there to deposit the money into the fund account. On each occasion, he proceeded to complete several deposit orders, mostly in the sum of $9,000 (although a few were for lesser sums), signing each deposit order with his own name. At present, no information is available regarding the actual source of the currency deposited.

Between August 19, 2008, and June 24, 2009, a total amount of $492,000 was deposited in this account. Most of this money was 48 deposits of $9,000. Money was deposited as follows:

Date	Number of deposits	Value/deposit ($)
08/19/2008	5	9,000
09/05/2008	20	9,000
09/05/2008	1	10,000
09/05/2008	3	5,000
09/06/2008	20	9,000
09/06/2008	7	5,000
09/20/2008	2	9,000
10/03/2008	1	9,000

There were roughly 59 transactions in the **fund account.** Most of the roughly **48 cash deposits** were for $9,000, and were deposited by one individual. The NGO **John Smith Charity Fund** opened accounts in all banks that operate in the Smith Islands. **Anthony SMITH** is an authorized person on all of the accounts. Since **January 1, 2008,** the total turnover in these accounts is roughly $1,766,039.47.

Appendix D. Planning the Execution of a Search and Seizure Warrant

- Identify assets in bank accounts and take steps to secure them, either in advance of the search or simultaneously (for example, through freezing orders).
- Identify the type of location to be searched—residence, business.
- Determine the probability that civilians or non-targets will be present, and plan accordingly. Avoid peak business times, if possible.
- Consider closing the business during execution of the warrant, if appropriate.
- Determine the number of officers required to conduct a safe and thorough search.
- Take necessary precautions to maintain operational integrity. Don't let the target(s) get word of an impending search.
- Execute the warrant in accordance with the authorization—that is, during normal business hours.
- If permitted by law and if beneficial to the investigation, consider executing the search warrant after normal business hours.
- Determine if the location is outfitted with an alarm system or has armed security personnel, cameras, canine patrol, and the like. Plan the operation accordingly.
- Provide a comprehensive briefing to all officers involved in the execution of the warrant.
- Include in the briefing any relevant intelligence about the target(s) and location(s) to be searched.
- Provide maps, schematic drawings, or other pertinent information about the residence(s) or business(es), if available.
- Assign a role to each officer involved in the warrant execution. Assignments should be made by the lead investigator. Some of these roles include the following:
  - An *entry team* enters first and secures the premises so that other officers can conduct a safe and thorough search. This team should disconnect telephone lines when it enters the premises.
  - A *perimeter team* may be useful when conducting a search in a hostile environment. These officers provide security in the area and allow the search team to conduct a safe and thorough search.
  - *Search officers* work in teams of two, if possible, to help avoid or refute any accusations of evidence planting. The lead investigator may identify specific places to be searched by each team.
  - A *videographer/photographer* records the execution of the warrant and documents where evidence is discovered. Where it is appropriate, remember to

demonstrate scale when taking photos: place a ruler or other object that indicates size alongside object(s) being photographed.

- An *evidence custodian* receives and records all evidence discovered and seized by search officers, thus maintaining a chain of custody record.

- An *interview team*, including the lead investigator, should be identified during the planning stage. If target(s) are present and agree to be interviewed, questioning should occur in an area that is conducive to interviews and does not impede the ongoing search.

- A *computer forensic specialist* may be helpful in gathering and securing evidence. Electronic and computer data must be gathered in a manner that avoids its loss, destruction, or damage; and that avoids potential claims by the suspect that the data were subsequently manipulated by law enforcement officials (for example, by preparing a mirror copy of the data). If there are no trained computer forensic experts within the investigator's unit or other related units, the investigator should consider securing such services from the private sector or requesting assistance from other jurisdictions that have this capacity.

Appendix E. Sample Document Production Order for Financial Institutions

Document Production Order to BANK ABC to Be Served on an Authorized Official of BANK ABC

Re: Investigation of

- Account number 12345678 at BANK ABC in the name of John Doe
- XYZ Company incorporated in Delaware, United States; with a registered agent in Douglas, Isle of Man; and an office in London, England.
- Unknown beneficial owners of accounts or funds related to the persons and entities above.

The Order to Produce Documents

In accordance with *[applicable law]*, the authorized representative of BANK ABC is commanded to produce the documents identified below to the public prosecutor's office *[judge, investigating magistrate, or other appropriate authority]* on *[date]*. An intentional failure to comply with this document production order is a criminal offense punishable by fine, imprisonment, or both.

[Where authorized by law] BANK ABC is ordered not to disclose to anyone outside of BANK ABC the fact of this production order, the identity of the subjects of the production order, or the documents ordered produced. Nor is it to disclose what is produced to the public prosecutor's office *[judge, investigating magistrate, or other appropriate authority]* until further order.

This order shall cover the time period from *[date]* to *[date]* or beginning the date this order is received by BANK ABC.

The order shall cover all documents related to the individuals, legal entities, and beneficial owners listed above, either individually or in combination with any other individual or legal entity; and documents for accounts for which these individuals are/were trustees, have/had signature authority, power of attorney, or the authority to transact business. This includes but is not limited to the following:

Account Opening, Client Identification, and Instructions

1. Account opening documents for any service or line of business provided by BANK ABC, including but not limited to any subsidiary and correspondent institution;

and, if applicable, closing documents for all accounts related to the individuals and legal entities listed above. For XYZ Company, the documents should include articles of incorporation, corporate resolutions and minutes, partnership agreements, powers of attorney, and signature cards (front and back) related to any person or beneficial owner referenced above.

2. Bank statements, periodic statements, and transcripts of accounts for any person or beneficial owner referenced above.

3. The identity of the beneficial owner of any account related to any person referenced above, and the documents in which this information appears. This is to include but is not limited to all supporting documentation submitted by the contracting party or beneficial owner or prepared by any financial institution, employee, or third party on behalf of the contracting party or the beneficial owner.

4. Information obtained by BANK ABC relating to the identification and verification of any person or beneficial owner referenced above.

5. National identity numbers, tax numbers, customer identification numbers, date and place of birth, and any reference number or method (other than the account number) used by BANK ABC to identify any person or beneficial owner referenced above.

6. For any person referenced above, any safe deposit box contract, identity of all persons with access to the box, documents showing dates when the safe deposit was accessed, and any video or other electronic medium showing the authorized person(s) who visited the safe deposit box area.

7. Client instructions regarding when and how account statements are to be delivered; and client instructions regarding mail, electronic, or voice contact by BANK ABC.

8. The identity of any BANK ABC employee who has or had any responsibility for dealing with or handling the accounts of any person or beneficial owner referenced above.

9. All records of charges for local and long-distance telephone calls, including telephone bills; and all records of charges for other communication services, telexes, courier and mail services incurred by or on behalf of any person or beneficial owner referenced above. In each case where there has been contact, the bank official who had the contact is to be identified; and any notes, documents, and information given or received during the contact or the sending or receiving of packages, letters, faxes, and e-mails are to be produced.

Due Diligence Documentation

10. The "know your customer" due diligence documents prepared by BANK ABC on any person or beneficial owner referenced above.

11. Where a person related to a transaction, account, wire transfer, Society for Worldwide Interbank Financial Telecommunications (SWIFT) message, or other action identified by this order has been identified by BANK ABC as a beneficial owner or a politically exposed person (PEP) (as defined in your bank policies and procedures), provide

a. all due diligence and enhanced due diligence files created;
b. documents identifying the rules and alerts placed in your processing and compliance systems to identify and segregate transactions related to the clients, accounts, identified PEPs, other public officials, those who have recently left public office, and beneficial owners; and the documents related to any transactions or question that triggered an alert; and
c. the identity of any BANK ABC employee handling the due diligence files and the alert systems related to this order.

Incoming and Outgoing Wire Transfers and Related Documents

12. Documents related to incoming and outgoing, domestic or cross-border funds transfers (for example, by Fedwire, CHIPS, or CHAPS) for or on behalf of any person or beneficial owner referenced above, including but not limited to, wire transfer request forms, advice statements, confirmation statements, debit memos, journal entries, or internal logs.
13. Documents related to SWIFT messages originating, terminating, or passing through BANK ABC and any related intermediary or correspondent institution, for or on behalf of any person or beneficial owner referenced above, including but not limited to
    a. SWIFT messages, including but not limited to SWIFT MT 100, MT 103, MT 202, MT 202 Cov, MT 199, and MT299 messages and any other SWIFT message (including those related to securities and trade transactions);
    b. fax, mail, e-mail, or telephone instructions; wire transfer request forms; advice statements; confirmation statements; debit memos; journal entries; or internal logs; and
    c. any "repair items" or rejected funds transfers or SWIFT messages; and any documents related to the repair and retransmission of the funds transfer or SWIFT message related to the persons, legal entities, and beneficial owners referenced above.
14. SWIFT bank identifier codes (BICs) for BANK ABC, including its business lines (for example, private banking), subsidiaries, and branches for which the codes differ from the main BIC code.
15. All names by which BANK ABC and its subsidiaries are identified.

Account Transactions

16. Documents related to funds that went into or out of any BANK ABC account related to any person or beneficial owner referenced above, including client orders, deposit slips, deposit items (front and back), withdrawal slips and cancelled checks (front and back), debit and credit memos, book transfers, and interbank transfer slips related to any person or beneficial owner referenced above.
17. Documents sent to or received from any intermediary or correspondent financial institution related to any person or beneficial owner referenced above.

Other Transactions

18. Copies of certificates of deposit, including interest payments, redemption records, and disposition of the proceeds regarding any person or beneficial owner referenced above.
19. Records of purchase or sale of bearer bonds or other securities by any person or beneficial owner referenced above.
20. Documents for purchase of manager's checks, cashier's checks, and bank money orders, together with the checks that were purchased by or on behalf of any person or beneficial owner referenced above.

BANK ABC Submissions to Financial Intelligence Units [where authorized]

21. Currency transaction reports relating in any manner to the persons or beneficial owners referenced above.
22. Currency and monetary instruments reports relating in any manner to the persons or beneficial owners referenced above.
23. Suspicious activity/transaction reports filed, relating in any manner to the persons or beneficial owners referenced above.

Include all additional documents that may have connection to the offense committed.

Definitions and Instructions

A. The terms "BANK ABC" and "XYZ Company" shall mean the business entity to which this order is addressed. It shall include all of the entity's affiliates, joint ventures, subsidiaries, subdivisions, and successors in interest; and all of its present and former directors, officers, partners, employees, agents, and other persons purporting to act on behalf of any of the foregoing.
B. The term "document(s)" means all written or printed matter of any kind, formal or informal, including the originals and all non-identical copies thereof (whether different from the original by reason of any notation made on such copies or otherwise) in the possession, custody, or control of the Company, wherever located, including, without limitation, papers, correspondence, memoranda, notes, diaries, statistical materials, letters, telegrams, minutes, contracts, reports, studies, checks, statements, receipts, returns, summaries, pamphlets, books, interoffice and intraoffice communications, offers, notations of any sort of conversations, telephone calls, meetings or other communications, bulletins, credit matter, computer printouts, hard discs, flash drives, removable hard drives, floppy discs, mainframe and personal computer databases, teletypes, telex materials, invoices, worksheets; all drafts, alterations, modifications, changes, and amendments of any nature or kind to the foregoing. Also included are all graphic and aural records or representations of any kind, videotapes, sound recordings, and motion pictures; any electronic, mechanical, or electrical recordings, including without limitation tapes, cassettes, discs, recordings, and films.

C. The term "document(s)" also means any container, file folder, or other enclosure bearing any marking or identification, in which other "documents" are kept; but it does not include file cabinets. In all cases where any original or non-identical copy of any original is not in the possession, custody, or control of the legal entity to which this production order is directed, the term "document(s)" shall include any copy of the original and any non-identical copy thereof.

D. The word "and" should be interpreted as including "or," and vice versa.

E. The term "person" shall mean any natural person, legal entity, proprietorship, corporation, partnership, joint venture, unincorporated association, and governmental agency; or any subdivision, affiliate, officer, director, employee, agent, or other representative thereof.

F. The term "beneficial owner" includes the natural person(s) who ultimately owns or controls a customer and/or the person on whose behalf the transaction is being conducted. It also incorporates those persons who exercise ultimate effective control of a legal person or arrangement, and relevant third parties.

G. The term "identity" shall mean the full name, including middle name; date of birth; place of birth; national identity or passport number; all positions held during employment; dates of service; responsibilities and duties in each position; termination date, if any; and the reasons for such termination.

H. "Public official" shall mean (1) any person holding a legislative, executive, administrative, or judicial office, whether appointed or elected, whether permanent or temporary, whether paid or unpaid, irrespective of that person's seniority; (2) any other person who performs a public function, including for a public agency or public enterprise, or provides a public service.

I. The terms "wire transfer" and "funds transfer" refer to any transaction carried out on behalf of a person through a financial institution by electronic means, with a view to making an amount of money available to a beneficiary person at another financial institution. The originator and the beneficiary may be the same person.

J. "Cross-border transfer" means any wire transfer for which the originator and beneficiary institutions are located in different countries. The term also refers to any chain of wire transfers that involve at least one cross-border element.

K. The "originator" is the account holder; where there is no account, the originator is the person who places the order with the financial institution.

L. "SWIFT" refers to the Society for Worldwide Interbank Financial Telecommunications.

M. "CHIPS" refers to the Clearing House Interbank Payments System.

N. "Fedwire" refers to the electronic funds transfer system owned and operated by the U.S. Federal Reserve System.

O. "CHAPS" refers to the Clearing House Automated Payments System, which offers same-day sterling and euro fund transfers.

Claim of Privilege

If any document is withheld by BANK ABC under claim of privilege, including the attorney-client privilege, BANK ABC shall furnish a schedule setting forth the date; the name and title of the author, addressee, recipient; and the subject matter of each such document, the nature of the privilege claimed, the basis on which it is claimed, and the paragraph of this order to which each such document is responsive.

Identifying Documents

To facilitate the handling of documents submitted pursuant to this order, to preserve their identity, and to ensure their accurate and expeditious return, it is requested that each document be marked with an identifying number and that the documents be numbered consecutively. Only the first page of multipage, bound documents should be numbered; and the total number of pages in a document should be noted. Documents should also remain within the file folders in which they were located at the time this order is served. Such file folders should also be numbered as if they were another document. Within each file folder, documents should remain in the same order they were at the time this order is served. Multipage documents should remain intact.

Document Production

The person appearing before the court or prosecutor in response to this order must be a person who is fully knowledgeable concerning BANK ABC's search for the documents responsive to this order, as well as one who can authenticate the documents as business records. Should the same person not be competent to perform both requirements, BANK ABC should designate such additional persons as may be necessary to appear on the same time and date.

Documents that exist in an electronic format should be produced electronically along with a paper copy certified by the BANK ABC custodian of records to be a true and accurate copy of the electronic original. All electronic documents should be produced in a form that is reasonably usable and searchable without the use of any specialized software.

Originals Required

This order requires the production of the originals of all documents ordered herein, except as particularly noted below. Submission of photocopies in lieu of originals shall not comply with this order.

Appendix F. Serial and Cover Payment Methods in Electronic Funds Transfers

Society for Worldwide Interbank Financial Telecommunications (SWIFT) messaging is an integral part of correspondent banking communication between financial institutions that do not have a direct account relationship with each other. SWIFT has developed fixed messaging formats for the two payment processing methods used between such institutions: the serial (or sequential) method and the cover method.

With the serial payment method, as figure F.1 depicts, a transfer is sent from the originating customer's financial institution through any correspondent banks and then on to the beneficiary customer's financial institution. The steps around this process are sequential in that clearing and settlement occur directly and at each point. Accordingly, relevant payment and customer information can be preserved along the way. The applicable SWIFT messaging format used for such a transfer is the MT 103—a direct payment order to a beneficiary bank that contains both originator and beneficiary information. MT 103s are the most heavily used message format on the SWIFT network, accounting for 15 percent of total SWIFT messaging volume.

The cover payment method also uses correspondent banks to intermediate transfers from one unrelated bank to another. However, as figure F.1 shows, the lack of a direct banking relationship requires correspondent accounts between banks to facilitate settlement. In this case, the originating bank may directly instruct the beneficiary bank to make payment to the customer and to advise that the transfer of funds to "cover" the payment obligation has been arranged through a separate interbank relationship. Settlement of the funds may then take place through another correspondent, if no relationship exists with the originating bank's correspondent bank and that of the beneficiary institution. In this way, the beneficiary customer can typically have his or her account credited by his or her own bank before interbank settlement is completed, especially where an established commercial relationship exists. Cover payments are also frequently used to help reduce overall transaction costs and the timing of commercial transactions for clearing banks.

In the context of SWIFT messaging, the bank-to-bank order to a correspondent bank to cover the originating bank's obligation to pay the ultimate beneficiary bank is effected through the use of an MT 202. These messages are used primarily for cover payments and settlement between financial institutions (for example, foreign exchange trades, payment of interest, and so forth). It is important to note that a correspondent bank that receives an MT 202 cover payment instruction does not receive an MT 103, which means that this bank is unable to monitor or filter payment details contained in an MT

Serial/Sequential Payment Chain

Originating Customer → Originating Bank — MT 103 → Originating Bank's Correspondent Bank — MT 103 → Beneficiary Bank's Correspondent Bank — MT 103 → Beneficiary Bank → Beneficiary Customer

Location: Country A | Location: Country B | Location: Country C

Cover Payment Chain

Originating Customer → Originating Bank — MT 103 → Beneficiary Bank → Beneficiary Customer

Originating Bank — MT 202 → Originating Bank's Correspondent Bank — MT 202[a] → Beneficiary Bank's Correspondent Bank — MT 9xx → Beneficiary Bank

Location: Country A | Location: Country B | Location: Country C

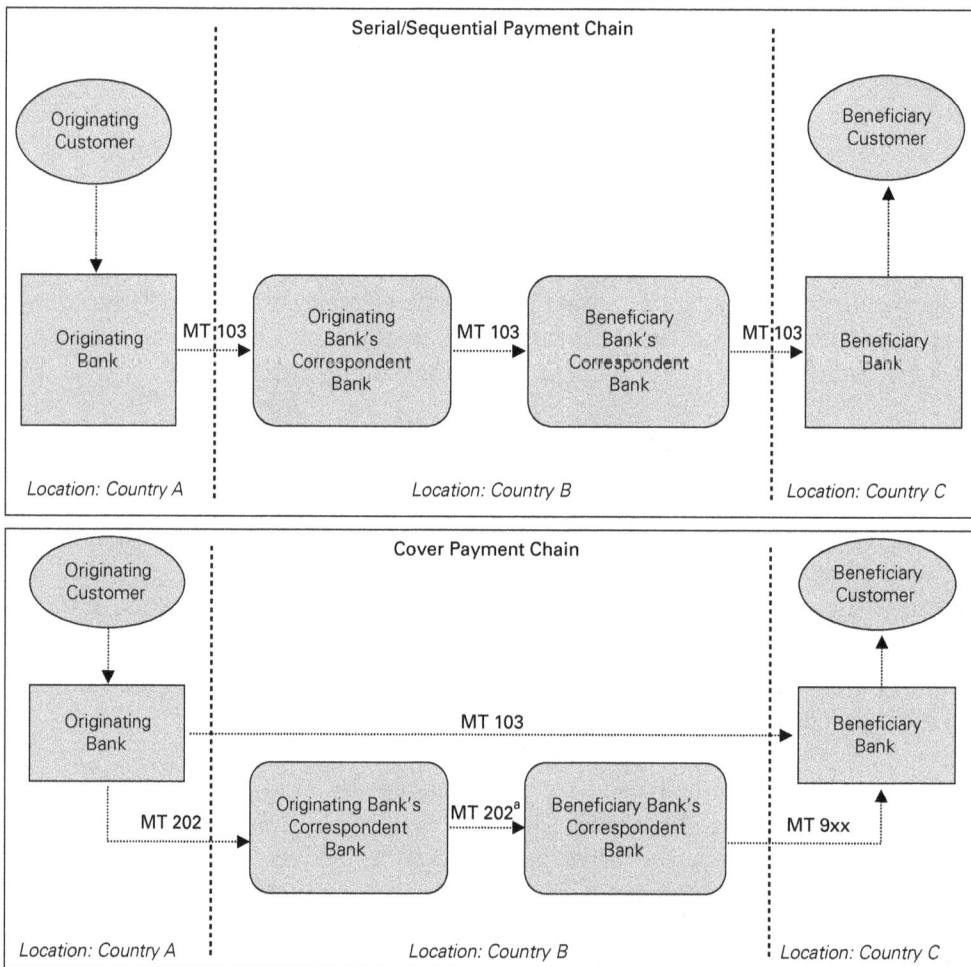

Source: Adapted from Basel Committee on Banking Supervision, "Due Diligence and Transparency Regarding Cover Payment Messages Related to Cross-Border Wire Transfers" (May 2009), p. 3.
a. Alternatively, this could be a local clearing system.

103 or to determine the purpose of the transfer (that is, cover payment or interbank settlement). For this reason, it is important that an investigator obtains all incoming and outgoing MT 103s related to a cover payment.

New Cover Payment Standards (MT 202 COV)

The Financial Action Task Force (FATF) has addressed only direct sequential payments (or SWIFT MT 103s) in which (as contemplated by FATF Special Recommendation VII on wire transfers) information sent to a beneficiary institution travels with the wire through the various intermediaries. The FATF has not dealt with cover payment scenarios in which payment information available to the originating financial institution is not communicated to correspondent banks involved in making the payments. As a

Hiding Originating Customer Information

To hide originator information, wire transfers may contain incomplete information, meaningless keystrokes, or false client names (such as "Mickey Mouse"). According to the Basel Committee on Banking Supervision, "[w]here fields are manifestly meaningless or incomplete, responses could include, for example, (i) contacting the originator's bank or precedent cover intermediary bank in order to clarify or complete the information received in the required fields; (ii) considering (in the case of repeated incidents involving the same correspondent or in the case where a correspondent declines to provide additional information) whether or not the relationship with the correspondent or the precedent cover intermediary bank should be restricted or terminated; banks should report such situations to their supervisor; and/or (iii) filing a report of suspicious activity with the local authorities, when the situation satisfies the local definition of reporting requirements."[a] These actions create internal bank records that will help the investigator trace and expose laundered funds.

Note: a. Basel Committee on Banking Supervision, "Due Diligence and Transparency Regarding Cover Payment Messages Related to Cross-Border Wire Transfers" (May 2009), para. 30.

Monitoring Records from Financial Institutions

Generally, financial institutions use two types of monitoring where wire transfers are concerned:

1. **Sanction screening.** Conducted automatically and in real time, the system will read the originator, beneficiary, and payment information; and will check for any name matching United Nations or other sanctions lists. If there is a match, the message will be segregated for review; and payment is either released for processing or the financial intelligence unit or other appropriate officials are notified. This entire process creates electronic and paper records that the investigator should subpoena from a bank and review.
2. **Back-end monitoring.** Performed after transmission, it uses a risk-based approach to look for patterns of activity that appear unusual or potentially suspicious. This process will also generate records that the investigator should subpoena from a bank and review.

result, particularly in the context of international funds transfers, the use of multiple financial institutions and reliance on interbanking relationships to facilitate transfers on behalf of a customer to a beneficiary located elsewhere (often in another country) has raised concerns about the preservation and transparency of information and possible implications for money laundering and terrorist financing activities (see box F.1 for further discussion of this issue).

As the leader in global interbank telecommunications, and in an effort to standardize international cover payment messaging practices in cross-border wire transfers, SWIFT developed new standards for all cover payments. These standards became effective in November 2009. The new MT 202 COV, which is simply a variant of the MT 202, is aimed at providing greater transparency by making all payment information available to the originating institution also available to other institutions in the payment process.

The MT 202 COV, which must now be used for all cover payments, replicates certain information fields from the MT 103 (namely, the originator and beneficiary information fields). The MT 202 may still be used for interbank settlement payments, but not for cover payments. The creation of this new standard now requires financial institutions, and specifically correspondent banks, to apply risk-based monitoring practices to customer and payment information to which they were not previously privy.

Although the MT 202 COV mandates the inclusion of all customer and financial institution identifying information, it is important to note that SWIFT does not play a role in validating or policing the standard. This responsibility falls to member institutions themselves. The SWIFT system will reject a transfer where the originator and beneficiary fields are blank; however, it is unable to determine if information entered in those fields contains false or incomplete data. Box F.2 describes two ways that financial institutions attempt to wire transfer information.

Appendix G. Sample Financial Profile Form

Financial Profile

Surname	URN

Last names	

Alias	Date of Birth

Address	

Commercial ☐   Drugs ☐

Criminal Case Officer ....   Team/Branch   ....
                                                Tel   ....

Financial Investigator ....   Team/Branch   ....
                                                Tel   ....

Criminal Case Solicitor ....
                                                Tel ....   Fax ....

Criminal Case Counsel ....
                                                Tel ....   Fax ....

Financial Solicitor ....
                                                Tel ....   Fax ....

Financial Counsel ....
                                                Tel ....   Fax ....

Forensic Accountant ....
                                                Tel ....   Fax ....

Financial Profile — Index & Check Sheet

Part 1: Personal Financial Profile

ASSETS	Cash/valuables seized	
	Bank accounts	
	Other bank/building society accounts	
	National savings	
	Premium bonds	
	Shares	
	Unit trusts	
	Life policies/endowments	
	Motor vehicles	
	Boats/caravans etc.	
	Other	
	Value of gifts to third parties	
LIABILITIES	Credit cards	
	Store cards	
	Credit agreements	
	Maintenance/CSA payment	
	Court judgments/fines/previous forfeiture orders	
	Other liabilities/debts	
	Overdraft current	
	Personal solvency	
DECLARED INCOME	Employment	
	Previous employment	
	Income tax details	
	Other sources of income in property	
PROPERTY	Property details	
	Occupiers	
	Rented property	
	Owned property	
	Value	
	Mortgage	
	Other property charges	
	Ground rent (leasehold)	
	Third-party interest	
	House contents	

UTILITIES (Property Liabilities)	Community charge	
	Water rates	
	Electricity	
	Gas	
	Telephone	
	Mobile telephone	
	Property insurance	

Part 2: Business Financial Profile

BUSINESS ASSETS	Bank accounts	
	Motor vehicles	
	Plant/machinery etc.	
	Office/trade fixtures and fittings	
	Other valuable property	
	Stock in trade	
	Work in progress	
	Fully secured debtors	
	Partly secured debtors	
BUSINESS LIABILITIES	Employees	
	Fully secured creditors	
	Partly secured creditors	
	Credit cards	
	Debit cards	
	Credit agreements	
	Direct debit/standing orders	
	Court judgments	
	Winding-up order/voluntary liquidation	
	Other contractual liabilities	
	Corporation tax/income tax	
	Value added tax	
BUSINESS INTEREST	Preliminary assessment	
	Trading partnership/company	
	Company directors/partners	
	Company's documentation	
	Interest in business	
	Realizable property held by business	

BUSINESS PREMISES	Assets	
	Other occupiers	
	Liabilities	
	Mortgage (business)	
	Other charges on property	
	Rates/business expenses	
	Water rates (business)	
	Electricity (business)	
	Gas (business)	
	Telephone (business)	
	Premises insurance (business)	
	Contents insurance (business)	
	Company insurance claims	

Part 1: Personal Financial Profile of ....

DECLARED INCOME

Employment

	Current Employment	Previous Employment
Name of employer or self-employed:		
Occupation:		
Net income:		
Weekly/monthly or annually:		
Commencement date:		
Leaving date:		
Notes:		

Income Tax Details

Period covered:	
Tax reference number:	
Tax paid:	
Tax office:	
Notes:	

Other Sources of Income

Source of income	
Notes:	

PROPERTY

Property Details

	Current Property	Previous Address
Full address and postcode:		
Date of purchase:		
Purchase price:		
Current value:		
Date last value:		
Valuer's name and address:		
Name in which property held:		
Mortgage/charges:		
Land registry office copy, attached (Y/N), and date:		
Notes:		

Mortgage

Name of mortgagee:	
Address of mortgagee:	
Account name(s):	
Account number:	
Amount borrowed:	
Date commenced:	
Balance of account:	
Payment week/month:	
Method of payment:	
Arrears:	
Notes:	

Other Charges on Property

Charge holder:	
Address:	
Amount of charge:	
Date of charge:	
Reason for charge:	
Notes:	

Ground Rent (leasehold property)

Name of landlord:	
Address of landlord:	
Payable month/year:	
When due:	
Method of payment:	
Notes:	

Third-Party Interest in Property

Status:	
Name:	
Amount:	
Contribution mortgage:	
Contribution expenses:	
Notes:	

House Contents (significant value only, antiques, paintings, jewelry, etc., and videos/photos)

Description	Value
Notes:	

UTILITIES (Property Liabilities) (include mortgage payments from above)

Community Charge

	Community Charge	Water Rates	Electricity	Gas
Authority paid:				
Payable annually:				
When and how paid:				
Current arrears:				
Notes:				

Telephone

	Telephone	Mobile Telephone
Telephone number:		
Authority paid:		
Payable annually:		
When and how paid:		
Current arrears:		
Itemized billing attached (Y/N):		
Notes:		

Property Insurance

Insurance company:	
Amount insured:	
Risks covered:	
Amount paid week/year:	
When paid:	
How paid:	
Any special risks:	
Notes:	

ASSETS

Cash/Valuables Seized by Police/Customs

Amount/value:	
Where deposited:	
Date of deposit:	
Deposit reference:	
From where seized:	
Restrained (Y/N):	
Notes:	

Bank/Building Society Accounts

Bank name:	
Bank address:	
Sort code:	
Account number:	
Type of account:	
Full name of account holder:	
Current balance:	
Annual credit turnover:	
Annual debit turnover:	
Notes:	

National Savings

Certificate numbers:	
Value:	
Where held:	
Amount held and dates of acquisition:	
Notes:	

Premium Bonds

Certificate numbers:	
Value:	
Where held:	
Amount held and dates of acquisition:	
Notes:	

Shares

	Quoted Shares	Nonquoted Shares
Name of company:		
Amount of holding:		
Location of certificates:		
Value of holding:		
Share transfer office:		
Notes:		

Unit Trusts

Description of trusts:		
Number of units held:		
Value:		
Name and address of holder:		
Notes:		

Life Policies/Endowments

Insurance company:	
Branch address:	
Policy details:	
Surrender value:	
Beneficiary:	
Premium amount week/month/year:	
How and when paid:	
Mortgage linked (Y/N):	
Notes:	

Motor Vehicles, Boats/Caravans, etc.

	Motor Vehicles	Boats/Caravans etc.
Make and model:		
Location:		
Registration mark (if applicable):		
Dealer's details (motor vehicles):		

	Motor Vehicles	Boats/Caravans etc.
Purchase price:		
Current value:		
(Registered) keeper:		
Hire purchase (Y/N):		
Name of company:		
Address of company:		
Date of agreement:		
Balance of agreement:		
Notes:		

Other Personal Property

Description	Holder	Location	Purchase Price	Value
Notes:				

Gifts to Third Parties

Description	Holder	Location	Purchase Price	Value

LIABILITIES

Credit Cards

Name of card, i.e., access:	
Amount owed or credit:	
Average payments:	
Name of holder:	
Notes:	

Store Cards

Name of card:	
Amount owed or credit:	
Average payments:	
Name of holder:	
Notes:	

Credit Agreements

Name of company:	
Branch:	
Purpose of loan:	
Amount borrowed:	
Amount owed:	
Monthly payments:	
Arrears:	
Notes:	

Maintenance Payment

Court/office:	
Date of order:	
Beneficiary:	
Amount of payment:	
When payable:	
Method of payment:	
Notes:	

Court Judgments/Fines/Previous Forfeiture Orders

Court:	
Date of order:	
Beneficiary:	
Amount of payment:	
When payable:	
Method of payment:	
Notes:	

Other Liabilities/Debts

Creditor:	
Creditor address:	
Amount of debt/liability:	
Particulars of debt:	
Notes:	

Actual Overdrafts

Bank:	
Address and telephone no.:	
Sort code/Account no.:	
Amount:	
Notes:	

Personal Solvency

Bankruptcy order (Y/N):	
Date of order:	
Trustee/official receiver:	
Address:	
Contact and telephone no.:	
Notes:	

Part 2: Business Financial Profile of . . . .

BUSINESS INTEREST

Preliminary Assessment

Sole trader and business premises are realizable property (Y/N):	
Substantial interest in partnership/limited company and interest is in itself realizable property (Y/N):	
Partnership/company holds realizable property (Y/N):	
Notes:	

Trading Partnership/Company

Name:	
Date commenced:	
Company registration no. (if applicable):	
VAT registration no.:	
Trading address:	
Registered address:	
Notes:	

Company Directors/Partners

Name:	
Address:	
Position:	
Notes:	

Company's Documentation

Company details (Y/N):		Dated:	
Financial accounts (Y/N):		Dated:	
Annual returns:		Dated:	
Notes:			

Subject's Interest in Business

Details	Value
Notes:	

Realizable Property Held by Business

Details	Value
Notes:	

BUSINESS PREMISES

Assets

Trading name:	
Business address:	
Freehold/leasehold/rented (if rented, see below):	
Registered land (Y/N):	
Title number:	
Purchase price:	
Date of purchase:	
Amount outstanding:	
Current arrears:	
Current value:	
Date last valued:	
Name of valuer:	
Address of valuer:	
Notes:	

Other Occupiers

Part of premises sublet (Y/N):	
Details of area 1 sublet:	
Name of lessee:	
Address of lessee:	
Amount paid:	
To whom paid:	
Details of area 2 sublet:	
Name of lessee:	
Address of lessee:	
Amount paid:	
To whom paid:	
Details of any third-party interest:	
Notes:	

Rented Premises

Landlord's name:	
Landlord's address:	
Rental week/month:	
How paid/by whom:	
Notes:	

Mortgage

Name of mortgagee:	
Address of mortgagee:	
Account number:	
Account name(s):	
Amount of loan:	
Payment week/month:	
How paid/by whom:	
Notes:	

Other Charges on Property

Name of charge holder:	
Address of charge holder:	
Amount of charge:	
Date of registration:	
Notes:	

Business Expenses

	Rates/ Business Charge	Water	Electricity	Gas	Telephone
Authority paid:					
Amount week/ month:					
Method of payment:					
Current arrears:					
Notes:					

Business Insurance

	Premises	Contents
Name of insurer:		
Address of insurer:		
Amount insured:		
Risks covered:		
Payment week/month:		
How/by whom paid:		
Notes:		

Company Insurance Claims

Insurance company:	
Date claimed:	
Claim type:	
Amount claimed:	
Amount paid:	
When paid:	
How paid:	
Copy of claim attached (Y/N):	
Notes:	

BUSINESS ASSETS

Business Bank Accounts

Name of bank:	
Branch address:	
Sort code:	
Account number:	
Account name(s):	
Current balance:	
Date of balance:	
Credit turnover:	
Debit turnover:	
Account signatories:	
Name:	
Notes:	

Motor Vehicles, Plant/Machinery, etc.

	Motor Vehicles	Plant/Machinery etc.
Make and model:		
Registration mark if applicable:		
Dealer's details (motor vehicles):		
Purchase price:		
Current value:		
(Registered) keeper:		
Hire purchase (Y/N):		
Name of company:		
Address of company:		
Date of agreement:		
Balance of agreement:		
Notes:		

Office/Trade Fixtures and Fittings

Make and model:	
Serial number:	
Purchase price:	
Current value:	
Lease purchase (Y/N):	
Name of lease company:	
Address of company:	
Date of agreement:	
Notes:	

Other Valuable Property

Details:	
Registration details if applicable:	
Purchase price:	
Current value:	
Keeper/location:	
Hire/lease purchase (Y/N):	
Name of company:	
Address of company:	

Date of agreement:	
Balance of agreement:	
Notes:	

Stock in Trade

Details	Value	Date of Value
Notes:		

Work in Progress

Details	Value	Date of Value
Notes:		

Fully Secured Debtors (Business)

Name	Address	Amount	Security
Notes:			

Partly Secured Debtors (Business)

Name	Address	Amount	Security
Notes:			

BUSINESS LIABILITIES

Employees

Full time:	
Part time:	
Outstanding wages:	
Notes:	

Fully Secured Creditors

Name	Address	Amount	Security
Notes:			

Partly Secured Creditors

Name	Address	Amount	Security
Notes:			

Credit Cards, Debit Cards

	Credit Cards	Debit Cards
Name of card:		
Amount owed or credit:		
Average payments:		
Name of holder:		
Notes:		

Credit Agreements (Business)

Name of company:	
Branch:	
Purpose of loan:	
Amount borrowed:	
Amount owed:	
Monthly payments:	
Arrears:	
Notes:	

Direct Debit/Standing Orders

Bank name:	
Branch details:	
Account number:	
Account name(s):	
Amount week/month:	

When due:	
Payable to:	
Notes:	

Court Judgments

Court:	
Date of order:	
Amount of order:	
Method of payment:	
Notes:	

Winding-Up Order/Voluntary Liquidation

Winding up (Y/N):	
Liquidation (Y/N):	
Date of order:	
Resolution:	
Notes:	

Other Contractual Liabilities

Details	Amount	When Payable
Notes:		

Corporation Tax/Income Tax

Tax inspector name:	
Tax inspector address:	
District:	
Reference number:	
Amount due:	
Notes:	

Value Added Tax

VAT office:	
Address:	
VAT registration no.:	
Amount due:	
Prosecutions pending (Y/N):	
Notes:	

Articles on Premises Controlled by Subject but Not Belonging to Subject (such as goods on hire, on loan, for repair, or otherwise claimed by some other person) (Supporting evidence of claim should be sought.)

Article	Value	Third-Party Interest
Notes:		

Source: Reproduced from Theodore S. Greenberg, Linda M. Samuel, Wingate Grant, and Larissa Gray, *Stolen Asset Recovery—A Good Practices Guide to Non-Conviction Based Asset Forfeiture* (Washington, DC: World Bank, 2009), 213.

Appendix H. Possible Discussion Points with Contacts—Informal Assistance Stage

Discussion Points

- Verify the information you have obtained.
- Obtain information and intelligence for asset tracing and investigation, including financial intelligence through financial intelligence units.
- Obtain background information to support mutual legal assistance (MLA) requests to trace and seize or restrain assets (for example, names, dates of birth, and addresses of witnesses; bank account locations; bank account numbers; link with the assets and the offense or offender).
- Confirm any requirements or procedures for obtaining noncoercive measures.
- Learn of any options for an emergency provisional measure (non-MLA) to avoid the risk of dissipation. If there are such options, what are the procedures and requirements?
- Define additional needs: urgency, confidentiality, procedures that must be followed.
- Review case strategy, including potential barriers to international cooperation, the best venue(s) for prosecution, the possibility of conducting a joint investigation or using case conferences.
- Where there are multiple investigative agencies, identify relevant agencies that could provide assistance.
- Review resource issues.
- Get guidance on next steps, including MLA requirements, processes, and contacts.

Issues to Keep in Mind (and Clarify with Counterpart before Discussing Substance)

- A memorandum of understanding may be required to share in some jurisdictions.
- Differences in legal traditions and confiscation systems may result in differences in what can be provided, what is required, and the process.
- Information you provide may be used by a foreign jurisdiction to open its own case.
- Information you request must be gathered lawfully in both the requested and the requesting jurisdictions.
- With large cases, consider joint investigation and a face-to-face meeting with counterparts.

Appendix I. Mutual Legal Assistance Template and Drafting Tips

Letter of Request

TO: [*Name and address of central authority in requested jurisdiction*]
FROM: [*Name and address of judge, prosecutor, central authority, or other competent authority under domestic law in requesting jurisdiction*]

[*I/we*] make this request pursuant to [*insert relevant domestic legislation authorizing request*]. [*I/we*] have the honor to request your assistance in relation to a criminal [*investigation or prosecution*] being conducted by [*name of agency*].

- *Include names and contact information of investigators and prosecutors leading the proceedings.*

Legal Basis

This request is made pursuant to [*cite legal basis (such as domestic or multilateral treaty)*].

Nature of the Criminal Matter

This request relates to [*prosecution against* or *ongoing investigation involving or restraint of assets suspected to be the proceeds of crime and subject to confiscation proceedings against*] the following individuals: [*list targets*]

- *Specify the assets to be restrained. Most often, it is best to list these assets in an appendix and reference that appendix here.*
- *List target(s), with as much information as possible—passport number, date and place of birth, nationality, address, employer.*

Assistance is sought in relation to the following offenses: [*list offenses with maximum penalty*].

- *For wording of offenses, it is best to use that which was used in the charge or proposed charge, with reference to the applicable statutory authority. Include extracts of relevant domestic law in an appendix and reference that appendix here.*

Purpose of the Request

In relation to this matter, the following is requested: [*state briefly the assistance required*].

- *Remember that MLA is a step-by-step process. Avoid asking for everything (documents, restraint, confiscation) in one request.*

Statement of Facts

[*Describe here the relevant facts of the case in a clear and concise manner.*]

- *There must be sufficient facts for the foreign authority to assess whether MLA requirements have been met (for example, dual criminality) and whether to grant the request. This necessitates a fact-gathering investigation in the requesting jurisdiction.*
- *Include an explanation of the link between the assets and the offense(s) or target(s).*
- *If requesting the use of coercive measures (for example, a search warrant or production order), include sufficient facts to show that the requirements in the requested jurisdiction are met. (For examples of requirements, see chapter 4.)*
- *Include in an appendix any documents that may assist in executing the request, and reference that appendix here. For example, certified court orders, affidavit or certificate supporting the application.*

Assistance Requested

[*State the assistance requested.*] We request that any mandatory court order or other order necessary to enable the provision of this assistance be sought.

- *The description of assistance should focus on what you are seeking—not the name of the measure for obtaining it—because measures used will vary among jurisdictions. For example, one jurisdiction will use a search and seizure order to obtain bank records, and another will use production orders.*
- *Provide sufficient justification for the request, particularly with coercive measures.*
- *Provide details of any procedures that must be followed in gathering evidence to ensure admissibility. Include oaths or warnings that are required or the format of the evidence— for example, witness statements must be taped, documents must be certified.*
- *For tracing efforts, provide as much information as possible on the location of the assets. Greater specificity will be required in requests for restraint and confiscation— name of account holder, account number, branch, amount to be restrained, location of property, and so forth.*
- *For restraint requests, it may be necessary to explain the risk of dissipation, confirm that a conviction likely will result in the assets being restrained (and listed in appendix), provide relevant statutory authority showing that the requesting country has extraterritorial jurisdiction over the assets, and explain any other restraint proceedings that have taken place.*

- *For interviews, consider including an appendix with a proposed line of questioning.*
- *To leave open the scope for additional information, an additional statement can be added (although it is not sufficient on its own). For example,* "It is also requested that such other inquiries be made and evidence gathered as appears to be necessary to further this investigation."

Confidentiality

[*If confidentiality is required, provide a statement requesting it and the reasons it is important.*]

Period of Execution

[*Provide details on when the information is needed. Include court dates, if applicable. Preserve "urgent" requests for cases of actual urgency.*]

Assurances or Undertakings

Reciprocity: The government of [*name of requesting jurisdiction*] undertakes that it will comply with a future request by the government of [*name of requested jurisdiction*] for similar assistance, by providing assistance having a comparable effect in respect to an equivalent offense to that requested from the government of [*name of requested jurisdiction*] in this case.

Limits on Use: [*It may be necessary to promise that information will be used only in the investigation specified.*[279] *Some jurisdictions will not require this assurance, and it may be possible to state explicitly that information can be used for other purposes.*[280]]

Prior Contact or Use of Other Channels

There has been previous contact between [*name of relevant agency or authority in requesting jurisdiction*] and [*name of relevant agency or authority in requested jurisdiction*].

Contact Information

The [*judge, prosecutor, or central authority officer*] who is in charge of this matter is [*name of officer*], and he/she can be contacted at [*street address, telephone number, e-mail address*].

---

279. An assurance regarding use of evidence may be stated as follows: "The government of [*name of requesting jurisdiction*] undertakes that all information, documentation, or other evidence obtained pursuant to this request will be used only for the purposes of the request in connection with the offenses described above. It should not be used for any other purpose, except with prior consultation with and the consent of the appropriate authorities of [*name of requested jurisdiction*].

280. In the United Kingdom, an MLA template includes the following phrase: "Unless you indicate otherwise, any evidence obtained pursuant to this request may be used in any criminal prosecution or other judicial proceedings connected with this investigation, including any restraint or confiscation proceedings, whether relating to the above-named subject(s) or to any other person who may become a subject of this investigation." See http://www.sfo.gov.uk/media/57234/sample%20letter%20of%20request%20for%20evidence.pdf.

The case officer in [*name of the enforcement agency or prosecutorial authority*] who has knowledge of this matter is [*name of officer*] and he/she can be contacted at [*street address, telephone number, e-mail address*].

| BOX I.1 | MLA Drafting and Execution Tips |

- Contact your counterpart (including through a face-to-face meeting, if possible) to
  - confirm general and evidentiary requirements;
  - discuss how thresholds might be met, and obtain examples of the types of evidence required;
  - confirm the format for evidence (for example, affidavit, signed statement, certified court documents);
  - discuss undertakings or assurances that may be required;
  - discuss needs of urgency, confidentiality, or procedure;
  - seek drafting assistance and templates;
  - determine if it is possible to participate in the execution of the request;
  - assess potential barriers in fulfilling the request, such as disclosure obligations; and
  - raise potential resource issues.
- Ensure general and evidentiary requirements are met.
- Exclude requests when property is of a *de minimis* value.
- Provide a clear and concise description of the facts and the state of proceedings in the requesting jurisdiction.
- If translation is required, use professional services.
- If tracing or freezing, include as much information as possible about the location of the assets and the link between the assets and the offense or offender.
- Do not ask for everything (trace, freeze, and confiscate) in one request. Start early and proceed step by step.
- Allow sufficient time for the request to be processed and action to be taken.
- Ensure that your domestic investigations and proceedings continue because a final order of confiscation will be required before funds can be returned. Also ensure that due process (including notice to parties and opportunity to appear) is followed.

Appendix J. Web Site Resources

Stolen Asset Recovery (StAR) Initiative

- StAR: http://www.worldbank.org/star

World Bank Group

- World Bank: http://www.worldbank.org
- Financial Market Integrity Group: http://www.worldbank.org/amlcft

United Nations

- United Nations: http://www.un.org
- United Nations Office on Drugs and Crime: http://www.unodc.org
- United Nations Mutual Legal Assistance Request Writer Tool (for justice system practitioners only): http://www.unodc.org/mla/introduction.html

International Conventions, Treaties, and Agreements

- United Nations Convention against Corruption (UNCAC): http://www.unodc.org/unodc/en/treaties/CAC/index.html
- United Nations Convention against the Illicit Traffic in Narcotic Drugs and Psychotropic Substances, 1988: http://www.unodc.org/unodc/en/treaties/illicit-trafficking.html
- United Nations Convention against Transnational Organized Crime (UNTOC): http://www.unodc.org/unodc/en/treaties/CTOC/index.html
- Organisation for Economic Co-operation and Development Convention on Combating Bribery of Foreign Public Officials in International Business Transactions: http://www.oecd.org/document/20/0,3343,en_2649_34859_2017813_1_1_1_1,00.html
- Southeast Asian Mutual Legal Assistance in Criminal Matters Treaty: http://www.aseansec.org/17363.pdf
- Inter-American Convention against Corruption: http://www.oas.org/juridico/english/treaties/b-58.html
- Council of Europe Conventions: http://conventions.coe.int
  - Council of Europe Convention on Laundering, Search, Seizure and Confiscation of the Proceeds of Crime, 1990; and revised Council of Europe Convention on Laundering, Search, Seizure and Confiscation of the Proceeds of Crime and on the Financing of Terrorism, 2005
  - European Convention on Human Rights

- ○ Convention on Jurisdiction and the Enforcement of Judgments in Civil and Commercial Matters (Convention of Lugano): http://curia.europa.eu/common/recdoc/convention/en/c-textes/lug.htm
- Council of the European Union Decisions and Regulations: http://eur-lex.europa.eu
  - ○ Council of the European Union Framework Decision 2003/577/JHA on the Execution in the European Union of Orders Freezing Property or Evidence and Corrigendum to Council Framework Decision 2003/577/JHA
  - ○ Council of the European Union Framework Decision 2005/212/JHA of 24 February 2005 on Confiscation of Crime-Related Proceeds, Instrumentalities and Property
  - ○ Council of the European Union Framework Decision 2006/783/JHA on the Application of the Principle of Mutual Recognition to Confiscation Orders
  - ○ Council Decision 2007/845/JHA of 6 December 2007 Concerning Cooperation between Asset Recovery Offices of the Member States in the Field of Tracing and Identification of Proceeds from, or Other Property Related to, Crime
  - ○ Council Regulation (EC) No. 44/2001 of 22 December 2000 on Jurisdiction and the Recognition and Enforcement of Judgments in Civil and Commercial Matters
  - ○ Council Regulation (EC) No. 1206/2001 of 28 May 2001 on Cooperation between the Courts of the Member States in the Taking of Evidence in Civil or Commercial Matters
- Southern African Development Community Protocol against Corruption 2001: http://www.sadc.int/index/browse/page/122
- African Union Convention on Preventing and Combating Corruption and Related Offences, 2003: http://www.africa-union.org/Official_documents/Treaties_%20Conventions_%20Protocols/Convention%20on%20Combating%20Corruption.pdf
- Commonwealth of Independent States Convention on Legal Assistance and Legal Relations in Civil, Family and Criminal Matters: http://www.hcch.net/upload/wop/jdgm_info01e.pdf

Financial Action Task Force (FATF) on Money Laundering

- FATF: http://www.fatf-gafi .org
- FATF 40+9 Recommendations: http://http://www.fatf-gafi.org/pages/0,3417,en_32250379_32236920_1_1_1_1_1,00.html

G-8 Best Practice Principles

- G-8 Best Practice Principles on Tracing, Freezing and Confiscation of Assets: http://www.justice.gov/criminal/cybercrime/g82004/G8_Best_Practices_on_Tracing.pdf
- G-8 Best Practices for the Administration of Seized Assets: http://www.apgml.org/issues/docs/15/G8%20Asset%20Management%20Best%20practices%20042705%20FINAL.doc

European Union and Council of the European Union

- Main sites: http://europa.eu/index_en.htm and http://www.consilium.europa.eu/showPage.aspx?lang=EN
- Civil and commercial matters:
  - ° Civil and commercial matters: general framework for community activity; European judicial network; judicial cooperation between member-states; service of documents; taking evidence; jurisdiction, recognition, and enforcement of judgments:
    - ▪ http://ec.europa.eu/civiljustice/index_en.htm
    - ▪ http://ec.europa.eu/justice_home/doc_centre/civil/doc_civil_intro_en.htm
    - ▪ http://europa.eu/legislation_summaries/justice_freedom_security/judicial _cooperation_in_civil_matters/index_en.htm
- Criminal matters:
  - ° General Framework for Community Activity: http://ec.europa.eu/justice_ home/doc_centre/criminal/assistance/doc_criminal_assistance_en.htm
  - ° Green Paper on Obtaining Evidence in Criminal Matters From One Member State to Another and Securing Its Admissibility, November 2009: http://eur-lex .europa.eu/LexUriServ/LexUriServ.do?uri=COM:2009:0624:FIN:EN:PDF

Country Legislation

- International Money Laundering Information Network: http://www.imolin.org
- UNCAC Knowledge Management Consortium and Legal Library: http://www .unodc.org (to be launched in fall 2010)

Asset Tracing Resources

Free sites (general information, public records, business records):

- http://www.google.com (general information, news)
- http://www.icerocket.com (blog search)
- http://www.archive.org/web/web.php (Internet archives)
- http://www.searchsystems.net ("invisible Web" search of public records, company records—worldwide)
- http://www.publicrecordfinder.com (public records, company records— worldwide)
- http://www.sec.gov/edgar.shtml (U.S. company records)
- http://www.zoominfo.com (people and company finder)
- http://www.superpages.com (people finder)

Subscription sites:

- http://www.worldlii.org (legislation, court decisions)
- http://www.lexisnexis.com (public records, court decisions, media, business records, people search)
- http://www.companydocuments.com (business records—worldwide)

- http://www.clear.thomsonreuters.com (public records, company records—worldwide)
- http://www.corporateinformation.com (company records)
- http://www.companieshouse.gov.uk (U.K. company records)
- http://www.pacer.gov (US court records)
- http://www.freeerisa.com (US employee benefits data)

Professional and international organizations:

- International Association of Prosecutors: http://www.iap-association.org/
- Camden Asset Recovery Inter-Agency Network: http://www.europol.europa.eu/publications/Camden_Assets_Recovery_Inter-Agency_Network/CARIN_Europol.pdf
- The Egmont Group: http://www.egmontgroup.org
- Latin American Association of Public Ministers (in Spanish and Portuguese only): http://www.aiamp.net
- MLA and Confiscation Information: http://www.aiamp.net/fichasaiamp/index.html

Country-specific Mutual Legal Assistance Resources

Australia:

- Information on mutual legal assistance, treaty agreements, and a checklist: http://www.ilsac.gov.au
- Information on civil processes, service of documents, taking of evidence, and model letter of request: http://www.ag.gov.au/www/agd/agd.nsf
- Ministry of Foreign Affairs: http://www.afp.gov.au/
- Attorney-General of Australia: http://www.ag.gov.au/
- Australian Transaction Reports and Analysis Centre (financial intelligence unit): http://www.austrac.gov.au/
- Commonwealth Director of Public Prosecutions: http://www.cdpp.gov.au/

Brazil:

- Department of Asset Recovery and International Legal Cooperation (within the Ministry of Justice): http://portal.mj.gov.br/drci/data/Pages/MJ7A4BFC59ITEMID401B422470464DA481D21D6F2BBD1217PTBRNN.htm
- Ministry of Foreign Affairs: http://www.itamaraty.gov.br/
- Ministry of Justice: http://portal.mj.gov.br
- Council for Financial Activities Control (financial intelligence unit): http://www.coaf.fazenda.gov.br/

France:

- Ministry of Foreign Affairs, Office of Conventions and Mutual Legal Assistance: http://www.Diplomatie.gouv.fr
- Ministry of Justice: http://www.justice.gouv.fr
- Tracfin (financial intelligence unit): http://www.bercy.gouv.fr

Germany:

- Information on civil processes, judicial cooperation, taking of evidence and mode of proof, service of documents, and enforcement of judgments:
  - ○ http://www.bmj.bund.de/enid/9de2c6dac41fc4c549b89d79e577a825,0/Legal_and_Justice_Policy/Judical_Cooperation_in_Civil_Matters_15b.html
  - ○ http://ec.europa.eu/civiljustice/homepage/homepage_ger_en.htm
- Federal Foreign Office: http://www.auswaertiges-amt.de/diplo/en/Startseite.html
- Federal Ministry of Justice: http://www.bmj.bund.de/enid/9de2c6dac41fc4c549b89d79e577a825,0/aktuelles_13h.html
- Financial intelligence unit: http://www.bka.de/

Hong Kong SAR, China:

- MLA information:[281] http://www.legislation.gov.hk/choice.htm#intro
- Foreign Ministry of Affairs (Commissioner's Office of China's Foreign Ministry in Hong Kong SAR, China): http://www.fmcoprc.gov.hk/eng/
- Department of Justice (International Law Division, Mutual Legal Assistance Unit): http://www.doj.gov.hk/publications/doj2010/en/international.html
- Independent Commission Against Corruption: http://www.icac.org.hk/
- Joint Financial Intelligence Unit: http://www.jfiu.gov.hk/

India:

- MLA information: http://www.mha.nic.in/uniquepage.asp?ID_PK=241&Search=mutual%20legal%20assistance
- Investigation assistance, letters rogatory, MLA treaties (Indian Central Bureau of Investigation): http://cbi.nic.in/interpol/assist.php
- Ministry of Justice: http://lawmin.nic.in/
- State anticorruption bureaus (for example, Anti-Corruption Bureau, Maharashtra): http://www.acbmaharashtra.org/
- Financial intelligence unit: http://fiuindia.gov.in/

Luxembourg:

- Information on civil processes, taking of evidence and mode of proof, and service of documents: http://ec.europa.eu/civiljustice/homepage/homepage_lux_en.htm
- Ministry of Foreign Affairs: http://www.mae.lu
- Ministry of Justice: www.mj.public.lu/
- Financial intelligence unit: http://www.gouvernement.lu/dossiers/justice/crf/index.html

Mexico:

- Information on letters rogatory: http://www.sre.gob.mx/english/
- Tracking service for letters rogatory: http://webapps.sre.gob.mx/rogatorias/

---

281. A manual for assisting countries is available from the International Mutual Assistance in Criminal Matters (IMAC) office in Hong Kong SAR, China.

- Ministry of Foreign Affairs: http://www.sre.gob.mx/english
- Attorney-General's Office (requests and receives MLA requests on criminal matters): http://www.pgr.gob.mx/
- Assistant Attorney General for Special Investigations and Organized Crime: http://www.pgr.gob.mx/prensa/2007/coms07/170407.shtm
- Financial intelligence unit: http://www.apartados.hacienda.gob.mx/uif/index.html

Singapore:

- MLA information and forms: http://www.agc.gov.sg/criminal/mutual_legal_asst.htm
- Ministry of Foreign Affairs: http://www.mfa.gov.sg
- Suspicious Transaction Reporting Office (financial intelligence unit): http://www.cad.gov.sg/amlcft/STRO.htm

South Africa:

- MLA treaties: http://www.justice.gov.za/docs/emlatreaties.htm
- National Prosecuting Authority (central authority for MLA): http://www.npa.gov.za/
- Department of International Relations and Cooperation: http://www.dfa.gov.za
- Department of Justice and Constitutional Development: http://www.justice.gov.za/
- Financial Intelligence Centre (financial intelligence unit): http://www.fic.gov.za/Default.aspx
- Public Service Commission (anticorruption authority): http://www.psc.gov.za/
- Asset Forfeiture Unit: http://www.npa.gov.za/ReadContent387.aspx

Spain:

- Information on civil processes, taking of evidence and mode of proof, and service of documents: http://ec.europa.eu/civiljustice/homepage/homepage_spa_es.htm
- Ministry of Foreign Affairs and Cooperation: http://www.maec.es/en
- Ministry of Justice: http://www2.mjusticia.es/
- Financial intelligence unit: http://www.sepblac.es/ingles/acerca_sepblac/acercade.htm

Switzerland:

- MLA information on civil and criminal matters: http://www.bj.admin.ch/bj/en/home/themen/sicherheit/internationale_rechthilfe.html
- Database of Swiss localities and courts: http://www.elorge.admin.ch/elorge/e/
- Swiss Foreign Ministry: http://www.eda.admin.ch/eda/en/home.html
- Office of the Attorney-General: http://www.ba.admin.ch/ba/en/home.html
- Federal Office of Justice: http://www.bj.admin.ch/bj/en/home.html
- Federal Department of Justice and Police, Section for Mutual Legal Assistance in Criminal Matters: http://www.rhf.admin.ch

- Money Laundering Reporting Office (financial intelligence unit): http://www .fedpol.admin.ch/fedpol/en/home/themen/kriminalitaet/geldwaescherei.html

United Arab Emirates (UAE):

- Ministry of Justice: http://www.elaws.gov.ae/DefaultEn.aspx
- Abu Dhabi Office of Public Prosecution: http://www.adjd.gov.ae/en/portal/public.prosecution.aspx
- Central Bank of the UAE, Anti-Money Laundering and Suspicious Case Unit (financial intelligence unit): http://www.centralbank.ae/AMLSU.php

United Kingdom:

- MLA information
    o Homes Office: http://www.homeoffice.gov.uk/police/mutual-legal-assistance/Assistance-from-UK/
    o Serious Fraud Office: http://www.sfo.gov.uk/about-us/what-we-do-and-who-we-work-with/international-collaboration.aspx
    o Crown Prosecution Service: http://www.cps.gov.uk/legal/l_to_o/obtaining_evidence_and_information_from_abroad/mutual_legal_assistance_(mla)_-_letters_of_request/
    o Serious Organized Crime Agency (financial intelligence unit): http://www .soca.gov.uk/

United States:

- Office of International Affairs, Department of Justice: http://www.usdoj.gov/criminal/oia.html
- Department of Justice Asset Forfeiture and Money-Laundering Section: http://www.justice.gov/criminal/afmls/
- Department of State: http://www.state.gov
- Financial Crimes Enforcement Network (financial intelligence unit): http://www .fincen.gov/

Glossary

Administrative confiscation. A non-judicial mechanism for confiscating proceeds of crime or assets used or involved in the commission of an offense.

Assets. Assets of every kind, whether corporeal or incorporeal, movable or immovable, tangible or intangible, and legal documents or instruments evidencing title to or interest in such assets.[282] The term is used interchangeably with **property.**

Bona fide purchaser. See **innocent owner.**

Civil action. See **private law action.**

Claimant. The party asserting an interest in the asset. This may include a **third party, innocent owner, defendant, target,** or **offender.**

Commingled assets. Proceeds or instrumentalities of an offense that have been mixed with other assets that may not be proceeds of crime.

Confiscation. The permanent deprivation of assets by order of a court or other competent authority.[283] The term is used interchangeably with **forfeiture.** The persons or entities that hold an interest in the specified funds or other assets at the time of the confiscation lose all rights, in principle, to the confiscated funds or other assets.[284]

Conviction-based confiscation. Describes all forms of **confiscation** that require the **defendant** to be convicted of an offense before confiscation proceedings can be initiated and confiscation can take place.

Criminal confiscation. See **conviction-based confiscation.**

Defendant. Any party who is required to answer the complaint of a plaintiff in a civil lawsuit before a court, or any party who has been formally charged or accused of violating a criminal statute.

Ex parte **proceedings.** Legal proceedings brought by one person in the absence of, and without representation or notification of, other parties.

Financial intelligence unit (FIU). "A central, national agency responsible for receiving, (and as permitted, requesting), analyzing and disseminating to the competent authorities, disclosures of financial information: (i) concerning suspected proceeds of

---

282. United Nations Convention against Corruption (UNCAC), art. 2(e).

283. UNCAC, art. 2(g). See also "Best Practices: Confiscation (Recommendations 3 and 38)," adopted by the plenary of the Financial Action Task Force (FATF), February 19, 2010.

284. FATF, "Interpretative Note to Special Recommendation III: Freezing and Confiscating Terrorist Assets," para. 7(c), http://www.fatf-gafi.org/dataoecd/53/32/34262136.pdf.

crime and potential financing of terrorism, or (ii) required by national legislation or regulation, in order to combat money laundering and terrorism financing."[285]

Forfeiture. See **confiscation.**

Freezing. See **provisional measures.** See also chapter 4.

Gatekeeper. Includes accountants, lawyers, financial consultants, or other professionals holding accounts at a financial institution and acting on behalf of their clients, either knowingly or unwittingly, to move or conceal the proceeds of illegal activity. A criminal may seek to use the gatekeeper to access the financial system, while remaining anonymous themselves.[286]

Hearsay. An out-of-court statement that is offered in court as evidence to prove the truth of the matter asserted. Whereas civil law jurisdictions do not usually exclude hearsay from proceedings, hearsay is inadmissible in common law (with a number of exceptions). If hearsay is admitted, the court must also consider the appropriate weight to give the evidence.

Informal assistance. Any activity or assistance that is provided without the need for a formal mutual legal assistance (MLA) request. There may be legislation that permits this type of practitioner-to-practitioner assistance, including MLA legislation.

Innocent owner. A third party with an interest in an asset subject to confiscation who did not know of the conduct giving rise to confiscation or, on learning of the conduct giving rise to confiscation, did all that reasonably could be expected under the circumstances to terminate use of the asset. The term is used interchangeably with **bona fide purchaser for value.**

In personam. Latin for "directed toward a particular person." In the context of confiscation or a lawsuit, it is a legal action against a specific person.

In rem. Latin for "against a thing." In the context of confiscation, it is a legal action against a specific thing or asset. See **property-based confiscation.**

Instrument or **instrumentality.** The assets used to facilitate crime, such as a car or boat used to transport narcotics or cash.

Know your customer. The due diligence and bank regulation that financial institutions and other regulated entities must perform to identify their clients and ascertain relevant information pertinent to doing financial business with them.

Letters rogatory. A formal request from a court to a foreign court for some type of judicial assistance. It permits formal communication between the judiciary, a prosecutor, or

---

285. Definition adopted at the plenary meeting of the Egmont Group, Rome, Italy, November 1996; as amended at the Egmont plenary meeting, Guernsey, June 2004.
286. FATF, "Guidance on the Risk-Based Approach to Combating Money Laundering and Terrorist Financing: High Level Principles and Procedures" (June 2007), http://www.fatf-gafi.org/dataoecd/43/46/38960576 .pdf; FATF, "Report on Money Laundering Typologies, 2000–2001" (February 2001), http://www.fatf-gafi .org/dataoecd/29/36/34038090.pdf.

law enforcement official of one jurisdiction, and his or her counterpart in another jurisdiction. A particular form of **mutual legal assistance.**

Mutual legal assistance. The process by which jurisdictions seek and provide assistance in gathering information, intelligence, and evidence for investigations; in implementing provisional measures; and in enforcing foreign orders and judgments. This handbook distinguishes between assistance that can be provided informally (see **informal assistance**) and formally (see **mutual legal assistance request**).

Mutual legal assistance request. Distinguished from informal assistance, an MLA request is typically a request in writing that must adhere to specified procedures, protocols, and conditions set out in multilateral or bilateral agreements or domestic legislation. These requests are generally used to gather evidence (including through coercive investigative techniques), obtain provisional measures, and seek enforcement of domestic orders in a foreign jurisdiction.

Non-conviction based confiscation (NCB confiscation). Confiscation for which a criminal **conviction** is not required.[287]

Politically exposed persons (PEPs). "Individuals who are, or have been, entrusted with prominent public functions, their family members, and close associates."[288]

Practitioner. Refers to law enforcement investigators, investigating magistrates, private lawyers, forensic accountants, financial analysts, and prosecutors. One or all of these roles may be involved in a component of the investigation, depending on the laws of the jurisdiction.

Proceeds of crime. Any asset derived from or obtained, directly or indirectly, through the commission of an offense.[289] In most jurisdictions, **commingled assets** are included.[290]

Property. See **assets.**

Property-based confiscation. A confiscation action that targets a specific thing or asset found to be the proceeds or instrumentalities of crime. Also known as *in rem* **confiscation** or a **tainted property system.**

Provisional measures. Temporarily prohibiting the transfer, conversion, disposition, or movement of assets or temporarily assuming custody or control of assets on the basis of an order issued by a court or other competent authority.[291] The term is used interchangeably with **freezing, restraint, seizure,** and **blocking.**

---

287. "Best Practices: Confiscation (Recommendations 3 and 38)," adopted by the plenary of the FATF, February 19, 2010.
288. Theodore S. Greenberg, Larissa Gray, Delphine Schantz, Carolin Gardner, and Michael Lathem, *Politically Exposed Persons: Preventive Measures for the Banking Sector* (Washington DC: World Bank, 2010), 3, http://www.worldbank.org/star.
289. UNCAC, art. 2(e).
290. See section 6.2.1 of chapter 6 for a discussion of commingled assets.
291. Adapted from UNCAC, art. 2(f).

Requested jurisdiction. A jurisdiction that is asked to provide assistance to another jurisdiction for the purpose of assisting a foreign investigation or prosecution or enforcing a judgment.

Requesting jurisdiction. A jurisdiction that asks for the assistance of another jurisdiction for the purpose of assisting with a domestic investigation or prosecution or enforcing a judgment.

Restraint. See **provisional measures.** See also chapter 4.

Seizure. See **provisional measures.** See also chapter 4.

Seller for value. See **innocent owner.**

Substitute assets. Assets that cannot be linked to an offense giving rise to confiscation, but that may be confiscated in substitution for such assets if the assets that are directly subject to confiscation cannot be located or are otherwise unavailable.

Suspicious activity report. See **suspicious transaction report.**

Suspicious transaction report (STR). A report filed by a financial institution about a suspicious or potentially suspicious transaction or activity. The report is filed with the jurisdiction's FIU. The term is used interchangeably with **suspicious transaction report.**

Tainted property. See **property-based confiscation.**

Target or **targets.** The suspect or suspects of an investigation.

Value-based confiscation. A confiscation action to recover the value of benefits that have been derived from criminal conduct and to impose a monetary penalty of an equivalent value.

Index

Boxes, figures, notes, and tables are indicated with b, f, n, and t following the page number.

MT 103 messages, 67, 205, 209–10
MT 202 COV standards, 205, 209–12
mutual legal assistance (MLA) requests. *See also* informal assistance
    asset recovery and, 9
    barriers to, 26–27, 126, 127*b*
    criminal investigations and, 11
    disclosure obligations, 127*b*
    fact gathering and, 20
    foreign jurisdictions, 99, 182*b*
    informal assistance vs., 124, 127–31, 129*t*, 131*f*
    in international cooperation, 6–7, 74, 122, 138–56, 158*b*. *See also* international cooperation
    in Montesinos case, 124*b*
    template and drafting tips, 237–40, 240*b*
    timing and coordination, 39

N
Namibia, asset confiscation funds in, 120
natural persons, 43
NCB confiscation. *See* non-conviction based (NCB) confiscation
net profits of contract, 109
networks, practitioner, 126*b*
net worth analyses, 73
New York Stock Exchange, 179*b*
Nigeria
    Alamieyeseigha case, 17–18, 160*b*, 169, 170*b*
    Dariye investigation, 46–47*b*
    Economic and Financial Crimes Commission, 17
    Metropolitan Police, 18, 18*n*26, 169
Nigeria, Federal Republic of v. Santolina Investment Corp., Solomon & Peters, and Alamieyeseigha (2007), 17–18, 160*b*, 169, 170*b*
noncoercive investigative measures, 128, 128*n*181, 131
non-conviction based (NCB) confiscation
    court proceedings and, 7
    domestic confiscation in foreign jurisdictions and, 177
    international cooperation and, 156–57
    retroactivity of, 29*n*39
    use of, 5, 9, 11–12, 106–7
no-say (gag) orders, 12, 170–71

O
Oakland County v. Vista Disposal, Inc. (1995), 165*n*244
objective confiscation. *See* non-conviction based (NCB) confiscation
obstruction of justice, 192

officials, immunity from prosecution of, 30
Oil-for-Food Program (UN), 185*b*
Okonjo-Iweala, Ngozi N., xi–xii
"ongoing proceedings," 126
orders, enforcement of, 7. *See also specific types of orders (e.g., no-say (gag) orders)*
"ordre public international," 167
originator information, 211*b*
Oyebanjo, Joyce, 46–47*b*

P
Pakistan, integrity pacts in, 168
Panama
    civil damages, 162*n*229
    restraint orders, 171*b*
"paper cases," 41, 45
partial control or interests in assets, 81, 82, 84*t*
PEPs. *See* politically exposed persons
periods of prescription, 31–32
perishable assets, 93, 98–99
personal connections, development of, 123–24, 124–26*b*
personal jurisdiction, 29
Pertamina (Indonesian state-owned enterprise), 161–62*b*
Peru
    Efficient Collaboration Act (Law 27.378), 15, 15*n*
    Montesinos case, 14–16, 32*n*51, 124*b*, 157*n*220
    plea agreements, 28, 28*b*
physical possession of assets, 82, 84–85
physical surveillance, 51
piercing the corporate veil, 80
plea agreements, 28, 28*b*, 185*n*
political activities, illicit financing of, 190
politically exposed persons (PEPs), 43*n*63, 62, 66
political will, 27
practitioner networks, 126*b*
precious metals, seizure of, 98
"preponderance of the evidence" standard of proof, 11, 13, 33, 106, 156
pre-restraint or pre-seizure planning, 79–85, 97
preservation of evidence, 56–57
presumptions of innocence, 115. *See also* rebuttable presumptions
pretrial discovery, 106*n*139
privacy rights, 52, 52*n*68
private law. *See* civil proceedings
privileged information, 207–8
"probable cause" standard of proof, 54, 77
procedural requirements for securing assets, 77–78
proceeds of crime, 42, 108–11, 108*n*142, 110*b*, 190–91

Siemens; United States v. (2008), 36*b*
Singapore, Pertamina case and, 161*b*
smuggling, 192
Society for Worldwide Interbank Financial
    Telecommunications (SWIFT), 64,
    66, 67, 68*f*, 205, 209, 212
South Africa
  Alamieyeseigha corruption scheme, 17, 18
  asset confiscation funds, 120
  Asset Forfeiture Unit, 18
  Prevention of Organised Crime Act, 3*n*12,
    92*n*119, 109*n*145
sovereignty, principle of, 121
Spain, asset confiscation funds in, 120
Special Recommendation VII on Wire Transfers
    (Financial Action Task Force),
    63*n*85, 210
spontaneous disclosures, 20
S.T. Grand, Inc. v. City of New York (1973),
    166*n*247
standards of proof
  account monitoring orders, 53*n*73
  "balance of probabilities," 9, 11, 13, 33, 106,
    156, 159
  "beyond a reasonable doubt," 9, 33, 106
  in case management, 32–33, 33*b*
  conviction, inability to obtain, 38
  evidentiary challenges, 37
  "intimate conviction," 33, 106
  "preponderance of the evidence," 11,
    13, 33, 106, 156
  "probable cause," 77
  "reasonable grounds to believe," 54, 77
  search and seizure warrants, 54
StAR Initiative. *See* Stolen Asset
    Recovery (StAR) Initiative
state responsibility, principle of, 167
statutes of limitations, 31–32, 32*n*49
statutory authorities, asset recovery
    pursuant to, 185–86
Stolen Asset Recovery (StAR) Initiative,
    2, 19*n*28, 42*n*62, 102,
    109*n*143, 126*n*
storage facilities, 82
strategic planning in case management, 39
"straw men," 42, 52
STRs. *See* suspicious transaction reports
subject profiles, creation of, 43, 44*b*
substitute asset provisions, 116–17
summary judgments, 173–74
summary testimony, 114
surveillance
  electronic, 59–60
  physical, 51

suspicious transaction reports (STRs), 13,
    20, 21*b*, 48–49, 61, 66, 89, 182*b*
SWIFT. *See* Society for Worldwide
    Interbank Financial
    Telecommunications
Switzerland
  asset return, 186, 186*b*
  disclosure obligations for MLA
    requests, 127*b*
  informal assistance, 128*n*180
  Montesinos case and, 14–15, 124*b*
  NCB confiscation, 157*n*218
  Swiss Bankers Association, 95*n*125
  Swiss Federal Tribunal, 30*n*45

T
tainted property systems. *See* property-based
    confiscation systems
task forces, 22–25, 122
taxation
  criminal violations, 192
  of illicit profits, 14, 15*b*
  real property seizure and, 96
  tax authorities, 50
team investigations, 22–25, 122
territorial jurisdiction, 29
Thahir, Haji Achmad, 161–62*b*
Thahir, Kartika Ratna, 161–62*b*
Thahir v. Pertamina (1992–94), 161, 161–62*b*
Thailand, NCB confiscation in, 29*n*39
third-party interests
  confiscation mechanisms, 118–19
  disclosure, 170–71
  in securing assets, 87–88
timing issues
  MLA requests, 39
  of provisional measures, 85–86
tort actions, 162–65
tort damages, 12, 163
tracing assets. *See* evidence and
    tracing assets
trading in influence, 37*b*, 188–89
transfers of assets, 116, 117
Transparency International, 167
trash runs, 51–52
treaties, asset recovery pursuant to, 185–86
trusts, constructive, 161*b*

U
Ukraine
  corruption in, 181*b*
  jurisdiction issues, 179*b*
UNCAC. *See* United Nations Convention
    against Corruption

www.ingramcontent.com/pod-product-compliance
Lightning Source LLC
Chambersburg PA
CBHW080520220326
41599CB00032B/6149